English for Diplor
Purposes

Full details of all our publications can be found on http://www.multilingual-matters.com, or by writing to Multilingual Matters, St Nicholas House, 31-34 High Street, Bristol BS1 2AW, UK.

English for Diplomatic Purposes

Edited by
Patricia Friedrich

MULTILINGUAL MATTERS
Bristol • Buffalo • Toronto

For my grandfather, José Goossens Marques
(in memoriam), who first, and to my great advantage, taught me what it
means to be a good person.

Library of Congress Cataloging in Publication Data
A catalog record for this book is available from the Library of Congress.

Friedrich, Patricia, editor.
English for Diplomatic Purposes/Edited by Patricia Friedrich.
Description: Bristol; Buffalo: Multilingual Matters, [2016] | Includes
bibliographical references and index.
Identifiers: LCCN 2015049063| ISBN 9781783095476 (hbk :alk. paper) | ISBN
9781783095469 (pbk :alk. paper) | ISBN 9781783095506 (kindle)
Subjects: LCSH: English language–Study and teaching–Political
aspects–English-speaking countries. | Intercultural
communication–Political aspects. | English language–Study and
teaching–Political aspects. | English language–Study and
teaching–Foreign speakers.
Classification: LCC PE2751 .E549 2016 | DDC 427–dc23 LC record available at http://
lccn.loc.gov/2015049063

British Library Cataloguing in Publication Data
A catalogue entry for this book is available from the British Library.

ISBN-13: 978-1-78309-547-6 (hbk)
ISBN-13: 978-1-78309-546-9 (pbk)

Multilingual Matters
UK: St Nicholas House, 31-34 High Street, Bristol BS1 2AW, UK.
USA: UTP, 2250 Military Road, Tonawanda, NY 14150, USA.
Canada: UTP, 5201 Dufferin Street, North York, Ontario M3H 5T8, Canada.

The policy of Multilingual Matters/Channel View Publications is to use papers that
are natural, renewable and recyclable products, made from wood grown in sustainable
forests. In the manufacturing process of our books, and to further support our policy,
preference is given to printers that have FSC and PEFC Chain of Custody certification.
The FSC and/or PEFC logos will appear on those books where full certification has been
granted to the printer concerned.

Typeset by Deanta Global Publishing Services Limited.
Printed and bound in Great Britain by Short Run Press Ltd.

Contents

Acknowledgments

What a great day it is when one can collaborate with wonderful peers to create a piece of work they truly believe is missing in the literature! From my first conversations with Danton Ford that generated the idea and identified the gap and the need that this book could start to fulfill, to the reading of the first drafts that taught me so much about facets of English when applied to diplomacy, I have enjoyed every minute of this process. My first thanks, therefore, could go to no other than the academics, scholars, and practitioners who made this project come to fruition. Their knowledge, enthusiasm, patience, and willingness to entertain my suggestions were the elements that made this volume possible. Special thanks go to Francisco Gomes de Matos, whose vision and wisdom first inspired me to pursue Peace Linguistics and issues of global understanding.

I would also like to thank Anna Roderick, our editor at Multilingual Matters, who saw the potential and the contribution of this volume. Her work and her team's dedication helped highlight the message and the teachings we wanted to share with the readers.

I would also like to thank my unit – The School of Humanities, Arts, and Cultural Studies – and my college – The New College of Arts and Sciences at Arizona State University – for the support I always receive from them. This great undertaking that is peace requires the commitment of all of us – at the institutional, professional, and personal levels.

I would like to acknowledge the instructors and students of diplomacy around the world, who are doing their part to establish dialogue with their diplomatic counterparts. Their job is of great importance and consequence, and I hope that in a way our effort here makes their work a little easier.

Finally, I would like to thank my family for their patience and belief in me, the very elements that always carry me through the writing of a book.

Patricia Friedrich
2015

Contributors

Danton Ford has worked in ESL teaching and training in the Republic of Korea since 1996. He is currently a full-time lecturer and curriculum developer at the Korea National Diplomatic Academy (KNDA) of the Ministry of Foreign Affairs, where he has been training Korean diplomats in English communication skills since 2005. The areas of his training include Negotiation, Debate, Presentation, Diplomatic Communication and Writing. In addition to his training at KNDA, he has lectured extensively on English negotiation and communication skills for various government organizations such as the Korean Intellectual Property Office, Korea Gas Corporation and Ministry of Environment. Danton completed his BA in English/Education from the University of Houston-Clear Lake and MA in North Korean Studies from Kyungnam University in Seoul. He also received training in negotiation from the Harvard Negotiation Institute and completed the Executive Education program in negotiation from the University of Notre Dame's Mendoza College of Business. Danton has co-authored a book on presentation skills and two English speaking books for ESL learners.

Patricia Friedrich (editor) is an Associate Professor of Rhetoric and Composition/Linguistics at Arizona State University in the United States, where she teaches courses on Writing, Sociolinguistics, the History of English, and topics in general Linguistics. Her main research interests include World Englishes, social and political aspects of the spread of English, cross-cultural communication, and Peace Linguistics. She is the author/editor of two books by Bloomsbury (*Language, Negotiation and Peace* and *Teaching Academic Writing*) and the editor of *Toward a Nonkilling Linguistics* (Center for Global Nonkilling). She was also an area editor for Wiley's *The Encyclopedia of Applied Linguistics*. Two new books on aspects of linguistic diversity were recently published: Palgrave-Macmillan's *The Literary and Linguistic Construction of Obsessive-Compulsive Disorder* and Routledge's *The Sociolinguistics of Digital Englishes* (with Eduardo H. Diniz de Figueiredo). Dr Friedrich has contributed about 30 journal articles and book chapters to such publications as *World Englishes* and *Harvard Business Review*. She is a published author of fiction as well.

Francisco Gomes de Matos is Professor Emeritus at the Universidade Federal de Pernambuco in Recife, Brazil. A peace linguist and a TESOLer, he has degrees in Law (UFPE), Linguistics (University of Michigan) and Applied Linguistics (Catholic University of São Paulo). He has taught in Canada, Mexico and the US. Dr Gomes de Matos is co-founder and president of the Board of ABA – Associação Brasil América in Recife and co-founder of the World Dignity University initiative. Among his publications are *Dignity: A Multidimensional View* (2013, DignityPress), *Nurturing Nonkilling: A Poetic Plantation* (2009, Center for Global Nonkilling), *Criatividade no Ensino de Inglês: A Resource Book* (2004, Editora DISAL, São Paulo), *Pedagogia da Positividade* (1996, Editora da UFPE, Recife). He co-authored, with Patricia Friedrich, the chapter 'Toward a Nonkilling Linguistics' in the volume *Nonkilling Linguistics: Practical Applications.* He has pioneered a chapter on 'Applying the Pedagogy of Positiveness to Diplomatic Communication' in the book *Language and Diplomacy* (2000). He is also the author of a pioneering Plea for a Universal Declaration of Language Rights (1984) and of a Plea for Communicative Peace (1993).

Noriko Ishihara holds a PhD in Curriculum and Instruction from the University of Minnesota and is Associate Professor of EFL/TESOL at Hosei University, Japan. She also leads language teachers' professional development courses at Temple University Japan and in the US. Her work in pragmatics centers on instructional pragmatics, in which she attempts to bridge research in interlanguage pragmatics and classroom practice to integrate culture into language instruction. Since her graduate studies, she has engaged in the development of instructional units in ESL/EFL, web- and classroom-based curricular materials in Japanese, and teacher education for instructional pragmatics. Her work in this area has led to co-authored teachers' resources: *Teaching and Learning Pragmatics* (with A.D. Cohen, Pearson/Longman, 2010) and *Advanced Japanese: Communication in Context* (with M. Maeda, Routledge, 2010). Her current research interests include pragmatics for language teachers and young learners, language and identity, and professional language teacher development.

Andy Kirkpatrick is Professor in the School of Languages and Linguistics at Griffith University, Brisbane. He was previously Director of the Research Centre into Language Education and Acquisition in Multilingual Societies at the Hong Kong Institute of Education, where he worked for six years. He has also worked for many years in tertiary institutions across Asia, including in China, Myanmar and Singapore. He is the author of *English as a Lingua Franca in ASEAN: A Multilingual Model* (Hong Kong University Press, 2010) and editor of the *Routledge Handbook of World Englishes* (2010). He is editor of the journal *Multilingual Education* and of the book series of the same name (both with Springer). His most recent books are *English as an International*

Language in Asia: Implications for Language Education, co-edited with Roland Sussex (Springer, 2012) and *Chinese Rhetoric and Writing*, co-authored with Xu Zhichang (Parlor Press, 2012).

Josette LeBlanc is a full time lecturer in the Department of English Education at Keimyung University in Daegu, South Korea. She has also worked as a curriculum developer and teacher trainer for intensive teacher-training programs offered to in-service Korean English teachers from the elementary and secondary sectors. In 2010 she received her Masters in TESOL from the SIT Graduate Institute where her culminating research focused on why teachers should develop their competence for communicative peace or compassionate communication. Her interest in this subject continues in her current practice where she aims to foster a space in which English language teaching, reflective practice, and compassionate communication coincide. Also very interested in writing, Josette has maintained a blog since 2009, *Throwing Back Tokens* (www.throwingbacktokens.wordpress.com), where she reflects on her experiences in teacher education. In addition to her interest in personal and professional development via such online forums, her extracurricular time is also shared with the Reflective Practice Special Interest Group she helps coordinate for her local teaching community.

Paul Kim Luksetich has over 15 years of training and instruction experience in negotiation, conflict resolution and sales, both in the United States and the Republic of Korea for companies such as Prudential Financial, Samsung, LG, Hyundai, and more. Paul carries a Bachelor's of Music from the University of Wisconsin, Madison campus and an MBA from the University of St Thomas, St Paul, Minnesota. Paul has also received an Executive Certificate in Global Negotiations at the Thunderbird School of Global Management. He is a Wilson Learning International certified trainer and served as the Officer of Employee Development for the Asian Pacific Americans Association at Prudential Financial where he facilitated numerous speeches and workshops on diversity. For the past seven years he has been teaching English to adults in Korea on subjects such as meetings English, correspondence, negotiation and conflict resolution. Paul is currently a full-time lecturer and curriculum developer at the Korea National Diplomatic Academy in Seoul, Korea, where he teaches diplomats on a wide range of subjects including negotiation. He has also co-authored two English speaking books for ESL learners.

Sophiaan Subhan is a Lecturer at the School of Languages and Linguistics, Griffith University, Brisbane, and a Senior Research Assistant for the Australian Research Council (ARC) Discovery project *Tense and Topic in English as an Asian Lingua Franca.*

Biljana Scott was trained as a linguist (BA in Chinese, M.Phil and D.Phil in Linguistics, University of Oxford). She is a Senior Lecturer in Political Language and Public Diplomacy at DiploFoundation (Geneva and Malta), and a Faculty Lecturer in Chinese Linguistics at the University of Oxford. All her research interests, both professional and personal, concern the way in which language influences the way we think about the world and act upon it. They include political rhetoric, public speaking, public diplomacy, photography and poetry. Dr Scott runs workshops on Language and Diplomacy for a variety of clients, ranging from the European Commission, Ministries of Foreign Affairs, Diplomatic Academies and Universities to the private sector. Topics covered include Building Relationships; Handling Disagreement; Understanding the Unsaid; Constructive Ambiguity; Force and Grace; and the Language of Negotiation and Persuasion.

Ian Walkinshaw is a Lecturer in English at the School of Languages and Linguistics, Griffith University, in Queensland, Australia. His research interests are in intercultural pragmatics, politeness/impoliteness, English as a *lingua franca* (particularly in Southeast Asia), and academic language and learning. He is the author of *Learning Politeness: Disagreement in a Second Language* (Peter Lang, 2009), and has published on applied linguistics in the *Journal of English as a Lingua Franca, English Australia Journal, TESL-EJ, RELC Journal*, and the *IELTS Research Reports* series.

Foreword

English is the global *lingua franca* of business and commerce. It is also almost everywhere the language of contemporary diplomacy. English seems exceptionally well suited to these roles. An enormous number of people speak it as a second language or are learning to do so.

One reason for the popularity of English is that it is a language that seems incapable of embarrassment. English asks only to serve as an effective means of communication and accepts widely varying accents with aplomb. There is no academy to punish its speakers for their shameless purloining of words and expressions from other languages. Their doing so enriches English (and thus international communication) while ensuring that speakers of other languages find many recognizable cognates in its vocabulary.

There are English-speaking nations on every continent but Asia and Antarctica. But, for most who use it to communicate with each other internationally, English is a second language they have in common, and an alternative to an interpreter. There are now many Englishes spoken with many accents and accompanied by many different styles of body language. But speakers of English – whether they are native speakers or not – are for the most part pragmatically concerned only with its efficacy as a means of communication, including cross-cultural communication, not its grammar. This focus creates a drive for mutual intelligibility that constantly pushes all the Englishes toward convergence when they diverge.

Unique among modern languages, English has become the international language of groups of states in which it is no member nation's native tongue and where it was not universally imposed by colonialism as a second language. The prime example of this is the Association of Southeast Asian Nations (ASEAN), whose member states include former Dutch and French as well as British and American colonies but which have made English the organization's official working language. Here, English is being used for diplomacy entirely in the absence of native speakers. (ASEAN English seems to be emerging as a distinctive dialect of the language.) The same is true in the South Asian Regional Cooperation (SARC) and the Southern African Development Community (SADC).

How English is used in such contexts and as a *lingua franca* in diplomacy in general is a matter of considerable interest and import. Diplomacy is an alternative to violent politics. It is the use of measures short of war to solve international problems. It is grounded in empathy as distinct from sympathy for the interests of others. Part of the ethic of diplomacy is keeping issues in a state of negotiability rather than allowing them to jell as military confrontation. This book advances our knowledge of how this can be done in English, which is the principal linguistic vehicle for diplomacy.

Diplomacy remains in many respects inchoate as a profession. Like members of the established learned professions, diplomats acquire a unique combination of specialized knowledge, experience and technique. But they have yet to achieve the level of professionalization of doctors, lawyers, or members of the clergy or armed forces. For the most part, diplomats learn through apprenticeship rather than through formal training in diplomatic history, the review of case studies, or the arts and techniques of peaceful persuasion and relationship management that define their role in statecraft. Many are amateurs trained in other professions. There is as yet no repository or professional mechanism for the development of diplomatic doctrine.

But diplomacy is ripe for professionalization. When that happens, the studies of English usage contained in this book will be an essential part of the corpus of professional knowledge and training for diplomats. Even before that, these studies are a delight to scholars and a stimulus to reflection for diplomats.

Ambassador Chas W. Freeman Jr (USFS, Retired).
Author, *Arts of Power: Statecraft and Diplomacy* and
The Diplomat's Dictionary.
October 2015, Singapore.

Introduction

The connection between language and diplomacy is a close one. Clearly, without language there is no diplomacy, and with careless language diplomacy is unable to achieve its goals. Yet this simplicity and straight forwardness masks its opposite – the complexity of finding ways to engage linguistically that enhance rapport rather than hamper it and to send the right messages at the right time. As I write this introduction, I am reminded of one favorite Buddha quote about the nature of the most worthy statements. While instructing the monks, the Buddha explained that right speech must have these five characteristics: 'It is spoken at the right time. It is spoken in truth. It is spoken affectionately. It is spoken beneficially. It is spoken with a mind of good-will.'[1] What is diplomacy, as a political art as well as the negotiation of everyday life, if not the talent of managing to tick all of these wish-list boxes at the same time while still pursuing one's interests?

Other ancient texts have also endeavored to enumerate the features of good communication. Kishan S. Rana (2001: 107) asks a very similar question to mine (I was pleasantly surprised that someone had made the same connection as me regarding a different ancient text). To him, the document in question is the Bhagwad Gita, a sacred text of the Hindus. The lines show uncanny similarity to the Buddhist wisdom above. Rana explains, with regards to the teachings of Krishna:

> Good speech should be marked by the following qualities, in ordered priority: it should not disturb the mind of the listener; it should be precise, with correct use of language; it should be truthful; if possible, it should be pleasing to the listener; and again if possible, it should be of utility to the listener.

A new version of this search for the features of perfect discourse – the kind that achieves its goals while (or because of) respecting the listener – is the ubiquitous acronym T.H.I.N.K. It has been produced and reproduced throughout social media to remind youth, and in reality all of us, to consider our words before speaking, so as to decide if what we are about to say is true, helpful, inspiring, necessary and kind.[2]

And yet, despite our centuries-old concern for discourse, finding that balance, the right language that will help us do that which we want to do while also respecting the needs of our audience, is no easy task. What is

xv

more, in the Tower of Babel world we live (to reference yet another ancient text, this time the Book of Genesis), one is often faced with the job of finding the right words that will fulfill the promise above in a language other than their so-called 'mother tongue.' To many, this adds to the complication and creates a situation of imbalance, where native speakers of languages of wider communication have a supposed linguistic advantage. But that is not universally the case, nor are we powerless in face of the need to use an international language.

Nelson Mandela, a wonderful negotiator, learned, against all expectations, to use Afrikaans during his imprisonment. Itziar Laka (2014) reminds us that Mandela knew (either by intuition of practice) about a phenomenon that Boaz Keysar and colleagues write of in a 2012 paper: they call it the foreign language effect. According to their perspective, the irrational, emotional connections that tend to affect our decisions when we use a first language are not present when another language is used, and their absence reduces biases and the fear of loss. The authors write:

> Two additional experiments show that using a foreign language reduces loss aversion, increasing the acceptance of both hypothetical and real bets with positive expected value. We propose that these effects arise because a foreign language provides greater cognitive and emotional distance than a native tongue does. (Keysar *et al.*, 2012: 661)

Mandela seems to have known this and used it in his favor. This is a revolutionary idea that should give hope and motivation to all of those who use, for example, English as a negotiating language despite not having English as a mother tongue. While English has become the primary language of international communication, business and in many respects diplomacy too, and many might believe that this means native speakers have an advantage, we as users of language can gather the tools and the skills to create a different reality.

In 2006, David Graddol, in his *English Next*, had estimated that within 10–15 years of his writing, the number of learners of English could have grown and peaked at 2 billion (we are now almost within the time range of his prediction). Since English has acquired the important role of *lingua franca* in several realms of life, many are the language users who seek the ability to communicate in it, which in turn creates a high demand for learning materials and new pedagogical ideas. In the last two decades, a lot has been written about international communication, particularly as far as business communication is concerned. In the realm of English teaching, for example, a reader/student can find a variety of very good sources and pedagogical materials that describe language that is appropriate for the many functions that a person performs in English. Writing memos, preparing presentations, dealing with cross-cultural differences and having a persuasive 'edge' all figure as frequent topics, as do necessary grammar, syntax and vocabulary lessons. The field of Teaching English to Speakers of Other Languages (TESOL) has expanded and developed dramatically, allowing people to find approaches and linguistic foci that fit their needs most of the time.

It has come to our attention, however, that the English language skills necessary for the more specific and at times quite delicate tasks performed by those who engage in diplomacy are not often addressed in the context of English language teaching. While overlap exists that allows teachers and students to adapt materials from general English courses and business English communication curricula, it is hard to find work that speaks directly to the English language features of diplomatic communication and to the challenges of finding language that inspires, convinces and asserts when English is used in this specific realm.

It is true that many worthwhile books exist that address cross-cultural communication and the potential clashes that may result from coming into a negotiation holding different cultural perspectives and beliefs. Nevertheless, these materials usually do not address the actual linguistic aspect of the knowledge necessary to make things work, much less in this precise context. Rather, they focus more exclusively on the dynamics of different cultural orientations and, to our knowledge, none was written with English and diplomacy specifically in mind. In diplomacy, it is our understanding that the considerations necessary for negotiations, talk and meetings to work are different from almost any other interaction we can imagine, and for that reason deserve their own field of study and practice.

The more we work toward linguistic understanding, the more we realize that the future belongs to those who can incorporate interdisciplinary views of phenomena into their areas of practice. In this sense the diplomatic worker, the negotiator and the international leader are well served by approaches to their language learning that integrate knowledge of language but also of cultural, human behavior and interaction, and social dynamics.

The contributors to this volume were given an important task: to write chapters that could be used by instructors, students and independent learners of diplomatic English to address the crucial linguistic and sociolinguistic considerations that need to take place when one is learning English for such specific purposes. They were to concentrate on the English language itself (being the many connections between language and culture a worthy addition) and on providing exercises, activities, or examples of application that could be used in the classroom by teachers and learners or for individual practice by those without access to an English classroom-learning environment.

The chapters in this book are designed to be used as materials that link theory and practice and that ground suggestions and activities in dynamic research. The contributors are a select group of researchers and practitioners, and their chapters thus exemplify the kind of dialogue that brings together academic scholarship and fieldwork.

In Chapter 1, Francisco Gomes de Matos and I situate the theme of diplomacy and English within the larger realm of peace linguistics, nonkilling linguistics and overall respect of language users. While we know that Diplomacy and Peace Linguistics are not the same, we encourage readers to consider what their language is doing to help establish harmonious communications. In Chapter 2, Noriko Ishihara shows how it is possible to disagree and still maintain elements of politeness that foster openness to dialogue and understanding. Ishihara demonstrates how balance between seemingly opposing forces can be achieved (e.g. directness and indirectness, assertiveness and empathy) and offers a chance for readers to analyze and discuss actual language use.

Chapter 3 presents us with a view on Compassionate English Communication (CEC) as seen by Josette LeBlanc. The focus is on three thorough activities, in which literacy in this important aspect of linguistic knowledge is practiced and linked to such essential elements of successful interactions as persuasion and compassion itself. As a matter of fact, compassion, peace and an understanding of others' motives are very important considerations throughout this book because several of us align our work with Peace Linguistics, World Englishes and Sociolinguistics, areas that see matters of linguistic rights as essential and intrinsically linked to human rights themselves.

In Chapter 4, Andy Kirkpatrick, Sophiaan Subhan and Ian Walkinshaw discuss the use of Diplomatic English in the more specific context of the member-countries of the Association of Southeast Asian Nations (ASEAN). As the chapter shows, language is context-dependent, and users of English who have not acquired it as a native or first language can also learn to use it for different functional purposes with great success. In a way, we all 'code-switch' between different varieties of language depending on the needs of the situation, and a rich repertoire and an understanding of the context of communication allow us to do that with varieties of a foreign or second language as well. Kirkpatrick and colleagues consider English in diplomacy to be one of the major functions performed by English as a lingua franca. They show how this happens through authentic samples of English interactions. They conclude with recommendations for language users who might find themselves in diplomatic situations.

I wrote Chapter 5 to bring together World Englishes (WE), Peace Linguistics and English for Diplomatic purposes. My contention is that WE is a wonderful framework through which to pursue English language studies for diplomacy because it already presupposes diversity, respect for difference and functional uses over prescriptive rules. I explain some basic premises of World Englishes and offer a number of activities to bring World Englishes awareness to the language and diplomacy classroom.

Chapter 6 offers an application of the principles of English for Specific Purposes (ESP) to English for Diplomatic Purposes (EDP) and especially to negotiating in English. In the chapter, Danton Ford and Paul Kim Luksetich present English language ideas for the different stages of negotiation. They describe how cross-cultural issues and translation interplay with language and offer practical activities and language samples throughout.

In Chapter 7, Biljana Scott explains how the interplay between grace and force works in diplomacy. She provides analyses of actual diplomatic discourse to show how force and grace are established and relates these concepts to the use of English in diplomacy and to strategies for being a gracious interlocutor and still maintaining assertiveness and poise.

Chapter 8 is a welcome application of Francisco Gomes de Matos's principles of Pedagogy of Positiveness to diplomatic English with a view to further highlighting the goal of peaceful interacting within the area. Gomes de Matos, the first and original peace linguist, offers many activities to enhance one's vocabulary and English use so as to foster peace and understanding. This chapter is particularly suitable for early learners.

Finally, in Chapter 9, I offer some concluding remarks to wrap up the volume. As with any uncharted or newly charted waters, we navigate the use of English for diplomacy with caution and hope. This important area of English language use is only beginning to be talked about as such, and we like to think of our contribution as the opening of a long conversation, of which we invite readers, teachers, scholars and learners to take part.

While a great deal of the instruction that we provide here is inspired by approaches to peace and language, we do not forward this perspective out of naivety. We do understand that diplomats and diplomatic workers negotiate to advance the interests of the nation states they represent. Chapters 6 and 7, for example, provide discussion and instruction on general elements of negotiations and the alternation of force and grace respectively, evidencing the need for different strategies and dynamics. Nonetheless, we believe that engaging with peace through language not only advances diplomatic interests but also makes for better humanistic outcomes, hence our emphasis on amity.

Our ultimate goal is that we can dream up a world where differences, disputes and conflicts are resolved through productive linguistic interactions and where we have realized the power and wisdom of the right words in the way texts since ancient times have been hinting at.

Although we hope to have created a cohesive whole within the book, its chapters can be read independently and in any order scholars, instructors and learners may choose. In some chapters activities appear at the end, whereas in others they are embedded in the text after the relevant sections or segments. We also wanted to offer chapters that cater to instructors, students and independent learners at different levels of communicative competence in both English and the practices of diplomacy. For this reason, the reader will find more elementary aspects of language use as well as more abstract nuances of meaning and connotation represented. While the chapters are independent, we reference one another's writing and we worked to make our individual contributions into a cohesive book. Although some chapters necessitate a more advanced understanding of language dynamics and linguistic features themselves, others, most notably Chapters 6 and 8, can be adapted to help beginners. In recognition of the different varieties used by contributors, an effort was made to keep the original English of each chapter.

While we wrote these chapters thinking of readers, instructors and students who work within the realm of diplomatic relations, we also believe that the lessons contained herein would be useful to those looking to enhance their English language teaching and learning by figuring out how to approach communication in more peaceful, compassionate and effective ways in other realms of English use. After all, everyone can do with a little more diplomacy in their professional and everyday lives.

Notes

(1) 'Vaca Sutta: A Statement' (AN 5.198), translated from the Pali by Thanissaro Bhikkhu. Access to Insight (Legacy Edition), 3 July 2010.
(2) For example, see The Free Dictionary http://acronyms.thefreedictionary.com/THINK

References

Graddol, D. (2006) *English Next*. London: British Council.
Keysar, B., Hayakawa, S. and Sun Gyu, A. (2012) The foreign language effect: Thinking in a foreign tongue reduces decision biases. *Psychological Science* 23, 661–668.
Laka, I. (2014) Mandela was right: The foreign language effect. *Mapping Ignorance*. See http://mappingignorance.org/ (accessed 1 August 2015).
Rana, K.S. (2001) Language, signaling and diplomacy. In J. Kurbalija and H. Slavik (eds) *Language and Diplomacy* (pp. 108–108). Malta: DiploProjects.

1 Toward a Nonkilling Linguistics[1]

Patricia Friedrich and Francisco Gomes de Matos

> *More than a universally avoided violence*
> *It's the constructing of peaceful permanence*
> *More than preventing the evils of violence*
> *Let's universally sustain Nonkilling sense.*
> (from 'Nonkilling Sense,' a poem by Francisco Gomes de Matos,
> dedicated by the author to Glenn D. Paige)

It is the age-old question: are human beings naturally predisposed to violence and therefore bound to a perpetual and elusive quest for peace, or are we a peaceful group falling prey to the traps of aggression and hostility?

In *Nonkilling Global Political Science*, Paige (2009 [2002]) raises the question of whether or not a nonkilling society is possible and what it would take to build such a society. He explains that a nonkilling society is a human community, smallest to largest, local to global, characterized by no killing of humans and no threats to kill; no weapons designed to kill humans and no justifications for using them; and no conditions of society depend upon threat or use of killing force for maintenance or change (2009: 21).

Paige (2009: 22) acknowledges that the answer to the first part of his question is a product of one's 'personal experience, professional training, culture and context'. The answer to the second, in case one agrees that such a society is possible, would, in our view, depend upon a collective effort in which each member of the society employs their expertise and special skills to contribute to the nonkilling paradigm. Our contribution to a nonkilling society would involve the responsible use of languages and the social power derived from such use.

In our nonkilling linguistics we can express our desire for languages to be employed in all of their peace-making potential. It is easy enough to observe that languages can sadly be employed as instruments of harm; a person can, for example, hurt with the words they choose or yet segregate and exclude those who share a different linguistic background. Thus, it seems intuitive to us that we need to tip the scale in the opposite direction by reinforcing instead those humanizing uses of language, which help

1

boost respect for human dignity and social inclusion. By doing so we may in some direct and indirect ways be advancing a nonkilling mentality.

The linguistic power conveyed by the juxtaposition of the negative prefix *non* and the noun *killing* recalls another felicitous combination, namely, *nonviolence*, a Gandhian concept-term, which according to *The Random House Dictionary* (1995: 891) originated in 1915, meaning 'the policy or practice of refraining from the use of violence, as in protesting oppressive authority.' That same source tells us that *violence* made its debut in written English at the beginning of the 14th century. How about *killing*, the reader might be wondering? The verb *kill* first appears in written form in 1175. According to the *American Heritage Dictionary* (2001: 469), *kill* can mean: 'To deprive of life; To cause to cease operating'. When, however, we add the prefix *non*, we positivize what would otherwise be destructive terms. Another history-making concept-term in that respect is, for example, that of *nonproliferation* as in the Nuclear Nonproliferation Treaty, signed in 1968 by the USA, the then USSR, the UK and over 80 non-nuclear-weapon states.

What these examples show is that language plays a significant role in the way we see and build the world because it has the power to transcend and transform. In the current state of affairs, Paige (2009: 30) argues, 'Language reflects and reinforces lethality, contributing a sense of naturalness and inescapability'. His examples are many; for instance, the way metaphors abound in the English language, which make reference to violence, war and conflict. He reminds us of expressions such as 'making a killing in the stock market,' or being 'stab[bed] in the back' or movie stars being dubbed 'bombshells.' We can add our own: Lou Dobbs's constant reference (2006, for example) to the 'war on the middle class,' the disagreements between men and women as 'the battle of the sexes,' or taking part in a discussion as engaging in a 'war of words.' There are also two ecolinguistically inappropriate – unfair! – nouns in English referring to animals: 'killer bee' (an African honeybee capable of stinging repeatedly) and 'killer whale' (a large carnivore, which is intelligent and relatively docile). Such labeling is biased against those species and again emblematic of our desensitizing toward the use of linguistically violent terms. English is not the only language through which we display violence-inspired metaphors. In Portuguese, for example, the combination of either 'morrer' or 'matar de vergonha' (to die or kill of embarrassment) fits this description as well (see also Arabic and Chinese for languages that extensively use linguistically violent terms). The existence, in several languages, of reference works on insulting words and expressions attests to the near-universal omnipresence of violent or *killing* communication across languages-cultures.

Because we live in a world which has, to a certain extent, been the backdrop for a rather unfortunately indifferent attitude toward killing, allowing language users to become also somewhat unmoved by it, linguists might be interested in mapping the lexicon of violence, an area which is in need of cross-cultural data collection. For a useful section on violence in a reference work, a starting point could be Glazier (1997: 634–638). That work features subsections on violent events, fights, attacks, violent actions and violent persons. The listing of over 300 types of violent actions provides evidence to support the hypothesis that human beings can be the most destructive creatures on Earth. However, we must also ask what listing would be made to exemplify the opposite, that is, the fact that human beings can/could be incredibly constructive creatures as well.

Other contexts of use also evidence this indifference and actually give away a certain unnecessary acclamation of violence. A quick search through a movie guide (Maltin, 2008) for example revealed the popularity of such titles as *Kill Bill* (2003), *The Matador* (2005) and *A Time to Kill* (1996). An interesting challenge could be to try to find an equivalent number of titles displaying peace-fostering terms. This challenge could be a desirable practice among conscientization (to use a Freirean term) activities aimed at communicatively enhancing constructive vocabulary, humanizing uses of languages and linguistic activism.

Of course the role of language in both the maintenance of peace and unfortunately the pursuit of violence is not restricted to its more metaphorical or purely linguistic uses. Effective diplomacy through peace talks, for example, can mark the divide between practicing peace through constructive dialogue or engaging in war through armed conflict. Further pacific pursuit of agreement and understanding can be exemplified by the growingly researched phenomenon of public peace dialogue (Saunders, 1999).

At the micro-level, the use of language can signal a language user's desire to respect and honor human dignity on the one hand, or to offend and attack one's self-esteem on the other. Recently, a friend of the senior author received a phone call from a stranger telling her that her daughter had been kidnapped. What ensued was a near-killing communicative exchange. The would-be kidnapping turned out to be a horrible prank, that is, an instance of *killing* use of Portuguese. For the mother, in this case, had to receive medical treatment to overcome the shock. Whereas this is an extreme example of both physical and psychological harm through language, human beings do indeed have the capacity to use linguistic boundaries to segregate, to deny membership, to belittle or conversely to educate, to empower, to establish contact and to elevate.

Surprisingly enough, given the ubiquitous nature of language, it took linguistics quite a long time to be more formally recognized as an important element of peace and the establishment of fairer social institutions. Luckily for us and our contemporaries, Peace Linguistics (Gomes de Matos, 1996 & 2008; Crystal, 1999 & 2004; Friedrich, 2007a & 2007b) now figures alongside Peace Psychology, Peace Education and other disciplines, among the contributing subjects helping in the development of interdisciplinary

Peace Studies, which in turn can inform those interested in the building of a nonkilling society.

However, the task ahead for linguistics scholars, teachers, language policymakers, government officials and language users themselves is not a small one. Language is so intricately connected to human experience that it can be said to permeate all aspects of our lives, from school to work, from entertainment to family relations, from conflict to diplomacy and governmental action. Yet, language users often take language for granted, fail to recognize its power and reach, and often trivialize its use. They neglect to engage in peace-fostering dialogue or become cocooned in their own silence. Language users often find it hard to say 'I am sorry,' to yield to the other speaker, and to choose their words according to their potential for peace. They at times fall short of recognizing situations in which language, if used constructively, could avoid serious conflict both at the personal micro-level and at the global macro-level.

In a nonkilling society, language must play a pivotal role as a tool for peace, as it needs to be widely engaged. Language users need to be empowered, and constructive dialogue needs to replace violence. This chapter is organized around the idea that several elements related to language are central to the establishment of a nonkilling society. We will visit but a few. While these elements relate to linguistics in its more abstract form, which means that they do not refer to any one particular language and at the same time include all languages, examples of their applicability are given vis-à-vis existing languages and the dynamics of power that unite and unfortunately also divide them. While many of our examples come from English, we do not in any way mean to imply that the use of English is more 'harmful' than the use of any other language. We truly believe that the power to change a language as a vehicle of peace and nonkilling power lies within the realm of the users (i.e. language as an abstract entity cannot be to blame). Therefore, the list, which includes many instances of uses of English, is simply an acknowledgment that we share English with the readers and thus can rely on an understanding of our examples. Whereas the list is not exhaustive, it is guided by two encompassing, fundamental principles and two general pleas as follows:

-   **First fundamental principle**: 'Language is a system for communicating in nonkilling ways.'
-   **Second fundamental principle**: 'Language users should have the right to learn to communicate nonkillingly for the good of humankind.'
-   **First plea**: 'Let us be communicative Humanizers, treating all language users with compassion and dignity.'
-   **Second plea**: 'Let us opt for communicatively nonkilling uses of language.'

Respect for Language Users and the Uses they Make of Language

Languages are not autonomous entities. They exist to serve the perceived needs of the societies that build them. They are made into tools or weapons depending upon their users. They are not intrinsically good or bad: however, they are used as vehicles of good or evil by the people who utilize them. Each user of language impacts the language in many ways by modifying, creatively applying, denying, or embracing it. Each language user is also unique because no one's experience with language and with the world is the same as anyone else's. Even considering identical twins, obviously born to the same parents in the same place and roughly at the same time, we will come to realize that the twins' experiences with language are unique: each will speak to different users, read different books and develop unique interests which in turn will help shape language use differently. Recognition of the multiplicity of users, realms of use, cline[2] of proficiency and educational environments of different languages and language varieties is paramount to building a nonkilling society.

Multiple users will present different linguistic features. Pronunciation will vary, and choice of vocabulary and type of variety will also oscillate according to the situation of communication, educational background, geographical location, gender and age of participants. While we must recognize and seize such diversity, we must also learn to refrain from using it against language users. How many times has violence resulted from denied membership due to linguistic separatism? How often do negative attitudes toward users or groups of users of specific dialects end up unfairly impacting people in nonlinguistic realms of life? Fought (2002: 127) provides an example of such attitudes. In a study conducted with college students from California about attitudes toward the various regional dialects of the United States, she found that 'the South was labeled as a separate geographic area more frequently than any other region.' In addition, 'a majority of terms associated with the South are negative.' The same stigmatization of regional dialects is true for Japanese (Gottlieb, 2008).

Scientifically speaking, no evidence exists that using a certain linguistic variety correlates with accomplishment, intelligence or skill. Yet, people are often stereotyped and pigeonholed with dialectal variation and language proficiency as criteria, and these criteria are then later wrongly reapplied to include or to exclude users. In a nonkilling society, multiple linguistic expressions exist in harmony, and people have a chance to develop their full potential regardless of the native status of their language use (i.e. whether they are native speakers or not), the regional origin of their dialect, or the functional range of their language use.

Additionally, in a nonkilling society notions about cline of proficiency and frequency of use are not employed judgmentally. Some people will use a certain language for a variety of functions (e.g. the speaker of English who uses the language in his medical practice, to talk to his kids, to write in academic journals and to chat with friends) while others will use it for only one (e.g. the airport controller in a primarily Spanish-speaking country who uses English for a specialized function at his workplace). In a nonkilling society, all kinds of users have a right to use such languages, and for those languages to be recognized and revered. They feel they are valuable members of their linguistic communities, and other members of such societies are grateful that because of those people's linguistic skills others have access to, for example, a medical diagnosis or the safe landing of their plane.

Thus, in a nonkilling society, beside the respect for dialectal variation, the questionable deficit approach to language use (i.e. the view which focuses on language users' shortcomings) is replaced with support for the further development of their skills and appreciation for the skills they already possess.

Respect for a Healthy Ecosystem of Languages

A few year ago, *The Economist* (23 October, 2008) published an article on endangered languages. The renowned publication reflected on the fate of thousands of languages which may disappear by the end of the 21st century, languages such as Hua, spoken in Botswana, and Manchu, from China. The most optimistic estimates foreshadow that about 50% of the almost 7000 languages of the world are endangered (Austin & Simpson, 2007; Gordon, 2005; Wurm, 2001); the most pessimistic bring the number of those endangered up to 90% (Krauss, 1992).

Disagreements aside, most specialists concur that the rate at which languages are disappearing is unprecedented, and part of our inability to know what to do is intimately connected to its uniqueness – no historical antecedent tells us what needs to be done. Austin and Simpson (2007: 5) point out that besides being unparalleled, '[l]oss of linguistic diversity on this scale … represents a massive social and cultural loss, not only to the speakers of particular languages but to humanity and science in general.' Scanlon and Singh (2006), referring to Maffi's scholarship (2001), cite colonization, the rise of the nation state, globalization and environmental degradation as the most important phenomena contributing to the disruption of linguistic diversity and a healthy ecosystem of languages (see also Mühlhäusler, 2003).

The fact that many languages are currently endangered has to be juxtaposed with the fact that languages also do fade away more 'naturally' too and that some of the sociolinguistic phenomena accounting for such disappearance is beyond our scope of action. Nevertheless, despite the fact that we might not be able to save all endangered languages, we do not need unnaturally to push for their demise. In a nonkilling society, the danger of languages displacing other languages is diminished because respect for language diversity also signifies that multilingualism is revered and encouraged (Phillipson, 1992). In that case, the need for languages of wider communication (which fulfill a pragmatic purpose) does not need to clash with the desire to build community and preserve local language and culture.

Notice, however, that the term 'preserve' is a tricky one; some preservation efforts are an attempt to catalog and document the language as it was last conceived. Such efforts are to a large degree undertaken by language preservationists when there is no hope of a language surviving (e.g. when the last few speakers are of an advanced age and no young users can be found). The other complementary effort is to preserve a language's ability to continue changing, that is, to continue to be used functionally by a community. In this case, policymaking, which includes sound educational policies, can be an important step to maintaining a language. Smith (2000: 174) argues '... mutual recognition of all linguistic heritage should be the goal. Without such mutual respect and tolerance, internal and international tension and hostilities may result.' While Smith is referring more specifically to languages indigenous to Europe, the researcher's reflection bears relevance to all relations among languages with regional and international status and those used only within smaller communities. It also establishes the connection between disrespect for linguistic diversity and social unrest (see also Fishman, 2001).

Therefore, as individuals interested in upholding the ideals of a nonkilling society, ideals which can be extended to the nonkilling of languages, we should take measures to preserve dying languages, counteract unnatural homogenizing forces when necessary, and recognize the necessity of lingua francas (but strive to establish them alongside local languages). In a nonkilling society, languages and speakers of languages are not purposefully exterminated. There is no effort of an educational, political or armed forces nature to decimate linguistic groups and extinguish their language and culture.

Focus on Diplomacy: Negative Peace

Galtung's (1964) widely known concept of 'negative peace' refers to the absence of war, thus the word 'negative.' Attempts to uphold peace in situations where conflict has already erupted fall within the realm of negative peace. Thus, a great deal of the effort to re-establish and restore peace is undertaken by diplomacy. In a nonkilling society diplomacy is also the primary vehicle used to resolve differences because armed conflict is not an option. The use of language in diplomatic talks is paramount to sustaining a nonkilling paradigm. Gomes de Matos (2001) has created a very thorough list of principles for diplomatic communication to be carried out 'constructively.' Some highlights include:

- Avoidance of dehumanizing language.
- Investment in handling differences constructively.
- Emphasis on language with a potential for peace rather than language employed with a strategic agenda.
- Focus on agreement rather than on polemics.
- Avoidance of pompous language used to separate and hide.

Gomes de Matos (2001) also speaks of the importance of upholding the ideals of diplomacy to the utmost degree and believing in the ability of diplomats and other representatives to pursue their ideals through pacific and honorable means. We would add that in a nonkilling society efforts need to be undertaken and investments made in research and education so that we can increasingly understand which features of languages make them more apt to generating peace in diplomatic talks. As Gomes de Matos (2001) similarly points out, our efforts should not be to take advantage of language to 'win' peace talks but rather to arrive at the kind of understanding which will lead to longer-lasting peace.

Focus on Building Strong Social Institutions: Positive Peace

Galtung's (1964) other form of peace, 'positive peace,' can also be framed in terms of language use. Positive peace refers to the building of strong social institutions, which would help prevent war in the first place. As pointed out elsewhere (Friedrich, 2007b), language, as a uniquely human institution, can largely contribute to this effort because, if individuals see their linguistic rights respected, they will be less likely to engage in violent conflict. Among the necessary steps to building a strong language institution, we can highlight efforts to offer sound, peace-promoting education with a curriculum that emphasizes rights and duties, moral values and ethics, and sound linguistic skills. Complementarily, a solid linguistic structure also relies on access to resources, information and opportunities by speakers of different languages and by users of various dialects. In a nonkilling society, individuals are encouraged to use their language-related skills for the development of society as a whole and for the upholding of human dignity.

Peace educators, peace psychologists, peace linguists and all those concerned with the nonkilling education of language users are urged to exercise their right to be communicatively creative for peaceful purposes and, in such spirit, to add, adapt, expand, refine and probe the practices found most relevant to specific socio-cultural contexts. The overall goal should be to make learners aware of the open-ended practical activities aimed at enhancing one's nonkilling communicative potentialities. Group discussion of results achieved is desirable since communicating is above all an act of sharing. Examples of educational activities that could help fulfill this goal are:

Practice 1. Answering the question 'When do language users kill a person linguistically?' by adding verbs or verb phrases to the list in the suggested answers.
Answer: When they antagonize, coerce, desecrate, frighten with threats of harm, intimidate violently, oppress, provoke in a violent way, exclude from a network.
Practice 2. Answering the question 'How can we humanize a person linguistically?' by adding verbs, phrases or sentences to the list of suggested answers.
Answer: When we refer to him or her in admiring respectful ways. For instance, when we call the person a peacebuilder, an expert, a connoisseur, a creative genius, a luminary, a mentor, a patriot, a prodigy, a role model, a trendsetter, a virtuoso, a visionary, a prophet.
Practice 3. Creating nonkilling sayings (adding to the challenge and the fun by using alliterations. rhyme, etc.). Examples: Wicked words wound the world/ Nonkilling words nourish nonviolence.
Practice 4. Creating constructive alliterations.
Example: Challenge yourself to add other letters:

> AAA = Activate life-Affirming Assertions
> MMM = Monitor Manipulative Messages (in the media)
> TTT = Transform Tension into Tranquility
> VVV = Value a Vital Vocabulary

Practice 5. Creating a poem celebrating the power of nonkilling communication or celebrating the vision of a nonkilling 'planetary patriot', such as Mahatma Gandhi or Johan Galtung.
Practice 6. Creating some entries for a dictionary of encouragement and praise, so conspicuously absent in the literature (there are dictionaries of insults even in Portuguese) or a dictionary of (name of language) for nonkilling purposes.
Practice 7. Paraphrasing inspiring statements by Glenn Paige in his seminal book.
Practice 8. Adapting famous quotations to a nonkilling perspective. For example: Confucius' statement 'Without knowing the force of

words, it is impossible to know men' could become 'Only by knowing the nonkilling power of words it is possible to humanize human beings communicatively.' Another example: 'Beauty is eternally gazing at itself in a mirror' (Kahlil Gilbran, *The Prophet* (1923), 'On Beauty') could become 'A nonkilling society is Humankind swimming in a Sea of Serenity.'

Practice 9. Listing more reasons for not killing, besides those mentioned by Glenn Paige.

Practice 10. Creating practical, transforming communicative alternatives. Examples: Turning an intended threat into a thought-provoking text; turning an intended intimidation into an invitation. In these two examples, the belief in loving one's linguistic neighbor is challengingly applied.

Practice 11. Composing a poem on 'Why more nonviolent people are needed.'

Practice 12. Completing a Nonkilling paradigmatic set with nouns in -ation. Example: nonkilling is (a) moral obligation, spiritual elevation, humanizing conscientization, global salvation, life-affirming education, planetary cooperation, vital preservation, etc.

Practice 13. Engaging your students in this creatively humanizing activity of transforming a repertoire of actions to avoid, with the use of non+noun words in an alphabetically arranged paradigm (for a complete list, see Appendix): nonaggression, nonanimosity, nonantagonism, nonattack(ing), nonbelligerence, nonbrutality, nonbombing, nonbombarding, nonconcealment, nonconspiracy.

When will educational systems include the systematic learning of nonkilling language in their language programs? How can *peace* educators, psychologists, linguists and other peacebuilding humanizers get together and help design *nonkilling language* programs for use in schools at all levels? Herein lies a formidable universal educational challenge. Besides learning to systematize one's nonkilling vocabulary, every planetary citizen could be educated in a critical nonkilling linguistics framework, or in other words, learning to question *killing* uses of language(s). In such spirit, human beings would learn not to *kill* their 'linguistic neighbors' communicatively, by avoiding linguistically violent actions.

If we take the above considerations about education seriously, it becomes clear that a curriculum of nonviolence and peace should be the next step to fostering a nonkilling mentality. Such a curriculum should include teachings about communicative aspects of peace, linguistic ecology, peace linguistic terms and language appropriate for peace-fostering action. Crystal (2004) writes about the importance of fostering a curriculum of peace from the early grades. Alongside teachings about ecology, he explains, young students can receive education on linguistic ecology, linguistic rights and other language-related topics.

Other scholars have addressed the importance of the classroom as a site for all facets of peace education. Gomes de Matos (2002), reviewed by Rector (2003), explains aspects of his 'humanizing pedagogy' which integrates Dell Hymes' (1966) concept of *communicative competence* expanded to include *communicative peace*. He urges the reader to promote language uses, which reflect a preoccupation with the linguistic rights of others as well as respect for the participants in communicative acts regardless of their status or of the communication site.

In Friedrich (2007a & 2007b), an argument is found for the importance of linguistic peace education in promoting encompassing peace and for the appreciation of the classroom as a prime environment for education about peace (Peace Education), education about linguistic forms which enhance peaceful communication (Peace Linguistics) and education about all things sociolinguistic, which impact the ways in which we communicate (Peace Sociolinguistics).

In a nonkilling society, classroom education, as well as lifelong education in all of these language-related aspects of peace, is taken very seriously and given a position of relevance and influence alongside other disciplines.

Respect for Individual Linguistic Choices

The matter of linguistic choices has largely become a political one. Whether one chooses to remain monolingual, embrace bilingualism or multilingualism, or primarily use a language other than one's native tongue has social implications. Furthermore, these choices are usually framed by critics in terms of group membership rather than individual decisions. The widely debated phenomenon of linguistic imperialism (Phillipson, 1992) is an example of how choices are made into political entities. Phillipson argues that the global use of English is a result of linguistic imperialism and that people in the 'periphery' (countries where English is acquired as a second or foreign language) are victims of the imperialistic moves by countries such as the US). However, what theories of imperialism fail to recognize (among the many other elements brought forth by non-supporters of this view) is that whether or not to use English or another language is ultimately a matter of personal choice and that individuals in the so-called periphery make these choices consciously based on weighing the benefits and drawbacks of using a given language[3] (regardless of the original intentions of leaders in the alleged imperialistic countries).

In a nonkilling society, these choices are easier to make because language use is not seen as part of an 'either/or' paradigm in which languages are disseminated (rather than spread) for purposes of domination. Since human beings have an infinite capacity for language acquisition, if we could remove the fear that language could be used as a weapon of domination and subjugation, then individuals would be free to make these choices based on functional needs and personal interests. In that kind of society, we would also be able to abandon all metaphorical references to killing vis-à-vis languages of wider communication, e.g. 'killer languages,' as used by Skutnabb-Kangas (2000) to refer to English and other dominant languages, and we would focus on a language's capacity to bring people together instead while maintaining diversity and a healthy ecosystem of languages.

Respect for Language Change

Languages go through a natural process of birth, change and death. Many times the 'death' of a language actually means that it changed so much that it gave birth to new varieties, which in time became so independent (and ultimately partially or totally unintelligible) that these varieties originate new languages.

Geopolitical phenomena also contribute to such a development because these new languages, by virtue of being embedded in different societies with different state-ruling and outside influences, continue the process of differentiation and modification. That was the case, for example, of Latin and such languages as Portuguese, Spanish, French, Italian and Romanian. Because of spread and then concentration in different regions, different outside influences and even different climates, what was once one (Latin) became many (Romance languages). So languages also die because their functional uses have ceased, no new native speakers exist and, as a consequence, linguistic change within that language becomes stagnated.

Language change will occur whether we like it or not. In a nonkilling society, however, the process of language death is not accelerated unnaturally because linguistic decisions are forced upon language users; nor is language change arbitrarily stopped in the name of language purism. In a nonkilling society, there is no policy impeding users to employ a given language and no violent and unnatural attempts to impact the ecosystem of languages. Legislation exists to protect individual linguistic choice but not to forbid it (see also the section on North Korea in Kaplan & Baldauf Jr (eds), 2003 and the work of Baldauf Jr & Kaplan, 2003).

On the other hand, in a nonkilling society individuals are not punished for engaging in linguistic change processes. Change is not seen as corruption, impurity, or error. It is seen as a natural process of linguistic evolution, one that is brought about by social transformation and/or one which aims at transforming society as well.

Respect for Language Teachers, Language Learners and Users with Special Language Needs

Language learning environments are not immune to some of the problems that plague other spheres of our society. In fact, in many cultures, learning settings suffer from a lack of resources and conditions because education has yet to be recognized in real and concrete terms as an important part of the foundation of any society that values human development. As a result, too often we see teachers working from a position of scarcity, with fewer resources than minimally necessary to perform their duties adequately. In other places, while the infrastructure is adequate, educational decisions are made capriciously or in the name of political interests.

In a nonkilling society, educators are given a prominent social role because members of such a society recognize that violence is to a great degree a result of ignorance. Once we empower (the term is used in the *Freirean* sense) individuals to the point that they feel the safety of being in control of their own future (and education can do just that), they can feel less inclined to resort to violence.

In a nonkilling society, we empower language teachers, and in fact all teachers by offering them a safe, clean and appropriate environment in which to work. We compensate them with fair wages for the important service they provide, and we encourage them to make pedagogical decisions based on sound knowledge and experience, not on their political impact.

By supporting the work of teachers, we directly affect the lives of students and consequently the whole social structure in which they are embedded. The classroom has been shown to be a perfect site for peace education, peace linguistics education and for discussing ecological concerns vis-à-vis languages with the students (Crystal, 2004). Any society that places education anywhere but in a prominent position is bound to be faced with ignorance, which in turn breeds violence, disrespect for human dignity and a relentless sense of underdevelopment. On the other hand, any society that values education and places it among the strategic elements greatly contributing to social justice and dialogue (also as understood by Freire, 1970), is on its way to greater social inclusion and ultimately nonkilling potential.

People with language-related disabilities (e.g. hearing and speech impairment and impediment, paralysis impacting speech production, aphasia) also have a right to education and communication in a dignified manner. We have the opportunity to provide them with tools, adaptive technology and other forms of support to allow them to express themselves, to claim their rights, and to contribute to their communities. In a nonkilling society the rights of all language users, including those with language-related disabilities are not only acknowledged but also, and more importantly, observed.

Upholding of a Vocabulary of Peace rather than One of War

Because language changes both to *reflect* social transformation and to *affect* such transformation (e.g. we created the word 'computer' because society had changed and needed it, but we employ politically correct terms because we want to change society), revising our metaphors to express a preoccupation with peace is a necessary step to becoming nonkilling. In that paradigm, as mentioned elsewhere in this chapter, terms such as 'killer languages' (Skutnabb-Kangas, 2000: 46), which is attributed to Singaporean linguist Anne Pakir, are replaced with peace fostering ones. We stop the 'fight' for human rights and start the educational process toward upholding such rights. We do not scare social groups into action by denouncing the 'war on the middle class' but instead establish a dialogue in which different constituencies in society can pursue social justice.

Within that paradigm we also avoid resorting to 'scare tactics' or appeals to fear to sell products or change one's mind. Everywhere, from political campaigns to television commercials, we emphasize the positive rather than the negative. Fear tactics only make people perceive reality as one of danger rather than harmony, and fear only fuels violence. On the other hand, wise linguistic choices can help change our perception and act more sensibly toward one another.

Forging of New 'Humanizers'

Although linguists kept refining their enumeration of aspects of language, one trait was conspicuously absent: the humanizing nature of language use. Thus, in Gomes de Matos (1994) a plea was made for such a conceptual gap to be filled, since by merely stating that language is human we do not do justice to its humanizing power. Humanizing has to do with both acknowledging language as a system shared by human beings as well as investing in making language humane. Realistically, such characterization of language would be worded so as to cover both its humanizing and dehumanizing power; after all, linguists such as Bolinger (1980) and Crystal and Crystal (2000) have already expressed that language unfortunately can be employed as a weapon (Gomes de Matos, 2006: 159).

Humanizers are persons imbued with the ideals of human rights, justice and peace and who apply such values in everyday interaction. In such spirit, language users, depending on their humanizing or dehumanizing uses of languages, can be described as humanizers or dehumanizers, and of course we need many of the former. While language is a mental marvel for meaning-making used by members of one or more communities in varied socio-cultural contexts for humanizing or dehumanizing purposes, the latter dimension seems to have received the most interest by linguists, especially when dealing with detrimental effects of language use. Jay (1999), for example, adopts a neuro-psycho-social approach for developing a theory of speech that can be explanatory of cursing. Of interest to researchers in nonkilling linguistics is his section on 'Do words wound?' in which he summarizes research on harmful, psychological effects of words on listeners. It seems appropriate for us as humanizers to ask that linguists take further interest in investigating the neurological, psychological and social makings of a theory of language, which explains positive uses of language such as praising, comforting and reassuring. Additionally, we need linguists, psychologists, sociologists and language users in general to employ their time, energy and knowledge in becoming humanizers themselves.

Implications for an Applied Peace Linguistics

An awareness of or conscientization about the need for a nonkilling society not only helps shed light on an equally needed nonkilling linguistics but also provides insights on actions to be implemented, which can contribute to the rise and development of an Applied Peace Linguistics. Among the implications that could be drawn, derived from an initial study of nonkilling linguistics as presented here, five stand out:

(1) Nonkilling linguistics prioritizes nonkilling, peaceful, humanizing uses of languages at the individual, group, community, national and international levels.

(2) Nonkilling linguistics needs to interact with many other fields so as to help build an interdisciplinary approach to nonkilling communication, in varied types of societies.

(3) The preparation of nonkilling linguists calls for a keen perception and thorough analysis of both constructive and destructive ways of interacting intra- and internationally, in face-to-face or online situations.

(4) Nonkilling linguistics can also be thought of as a humanizing realization of an Applied Peace Linguistics. As such, it should be able to join other interdisciplinary areas within the ever-growing macro-field of Applied Linguistics. For an overview of the latter, see Kaplan (2002).

(5) A steady, universal increase in conflict and violence – sometimes deplorably labeled 'justifiable' – calls for immediate nonkilling action by all individuals and organizations committed to protecting and preserving human linguistic health and life.

May we close this section with a plea for the systematic application of principles and practices of nonkilling linguistics all over the world. May Glenn Paige's prophetic, transformative wisdom of a nonkilling society also influence the work of linguists committed to helping improve the living conditions of human beings as language users at the service of universal, communicative peace.

Conclusion

Our list of elements connecting language and peace or language and nonkilling ideas could go on for a long time. It would come to include the importance of empathy and sensitivity to different rhetorical patterns in cross-cultural communication (e.g. Friedrich *et al.*, 2006; Hofstede, 1980; Kaplan, 1966). It would also describe the need to respect and preserve linguistic artifacts, from books to original manuscripts, so often destroyed for political reasons. What all of the elements above and the many still missing from the list have in common is their central role in making human beings, in their uniqueness as producers of complex linguistic expression, feel included, valued and reverenced (see also Lee *et al.*, 2009). Respect for human communication and human dignity is paramount to building a nonkilling society and as such should be pursued in all aspects of our lives.

> *Languages per se are not dehumanizing, lethal, or killing*
> *It is the linguistic choices made by the users that may be*
> *The new, universal challenge school systems could be facing*
> *Has to do with why and how nonkilling language uses should be*
> *May all education systems their citizens prepare*
> *As communicative beings of an unprecedented kind*
> *By assuring them of a human right beyond compare*
> *Learning to use languages for the good of humankind.*

Notes

(1) This chapter first appeared in the volume *Toward a Nonkilling Paradigm* edited by Joám Evans Pim for the Center for Global Nonkilling.
(2) The continuum that extends itself from 'not proficient at all' to 'fully' competent.
(3) It is our belief that in former colonial contexts, the languages first introduced through imperial power have come to change so as to express the culture, values and linguistic choices of their users and have therefore defied the colonial structures that first brought them there (see also Mufwene, 2001).

References and suggested further reading

American Heritage Dictionary of the English Language (2001) Boston: Houghton Mifflin.
Austin, P.K. and Simpson, A. (2007) Introduction. In P.K. Austin and A. Simpson (eds) *Endangered Languages*. Hamburg: Helmut BuskeVelarg.

Baldauf Jr, R.B. and Kaplan, R.B. (2003) Language policy decisions and power: Who are the actors? In P.M. Ryan and R. Terborg (eds) *Language: Issues of Inequality* (pp. 19–40). México, D.F: Universidad National Autónoma de México.

Bender, L., producer and Tarantino, Q., director (2003) *Kill Bill (Vol. I)* [Motion picture]. United States: Miramax Films.

Bolinger, D. (1980) *Language, the Loaded Weapon: The Use and Abuse of Language Today.* London: Longman.

Brosnan, P., Del Rio, R. and Furst, B. *et al.* (2005) *The Matador* [Motion picture]. United States: Stratus Film Co.

Crystal, D. (1999) *The Penguin Dictionary of Language.* London: Penguin.

Crystal, D. (2004) Creating a World of Languages, introductory speech presented at the 10th Linguapax Congress, Barcelona, FIPLV (International Federation of Language Teacher Associations), *World News*, 61: 22–35.

Crystal, D. and Crystal, H. (2000) *Words on Words: Quotations about Language and Languages.* London: Penguin.

Dobbs, L. (2006) *War on the Middle Class: How the Government, Big Business, and Special Interest Groups Are Waging War on the American Dream and How to Fight Back.* New York: Viking Adult.

Elvin, W., Grisham, J. and Lowry, H. *et al.* (1996) *A Time to Kill* [Motion picture]. United States: Regency Enterprises.

Fishman, J. (ed.) (2001) *Can Threatened Languages be Saved*? Clevedon: Multilingual Matters.

Freire, P. (1970) *Pedagogy of the Oppressed.* New York: Continuum.

Fought, C. (2002) California students' perceptions of, you know, regions and dialects? In D. Long and D. Preston (eds) *Handbook of Perceptual Dialectology*, Volume II. Philadelphia: John Benjamins.

Friedrich, P. (2007a) English for peace: Toward a framework of Peace Sociolinguistics. *World Englishes* 26 (1), 72–83.

Friedrich, P. (2007b) *Language, Negotiation and Peace: The Use of English in Conflict Resolution.* London: Continuum Books.

Friedrich, P., Mesquita, L. and Hatum, A. (2006) The meaning of difference: Cultural and managerial homogeneity stereotypes of Latin America. *Management Research* 4 (1), 53–71.

Galtung, J. (1964) A structural theory of aggression. *Journal of Peace Research* 1 (2), 95–119.

Glazier, S. (1997) *Word Menu.* New York: Random House.

Gomes de Matos, F. (1976) *Linguistica aplicada ao ensino de inglês.* São Paulo: McGraw-Hill do Brasil.

Gomes de Matos, F. (1994) A thesis 20 years on: The theory-praxis of the rights of language learners. In L. Barbara and M. Scott (eds) *Reflections on Language Learning: In Honour of Antonieta Celani.* Clevedon: Multilingual Matters.

Gomes de Matos, F. (1996) *Pedagogia da Positividade: comunicação construtiva em Português.* Recife: Editora da Universidade Federal de Pernambuco.

Gomes de Matos, F. (2001) Applying the pedagogy of positiveness to diplomatic communication. In J. Kurbalija and H. Slavik (eds) *Language and Diplomacy.* Msida: DiploProjects.

Gomes de Matos, F. (2002) *Comunicar para o bem: rumo à paz comunicativa.* São Paulo: Editora Ave-Maria, 2002.

Gomes de Matos, F. (2005) 'Using peaceful language.' In *Encyclopedia of Life-Support Systems.* Oxford: EOLOSS Publishers.

Gomes de Matos, F. (2006) Language, peace, and conflict resolution. In M. Deutsch, P.T. Coleman and E.C. Marcus (eds) *The Handbook of Conflict Resolution.* San Francisco: Jossey-Bass.

Gomes de Matos, F. (2008) Learning to communicate peacefully. In M. Bajaj (ed.) *Online Encyclopedia of Peace Education*. See http://www.tc.edu/ centers/epe/.

Gordon, R.G., Jr. (ed.) (2005) *Ethnologue: Languages of the World* (15th edn) Dallas: SIL International. See http://www.ethnologue.com/.

Gottlieb, N. (2008) Japan: Language planning and policy in transition. In R.K. Kaplan and R.B. Baldauf, Jr. (eds) *Asia, Vol. 1: Japan, Nepal and Taiwan and Chinese Characters* (pp. 102–169). Clevedon: Multilingual Matters.

Hofstede, G. (1980) *Culture's Consequences: International Differences in Work- Related Values*. Newbury Park: Sage.

Hymes, D. (1966) Two types of linguistic relativity (with examples from Amerindian ethnography). In W. Bright (ed.) *Sociolinguistics* (pp. 131–156). The Hague: Mouton.

Jay, T. (1999) *Why We Curse: A Neuro-Psycho-Social Theory of Speech*. Philadelphia; Amsterdam: John Benjamins.

Kaplan, R. (1966) Cultural thought patterns in intercultural education. *Language Learning* 16 (1), 1–20.

Kaplan, R.B. (ed.) (2002) *The Oxford Handbook of Applied Linguistics*. New York: Oxford University Press.

Kaplan, R.R. and Baldauf, R.B. (eds) (2003) *Language and Language-in-Education Planning in the Pacific Basin*. Dordrecht: Kluwer.

Krauss, M. (1992) The world's languages in crisis. *Language* 68 (1), 6–10.

Lee, N., Mikesell, L., Joaquin, A.D.L., Mates, A.W. and Schumann, J.H. (2009) *The Interactional Instinct: The Evolution and Acquisition of Language*. Oxford: Oxford University Press.

Maffi, L. (2001) *On Biocultural Diversity: Linking Language, Knowledge, and the Environment*. Washington: Smithsonian Institution Press.

Maltin, L. (2008) *2009 Movie Guide*. New York: Signet.

Mufwene, S.S. (2001) *The Ecology of Language Evolution*. Cambridge: Cambridge University Press.

Mühlhäusler, P. (2003) *Language of Environment, Environment of Language: A Course in Ecolinguistics*. London: Battlebridge.

Paige, G. (2009) *Nonkilling Global Political Science*. Honolulu: Center for Global Nonkilling.

Phillipson, R. (1992) *Linguistic Imperialism*. Oxford: Oxford University Press.

Random House Webster's College Dictionary of the English Language (1995) New York: Random House.

Rector, M. (2003) Review of Frascisco Gomes de Matos, *Comunicar para o Bem: rumo à paz comunicativa, Hispania. Journal of the American Association of Teachers of Spanish and Portuguese* 86 (3), 529–531.

Saunders, H.H. (1999) *A Public Peace Process: Sustained Dialogue to Transform Racial and Ethnic Conflicts*. New York: St. Martin's Press.

Scanlon, C. and Singh, M. (2006) Theorizing the decline of linguistic diversity. *International Journal of the Sociology of Language* 182, 1–24.

Smith, R.K.M. (2000) Preserving linguistic heritage. A study of Scots Gaelic. *International Journal of Minority and Group Rights* 7 (3), 173–187.

Skutnabb-Kangas, T. (2008 [2000]) *Linguistic Genocide in Education - Or Worldwide Diversity and Human Rights*? London: Longman Orient.

Wurm, S. (2001) *Atlas of the World's Languages in Danger of Disappearing*. Paris: UNESCO.

Appendix

Here is the full list of terms positivized by the prefix NON. We invite you to add your own contribution to the list.

NONaggression, nonanimosity, nonantagonism, nonattack(ing), nonatrocity

NONbelligerance, nonbrutality, nonbombing, nonbombarding

NONconspiracy, nonconcealment

NONdestrution, nondevastation, nondiscrimination, nondomination

NONexploitation, nonexplosion, nonextermination, nonescalation

NONfrightening, nonfear

NONgore

NONharassment, nonhatred, nonhumiliation

NONintimidation, noninvasion, nonintervension

NONjeopardy, nonjeer

NONKILLING

NONlethality

NONmurdering

NONnegativity, nonnegativism

NONoffending, nonoppression

NONpersecution

NONquarreling

NONretaliation

NONslandering, nonslaughter

NONterror(ism), nontorture, nonthreat(ing)

NONusurpation

NONVIOLENCE, nonvillainy, nonvillification, nonvengeance

NONwar, nonwarmaking, nonwickedness

NONxenophobia

NONzealotry

2 Softening or Intensifying Your Language in Oppositional Talk: Disagreeing Agreeably or Defiantly

Noriko Ishihara

Introduction

In today's globalized world, when mediators attempt to advance national interests in diplomatic negotiations, they are bound to encounter conflicts and disagreements. Much of the peace-keeping effort aimed at resolving or avoiding conflicts may be made by way of language in the context of diplomacy. This chapter explores how concepts from the area of pragmatics come together with the notions of openness, cultural sensitivity and compassion promoted in the area of peace linguistics (also see LeBlanc and Friedrich & Gomes de Matos, this volume) and demonstrates how this awareness can be used for the professional development of diplomats.

To maintain or cultivate amicable relationships, trust and openness in diplomatic negotiations on the one hand and to further the aim of peaceful conflict resolution on the other, negotiators must first develop openness to different cultures, acceptance of different points of view, tolerance for alternative histories and above all, the willingness to deal with various cultural and professional practices (Friedrich & Gomes de Matos, this volume). Simultaneously, the language that nonviolent negotiators may wish to use for diplomatic purposes would be required to strike a fine balance between being direct and indirect (e.g. Bjørge, 2012), assertive and empathetic, and persuasive and compromising. In this challenging meaning-making endeavor, it is evident that verbal and nonverbal language assumes a crucial role if negotiators are to be contextually and interculturally tactful. Diplomats must not only be professionally persuasive and constructive in producing language, but they are also required to understand their international counterparts' true intentions, which may be conveyed in a non-literal and culturally-laden manner.

The aim of this chapter is threefold: (1) to raise diplomat readers' awareness of mitigated (softened) language in oppositional talk in English in relation to the concepts of *face* and *(im)politeness*; (2) to promote an understanding of the interconnectedness of language and context; and (3) to develop meta-cognitive strategies for analyzing expert diplomats' use of English for diplomatic purposes. First, relevant concepts from pragmatics, the study of socio-culturally preferred use of language, will be introduced and explored in the context of oppositional talk. You will be guided to notice how mitigators (softeners) are used in complex interactions with crucial contextual factors such as the relative social status of the interactants and the distance between them as well as the stakes involved in the immediate context.

In the second part of the chapter, excerpts of spoken and written English will be presented in a case study format. The samples will be drawn from empirical studies of *face-threatening* oppositional talk such as disagreement. You will be invited to analyze potential face threats embedded in these contexts as well as *face-saving* or *face-aggravating* language strategies (see the following section for more information about these terms).

Finally, I will introduce a 'learner-as-researcher/ethnographer' approach (Roberts *et al.*, 2001; Tarone & Yule, 1989) consisting of observing oppositional talk used by expert diplomats or that represented in language corpora. You will have opportunities to analyze the language in relation to the context and consider why certain strategies were selected in that context. You will also be invited to interview any effective diplomats regarding the justifications for their own language choices, which will provide you with an insider perspective of these experts in their community.

Face and (im)politeness

In considering diplomatic negotiations, the notions of *face* and *(im)politeness* in pragmatics become useful. According to Goffman (1967), face is the positive social value or public identity that we strive to maintain both for ourselves and each other in interaction, a concept similar to respect or dignity. Based on Goffman's work, Brown and Levinson (1987) argue that in general, the participants in an interaction tend to share a wish that face be respected, but because face is always at risk, constant attention and the cooperation of all interactional participants during interaction is necessary (i.e. *facework*). Face is what we protect, defend, save (Bremner, 2013) and possibly even threaten and aggravate (Locher, 2012), deliberately or inadvertently. *Facework* can be achieved through the various strategies language users employ, allowing them to negotiate their place in a given social practice, their human dignity, and integrity in interaction with others.

Goffman (1967) distinguishes between the concepts of *positive* and *negative politeness*, though in this context positive and negative are not related to good and bad. To address an interactional partner's negative face wants, which consist of the need for independence and freedom, we use *negative* politeness strategies, typically by showing deference, emphasizing the importance of the other's time and freedom, or apologizing for an imposition or interruption. For example, to convey that we need a ride, we might say or write from a seemingly negative or pessimistic standpoint: *Ms Miller, I'm sorry to be a bother, but you couldn't possibly give me a ride on Wednesday, could you*? In this example, the use of a formal term of address (*Ms*), an expression of apology (*I'm sorry*), a negative and courteous outlook (*couldn't possibly*) and linguistic construction (the question form), and a tag question (*could you*) can be viewed as manifestations of negative politeness. In expressing oppositional views such as disagreements, challenges, denials, or accusations, negative politeness strategies function to minimize potential face threats (i.e. discomfort, embarrassment, or humiliation caused by the oppositional views) through the use of a variety of mitigating devices and stance markers (see the following section for more detail and examples).

On the other hand, to satisfy others' positive face wants, which consist of the need to belong, to be connected, and to share a common goal, we use *positive* politeness strategies, that is, we show solidarity and emphasize that both speakers are close, that they have a common goal (Goffman, 1967). As a result, language may often be positive in the sense of optimistic and forward-looking, as in: *Hey, pal, what if I rode with ya on Wednesday*? or *Jen, you wanna pick me up then*? Here, positive politeness is manifested in the use of an informal term of address *pal*, and a casual attention getter, a positive outlook and linguistic construction, and a friendly tone created by informal word choices and contractions. In oppositional talk, since disagreement essentially suggests disapproval, it is likely to threaten positive face needs. While expressing oppositional stance, interactional partners often stress commonality of opinion and inclusiveness within a general membership in an attempt to preserve the speaker's face wants by way of positive politeness strategies such as jokes, partial agreement and the use of inclusive pronouns such as *we* and *us* (Holtgraves, 1997; Johnson, 2006; Malamed, 2010). The following section will introduce a series of face-saving strategies used in an attempt to ease a potential threat.

The preference and acceptability of the choice of positive or negative politeness strategies in a given context varies across cultures and communities. Spanish and Greek cultures, for example, are oriented toward positive politeness in general, whereas British culture tends to rely more extensively upon negative politeness (Johnson, 2006). Preferred politeness strategies can also vary between varieties of the same language spoken within a single country. In Johnson's (2006) study of British West African and British White English, the former tended to emphasize positive politeness through interpersonal involvement, for example by frequently overlapping during both agreement and disagreement. In contrast, the latter displayed a stronger concern for negative face favoring non-imposition, for example by resorting to mitigation, hesitation and self-deprecation.

Misunderstandings are bound to occur where there are differences in politeness orientations. Unfortunately, these differences can readily be attributed to flaws in personality rather than to differences in communication styles, possibly leading to negative cultural stereotypes and animosity. In diplomatic negotiations involving interactants from a wide range of cultural backgrounds, positive politeness strategies that may be intended as amicable, friendly and pleasant may be misinterpreted as intrusive, overly informal, or simply rude. In turn, well-intended negative politeness strategies could create the misguided impression as being overly distant, alienating, or aloof. In diplomatic negotiations, being aware of various cultural orientations in the use of politeness strategies may be conducive to remaining open and compassionate toward other cultures that may prefer different linguistic and social conventions.

While these expressions of mitigation are associated with certain levels of (im)politeness and (in)directness, it is important to note that no language is in itself polite or impolite, formal or informal, direct or indirect and so forth (Locher, 2012; Locher & Watts, 2005). As interactional partners discursively co-construct meaning within contextual constraints, what seems acceptable and tactful in one context may be interpreted as excessively formal or informal in another. In assessing the acceptability or appropriateness of certain linguistic expressions, it is crucial to consider the impact and constraints of the local context since the context influences language choices while language use itself simultaneously shapes the context as interactants negotiate meaning.

The context of communication can be analyzed from the perspectives of the following three contextual elements:

- Social status (*Is your interactant of higher or lower status than you, or is he or she equal to you?*)
- Distance (*How distant or close is the other party?*)
- Stakes involved (*What stakes are involved in the given situation and its purpose? How serious or consequential is the outcome of the interaction?*) (adapted from *power, distance* and *imposition*, Brown & Levinson, 1987)

Social status refers to the relative social hierarchy of the listener or the addressee from the perspective of the speaker or the writer. *Distance* concerns perceived relative social and psychological familiarity between the speaker/writer and the listener/reader. Perceived distance may depend on the actual extent of the acquaintance (e.g. whether it is someone you have not met before or know slightly, well, or intimately) as well as on the perceived sense of familiarity due to certain social and psychological factors based, for example, on social identities and personalities. *Stakes involved* refers broadly to the seriousness, significance, or gravity of the situation and the outcome of the interaction. For example, how serious is the offense that might be caused by a conflict? What stakes, from very high to very low, are likely to be involved in the matter in question? How urgently does the conflict need to be resolved? What is the significance of the topic, and how much does it matter to the listener/addressee for the speaker/writer to agree or disagree on the given topic (e.g. low stakes involved in disagreeing about someone's taste for clothing vs. high stakes involved in disagreeing about a nation's diplomatic policy)?

As the diagrammatic representation of visualized contextual factors below shows, if the situation falls to the left of the three continua of social status, distance and stakes involved (e.g. as in speaking to someone of lower status whom the speaker knows well on a topic of little importance), the language is likely to be less polite, more informal and more direct. For example, two coworkers of equal social status who are familiar to each other may say, *Can you pass me that folder, please*? for a low-stake request with a minor imposition. Conversely, the level of politeness, formality and directness increases to the right side of the continua (e.g. as in interacting with someone of higher status with whom the speaker is not familiar in a high-stakes situation). If the same employee is asking a new boss a larger request, he or she may use more formal, more polite and less direct language like *I am sorry to bother you, but you couldn't possibly review this file for me this afternoon, could you*?

These three factors are likely to interact dynamically with each other in determining the level of (im)politeness, (in)directness and (in)formality of the language that is expected or socially preferred in each local context. Such language use assists in shaping the context, while the context simultaneously influences the language choices of the speaker/writer. This is an interconnected fluid process in which (im)politeness

Figure 2.1 Visualization of major contextual factors

and face are negotiated in the social practices in which the interactional partners engage, and the negotiated norms and expectations are acquired, shared and challenged in the process of socialization. As a result, deeply intertwined with the notions of face and (im)politeness are the language choices made in the negotiation. We now specifically explore the language of disagreement below.

The Language of Disagreement

Before embarking upon an in-depth data-based discussion on the language of disagreement in English, it may be beneficial to first look back on your own language use in your dominant language(s), especially if it is not English. In what contexts are you likely to express opposition in your language and culture? What are some consequences of oppositional talk? When would you rather avoid disagreeing with others and for what reasons? Does the choice of linguistic forms used for disagreeing change depending on your relationship with the other person? Are there some topics that are more appropriate to disagree on (Malamed, 2010)? In other words, how does the topic influence your choices and language of disagreement in your language or culture?

Turning now to actual English data, let us take an inductive approach by first presenting some excerpts representing disagreement sequences in a case-study format. Before reading the interpretation that follows each excerpt, you are invited to closely observe the potential face threats embedded in these contexts and analyze precisely what language forms function as mitigators, in what ways, and how successful the interactions seem to be. All excerpts are taken from naturally-occurring language data drawn from business and family discourses, representing the authentic language choices of users of English in New Zealand and the United States (see a later section for language strategies used by speakers of other World Englishes). Although these contexts may seem unrelated to English for diplomatic purposes, the aim is to enhance your awareness and ability to analyze specific language strategies as well as to develop critical insights into the interpretation of the context.

Case 1: The first conversation takes place in a regular monthly team meeting in a commercial production company in New Zealand (Riddiford & Newton, 2010: 72–73). The excerpt below involved approximately 11 employees in addition to the owner of the company. Jason and Rob are both managers. Jason has been working with the owner for a long time, while Rob is a relative newcomer to the company. The meeting is chaired by Jason. Read the transcript below, paying special attention to how Jason and Rob disagree with each other and why they use the particular language that they do given the context.

Excerpt 1

> **Turn 1. Rob**: If you bear the cost of their mistake, their screw ups, well, of course they'll leave it for you to find these.
>
> **Turn 2. Jason**: Well, it's not so much that, it's just we need to transfer that responsibility back to them.
>
> **Turn 3. Rob**: Well then, we need to transfer the cost of it back too.
>
> **Turn 4. Jason**: Yeah, but in, um, reality the industry has allowed that to happen, Rob.
>
> **Turn 5. Rob**: Not all.
>
> **Turn 6. Jason**: Um, for the most it has. And...

As Jason and Rob are both managers, they can be considered of roughly equal social status, although Jason may be viewed as being of slightly higher status due to his longer career in the company. We may imagine that the two feel relatively close to each other as they probably work together on a daily basis. The fact that this is a monthly meeting coupled with the general level of informality in word choices (e.g. *screw ups*) lead us to infer that the stakes involved in any disagreements are rather low.

Taking a close look at the language of disagreement, we first notice the frequent use of hesitation markers, such as *well* (Turns 1, 2 and 3) and *um* (Turns 4 and 6). While *preferred* agreement (e.g. *I agree*) is typically accompanied by an immediate response that shows harmony and serves to maximize its effect, hesitation or a pause causes a delay and indicates that the response is *dispreferred* and to be distanced (Pomerantz, 1984; Schegloff, 2007). A delay device can signal an upcoming disagreement or rejection, psychologically prepare the hearer for the imminent face threat, and minimize the potential offense. For instance, a response to *let's go for a drink* may be an immediate acceptance, *sure, why not?* without a delay (a *preferred* response). Agreement components alone can occupy an entire turn, and this serves to emphasize the agreement. In contrast, a hedged response, *well, you know* or an initial pause can alert the interactional partner to the fact that the speaker is taking time to prepare a face-saving response and perhaps a rejection of the invitation is in order. Or this delay can at least imply a lack of enthusiasm (a *dispreferred* response). Thus, a dispreferred turn tends to be structurally more complex and elaborate so as to downplay the intensity of the disagreement. The mitigation that prefaces a disagreement, such as delay devices including those described here and below, can soften the impact of the disagreement and help maintain the interactant's face.

Other mitigating devices include the use of *just*, a mitigated negation and *yeah, but*. In Turn 2, Jason expresses an alternative view to that stated by Rob in Turn 1 by saying, **well**, it's **not so much** that, it's **just**... Here, in addition to the delay device *well*, Jason softens the negation of Rob's idea (i.e. by saying **not so much** *that* rather than **not at all** *that*), and employs the cost-minimizer *just*, which functions to make the offense appear less serious and less face-threatening. A similar avoidance of the outright negation of Rob's idea can be found in Rob's Turn 5 and Jason's Turn 6. In these turns, by saying *not all* and *for the most*, each speaker leaves room for the other to be correct, thereby saving mutual face.

Finally, two more mitigating strategies can be found in Turn 4: the delay device *um*, and the address, *Rob*. The informal address expresses familiarity and camaraderie, thus attending to the addressee's positive face. Similarly, Jason's Turn 4 displays the combination of multiple mitigating devices. Besides the delay device *um*, the initial *yeah* expresses partial agreement and softens the upcoming disagreement prefaced by *but*.

The close analysis above reveals that both speakers use one or more face-saving devices in each of their turns even in this everyday situation in which the stakes involved in the disagreement may be viewed as rather low. While the perceived need for mitigation may appear minimal in this close working relationship, it is notable that both speakers frequently disagree indirectly or *off record* (Brown & Levinson, 1987) in the presence of nine other employees. Although the case above is based on a business context, what may be applicable to diplomatic talk is the role of language use in shaping collaborative dialogues and the value of mutual respect as well as the language representing such respect in building collaborative relations.

If you are a facilitator in a language program teaching English for diplomacy, you could introduce an activity in which participants practice softening their language of disagreement. You may prepare a list of controversial arguments (e.g. *we can justify the use of animals for research; climate change has nothing to do with global warming; enforcing a minimum wage increases unemployment*) and have a group of diplomats debate against each other. They can be encouraged to use face-saving language when they express oppositional stance as if they were speaking to someone of higher status they have just met. You may take close notes of their language to provide feedback later or tape the session for the participants' self- and peer-assessment. The participants can also come up with contentious topics in diplomacy on which they exchange their views.

Returning to the Case 1 interaction, alternatively, the speakers could have selected an aggravating strategy, intensifying the disagreement and being *bold on record* (Brown & Levinson, 1987). For example, instead of saying *not all* in Turn 5, Rob could have argued directly (e.g. *you're absolutely wrong*), had he perceived a need to stress and upgrade the force of his disagreement. We now turn to an example of more direct oppositional talk from the seemingly less relevant context of an everyday family interaction.

Case 2: In the following example, we examine language use in a conversation between an Italian-American mother and her teenage daughter at their home in the eastern United States. In the case below, the daughter previously used a particular medication for her skin trouble and as the mother now shows similar symptoms, she asks her daughter about the experience. The daughter maintains that her mother should not assume that they share the same problem (adapted from DelPrete & Box, 2014).

Excerpt 2

Turn 1. Mother: How long did it take to go away? How long did yours last?

Turn 2. Daughter: I don't know. It's different. Mom, it's… (walks away from mother) Why don't you call them up?

Turn 3. Mother: Because no one's in the office now.

Turn 4. Daughter: Then you have to wait.

Turn 5. Mother: No, but when you got the benzoyl peroxide thing going on, how long did you…

Turn 6. Daughter: It's not going to be the same thing with you, okay?

In Turn 2, the daughter appears to refuse to answer her mother's question in Turn 1 as she sees her condition as different from her mother's. There is no delay or mitigation in her language, and she physically and psychologically distances herself from the mother. Moreover, she even offers the unsolicited advice that her mother call the doctor's office with rather direct language. Unsolicited advice like this could be highly face-threatening in American culture in general, as it is often associated with criticism (Houck & Fujimori, 2010) and may be viewed as intrusion to privacy. In Turn 3, the mother disagrees by offering a reason indirectly without uttering a direct *no*. The daughter then offers another piece of unsolicited direct advice in an irritated tone of voice in Turn 4. Again, there are no mitigating devices in her language, such as hesitation, delays, pauses, or epistemic stance markers (e.g. *I think, in my opinion*). In Turn 5, the mother neglects the daughter's advice and persists with her previous question. The daughter's reaction in Turn 6 interrupts the mother's question in Turn 5, which expresses her unrestricted and unconcealed frustration.

The lack of mitigation in a series of direct disagreements represented in this example may be characteristic of a conversation between intimates such as family members, as in this particular case. Here, the mother and the daughter continue in a sharp tone of voice for a few more turns until the teenage daughter concludes the conversation by saying *you're so annoying*. Thus, the consequence of this type of direct disagreement appears to be upgraded personal criticism and unresolved conflict. It may be that the daughter's resistance, along with a lack of mitigation in her language, is linked to her identity construction (DelPrete & Box, 2014). Her direct opposition can be viewed as a face-*enhancing* act on her part rather than as a face-*threatening* one. Direct conflict and disharmony may be part of everyday interactions between parents and their teenage children, and as a result of their intimate relationship, minor cases of dissonance may be expected and can even be regarded as a positive sign of an open, uninhibited and trusting relationship.

In fact, it has been pointed out that on certain specific occasions in English, disagreements or rejections could serve as a preferred rather than a dispreferred response (Dippold, 2011; Fujimoto, 2010, 2012; Kotthoff, 1993; Pomerantz, 1984; Schegloff, 2007). For example, disagreements may be expected or even welcomed in academic discussions and debates as critical insights that could further the discussion or analysis. Moreover, an immediate and strong rejection of self-deprecation (e.g. A: *I'm so dumb!* B: *No, you are not*) would be interpreted as an affable preferred response.

While the conflict and disharmony that resulted from the language exchange in this example may not be desirable in diplomatic negotiations, it would be productive to ponder contexts in which direct language strategies such as those used here could be acceptable or tolerated. Between whom, about what topics, and on what occasions can unmitigated disagreements and a direct expression of oppositional stance be seen as appropriate, constructive, or even desirable? Are there any situations in which straightforward or jocular disagreements are tolerated or even encouraged in negotiations, small talk, or social events related to diplomatic duties? If so, why are direct expressions acceptable or even preferred in those contexts?

In a study of language use in authentic business contexts (Williams, 1988), speakers who were familiar with each other were occasionally quite blunt and neither excessively polite nor explicit. The speakers sometimes said *no, no, it's...* or simply, *but...* without prefacing their disagreement through partial or tentative agreement, as in *yes, but...* Likewise, members of an international consulting corporation in Hong Kong sometimes disagreed quite explicitly in English, using little mitigation with each other or even the CEO, actively co-constructing their expert identities and dynamically negotiating co-leadership (Schnurr & Chan, 2011). However, such preferences for direct language use may not apply to more formal occasions involving higher-stakes confrontations in diplomacy.

In order to instill the contextually dependent language use in diplomat participants in a language program, a facilitator could provide an additional classroom activity. In small groups, participants can come up with as many expressions of disagreements as possible within a short time and write each of them down on separate Post-it notes. The expressions should range from mitigated face-saving utterances (e.g. *I wasn't entirely sure about that; I could be wrong, but...*) to unmitigated face-aggravating lines (e.g. *no way; that's absolutely untrue*). When these are reported back to the whole class, the Post-it notes can be rearranged in the order of assertiveness or formality, and the class can discuss in what contexts each expression can be appropriate and why. This activity can serve to expand the participants' repertoire of linguistic strategies as well as to fine-tune their awareness of language-context relationship. The list of expressions provided below in a section following Case 3 may be a useful resource for this activity.

Case 3: Unlike the two cases of interactive spoken discourse discussed above, Case 3 involves written language data deriving from the medium of email. Returning to a business context, Catherine, the writer of the following group message, is the purchasing officer discussing the addressees' plan to buy new digital hardware (Riddiford & Newton, 2010: 75).

Excerpt 3

> I happen to oversee the buying of equipment for the department and in that capacity I have to remind you that that [sic] this purchase does not fit in with our department needs. Sorry to pour cold water on your plan.
>
> Catherine

In this case, Catherine appears to have more power in this particular context than those of the email recipients as she is entitled to make executive decisions for purchasing equipment in her department. There may be different levels of perceived social and psychological distance between Catherine and her colleagues. However, given the lack of formalities such as opening and closing salutations and an initial address, we can safely infer that Catherine must work relatively close to them or that this type of email communication is part of their work routine and does not require formality. Catherine appears to be aware of the stakes involved in this disapproval as she discusses it directly and apologizes for not being able to comply with her colleagues' proposal.

In terms of language, Catherine effectively uses two expressions, *happen to* and *have to* in order to minimize the force of her institutional power over her addressees in an attempt to equalize their perceived social status and distance. By stating that she *happens to* oversee the purchase of equipment, she attempts to minimize the face threat as it is rather by chance that she holds this executive power over them. She continues by saying that she *has to* remind them of a disappointing decision, implying that even if she wished to accommodate the addressees' purchasing plan, her departmental position would not permit her to do so despite her will. These strategies may be interpreted as attending to addressees' positive politeness wants as these linguistic devices allow the writer to emphasize common goals, collegiality and circumstances shared by all parties involved. Catherine also employs the negative politeness strategy of apologizing in response to the addressees' perceived need for independence and freedom. By doing so, she shows her awareness of potential stakes involved in her disapproval of the proposal and attempts to soften the potential offense.

In addition, let us consider the impact of the written medium of email on the discourse structure of this message. How are written disapprovals or disagreements likely to be different from those in interactive spoken discourse? One noticeable feature is that the written mode typically involves less turn-taking due to the asynchronous nature of the medium (i.e. replies are often not immediate). Discourse components that would be broken into multiple turns in speech may be bundled up together in one message, making the written message lengthier and more comprehensive than a spoken turn. For example, instead of presenting details of the reasons for the disagreement in multiple turns, an extended explanation is readily available in a single message. Even a word of apology may be included in an attempt to preempt the feeling of animosity. As a result, a more comprehensive and less interactive written message is likely to permit less room for immediate negotiation of the issue in question.

It is also important to consider the level of formality in the contexts of written and spoken discourse. The written discourse represented in this particular email example can be interpreted as a mode halfway between spoken and written, since many of the characteristics of more or less formally written messages are omitted. There are no mailing addresses and dates as in formal letters, no opening salutations (e.g. *Dear all*), no greetings (e.g. *Hi everyone*), no closing salutations (e.g. *best wishes*, *regards*) and no formal signature (e.g. complete name of the writer, title and contact information). On what occasions are these formalities required or favorable and why? In what other contexts are these unnecessary and for what reasons?

After such an awareness-raising discussion, a facilitator of a language program may wish to consider designing a classroom activity focused on written disagreements. You could begin by asking the participants to rewrite the Case 3 email with a maximum level of formality and mitigation and discuss who the writer and the addressee might be. A more challenging activity would be to ask the participants about the oppositional stance they take against their bosses or colleagues and have them write a letter or email expressing these views. The participants can send their mock emails of disagreements to you and to each other for feedback.

In summary, below is a list of linguistic strategies for expressing disagreement (Bjørge, 2012; Bouton *et al.*, 2010; Brown & Levinson, 1987; Cheng & Tsui, 2009; Fujimoto, 2012; Holtgraves, 1997; Houck & Fujii, 2013; Johnson, 2006; Locher, 2004; Maíz-Arévalo, 2014; Malamed, 2010; Pomerantz, 1984; Schnurr & Chan, 2011; Stalpers, 1995). Most of these are exemplified in the language data excerpted above in Cases 1–3, although there are a few that have not yet been introduced.

Mitigated disagreement

- Delay that prefaces the dispreferred response of disagreement through:
  - A pause or silence (e.g. A: *God, isn't it dreary.* B: [**pause**] *It's **warm** though.* [adapted from Pomerantz, 1984: 70])
  - Hedging (e.g. *um, uh, er*)
  - Discourse marker (e.g. *well, but and, or*)
- Understaters and downtoners (e.g. *maybe, perhaps, just, possibly, seem, a little, kind of, sort of*)
- Modal verbs (e.g. *I **may have to** admit, it **could** be that..., there **might** be some...*)
- Partial or conditional agreement often followed by *but* (e.g. *yeah but..., I would agree except that...*[Holtgraves, 1997: 230])
- An expression of appreciation (e.g. *thanks for that, but.., nice try, but...*), or apology/regret (e.g. *I'm sorry, but.., I'm afraid*) often followed by *but*
- A request for clarification by way of a question or repetition (e.g. A: *What's the matter with you? You sound happy.* B: ***I sound happy***? A: *Yeah.* B: ***No.*** [adapted from Pomerantz, 1984: 71])
- An explanation, justification, or elaboration serving as added support (e.g. *I don't er I don't agree at all with this **because furniture is the kind of product that people are not used to buy** [sic] **without seeing it and touching it*** [Bjørge, 2012: 420])
- A personal reason (e.g. *it's just me, but...*) or a personal view (e.g. *I think, I guess, I feel, it seems to me that...*) serving as a qualifier/softener
- Claiming a lack of access, knowledge, or ability (e.g. *I don't know, it's hard to say, I'm not sure but.., I can't express what I'd like to say* [Houck & Fujii, 2013: 126])
- Asking for others' opinion (*What do you all think?*)
- Emphasis on common ground (e.g. *you know*)
- Self-deprecation (e.g. *it's a dumb idea but...*[Holtgraves, 1997: 233])
- Indirect (off-record) disagreement
  - Joking (e.g. *sure, if you enjoy crowds and street gangs* [Malamed, 2010: 204])
  - Metaphors, irony and rhetorical questions (e.g. *What can I say?* [Brown & Levinson, 1987: 223])
  - Laughter
  - Gaze avoidance and posture
  - Unmitigated disagreement
- No delay and mitigating devices (e.g. *no that's not possible, no we can't* [Bjørge, 2012: 422])
  - Aggravated disagreement

- Upgraders/intensifiers (e.g. *absolutely, not at all, really, so, such, quite*) without delay and mitigating devices

Note that as these categories are borrowed from several different frameworks (e.g. speech act theory and conversation analysis), some of the concepts may overlap even without identical labels and it may be difficult to draw clear lines between them. You may also notice that agreement and disagreement are not necessarily dichotomous opposites but that they can be better situated along a continuum (e.g. disagreement with partial or conditional agreement) (Johnson, 2006; Mori, 1999). Moreover, what is left out of this list includes unstated disagreement or an oppositional stance the speaker elects not to express (Cheng & Tsui, 2009; Pomerantz, 1984), as well as the postponement of oppositional talk until later (e.g. choosing not to express disapproval or disagreement at the time of the face-to-face conversation but doing so afterward by phone or email).

Note also that mitigating devices are sometimes used in combination and can occur within a speaking turn or can be dispersed beyond one speaking turn or written sentence or paragraph, as shown in Cases 1 and 2 above. Studies of disagreement sequences have revealed how disagreement may be communicated, expanded upon, and abandoned in extended discourse. After disagreement is expressed as a way of challenging the preceding speaker's viewpoint, the response may be a concession resulting in a revision of the original claim, a reassertion or expansion of the original assertion, a topic shift abandoning the argument altogether, or a use of ambiguous language to restore harmonious rapport (Cheng & Tsui, 2009; Houck & Fujii, 2013). Disagreement can also elicit collaboratively constructed elaboration on the original idea and be followed by co-constructed alignment between cooperative conversation partners (Houck & Fujii, 2013).

The Language of Disagreement Employed by Global English Users

This section addresses the diverse ways in which the language of disagreement is used globally. Needless to say, English is not owned by its native speakers alone but used also as a *lingua franca* by many translingual users around the globe. Naturally, the language of disagreement adopted by native English speakers as well as World Englishes users may vary (Bouton *et al.*, 2010; Cheng & Tsui, 2009; Johnson, 2006) under the influence of complexly intertwined factors including the speakers' languages, cultures, identities, affiliations and personal dispositions. As mentioned earlier, we should note that even within the same language spoken within a country, the choice of rapport management strategies may show distinct tendencies across cultural communities.

In Bjørge's (2012) study of disagreement expressed by speakers of World Englishes from 14 countries during simulated negotiations conducted by business students, over two-thirds of the speakers' disagreement was mitigated. Among the mitigating strategies used, a great majority (96%) included delays, followed by added support (an explanation of the disagreement), or a combination of both. The negotiators' lexical choices largely relied on basic vocabulary items including *but, no, think, problem* and *well*. Although the speakers of World Englishes hardly used the expressions recommended by the 13 textbooks examined, they used the mitigation strategies they were exposed to implicitly through the textbook examples (e.g. using partial agreement followed by *but* and modal verbs). As there was no alignment between the linguistic choices of the speakers and their nationalities or cultural orientations, the author argues that the business students appeared to be participating in a community of practice (Lave & Wenger, 1990; Wenger, 1998), relying on a shared repertoire in the joint speech event.

Bjørge (2012) also argues that the speakers of World Englishes seemed to be aware of the intrinsic face-threat involved in the disagreement and thus utilized mitigation strategies to avoid the risk of communication breakdown. At the same time, as the negotiators constantly engaged in competition for the floor in the negotiations, excessive indirectness and elaborate expressions of politeness may have been viewed as a potential deterrent to effective negotiations and rapport management. Consequently, the speakers strove to strike a fine balance between linguistic directness and indirectness. These findings appear consistent with existing research characterizing World Englishes. World Englishes users may prefer rather straightforward expressions and avoid excessive politeness, indirectness, idioms and cultural innuendos, focusing on negotiating the main message and letting less important errors or details pass (i.e. a consensus- or message-oriented approach, Dippold, 2011).

Studies investigating the language of disagreement used by native speakers of American English found that although disagreement was expressed less frequently than agreement, when speakers did disagree, they tended to make linguistic attempts to minimize its challenge or threat (Pearson, 1986, cited in Bardovi-Harlig & Salsbury, 2004; Salsbury & Bardovi-Harlig, 2001). Similarly, learners of English (or speakers of World Englishes) were also found to largely avoid disagreement (Bardovi-Harlig & Salsbury, 2004; Beebe & Takahashi, 1989; Salsbury & Bardovi-Harlig, 2001). However, when they did disagree, their level of mitigation and (in)directness varied. For example, Salsbury and Bardovi-Harlig (2001) closely observed three beginning-level learners of English in authentic interactions and found that they developed a different range of linguistic strategies over time with which to mitigate disagreements through modal verbs (e.g. *can, could, will, would, might, have to* and *need to*), modal adjectives (e.g. *possible, necessary*) and lexical verbs (e.g. *think, hope,* and *prefer*) and used them at different frequencies. Even though a strong linguistic foundation did assist these learners in their pragmatic development, grammatical ability alone did not guarantee pragmatically preferred language use. With a larger corpus of longitudinal data from L1 learners of English from eight countries, the same authors propose a potential sequence of acquisition of disagreement, starting from direct disagreement using primarily *no* to mitigated disagreement prefaced by agreement, then to postponement of disagreement within a turn, and finally progressing to its postponement across a sequence of turns or even avoidance of disagreement altogether (Bardovi-Harlig & Salsbury, 2004). The learners' disagreements became more elaborate over time following these acquisitional stages. Therefore, depending on the status of your diplomat interactants, they may use a different repertoire of these linguistic strategies in expressing opposition.

On the other hand, even with advanced linguistic competence, some learners may progress little on the pragmatic acquisitional stage, employing unmitigated disagreement in a context where some sort of softener is generally expected. Some of the advanced Japanese learners of English in Beebe and Takahashi's (1989) studies often overtly criticized the proposal made by their assistants or even bluntly disagreed with their boss on a business plan in simulated written tasks. Moreover, some of the mitigating devices used by the learners were perceived as confusing or less effective. These findings contradict the prevalent stereotypes that Japanese speakers are indirect and American speakers explicit (Beebe & Takahashi, 1989). The misconception that may have been held by the learners that disagreement can or should be directly conveyed in English may have derived from the equal emphasis given to agreement and disagreement by many textbooks (Pearson, 1986, cited in Salsbury & Bardovi-Harlig, 2001), a stereotypical overgeneralization sometimes induced through instruction (Beebe & Takahashi, 1989), and limited linguistic ability (Ishihara & Cohen, 2010, see Chapter 5 for classroom activities for language learners). If your interactants are using fewer mitigation devices than expected in their oppositional talk, you may give them the benefit of the doubt and assume that their language choices may be influenced by factors related to the language instruction they have received rather than by a flawed personality or an offensive national character.

Developing Meta-Cognitive Strategies for Analyzing Expert Diplomats' Language

In the preceding sections, we have taken a close look at naturally occurring data in order to focus on the language of oppositional talk in both business and family contexts and reviewed some of the variation found in the language of disagreement used by English speakers around the globe. Although language textbooks abound, it has been found that their recommendations do not necessarily align with the actual language use in World Englishes (Bjørge, 2012; Williams, 1988). For example, in a study of language use in authentic business contexts (Williams, 1988), native English-speaking business associates taking part in informal meetings were found to carefully build up their main points with elaboration rather than expressing their views in isolation, as was often done in the language textbooks investigated in this study. In addition, there rarely seems to be a need to be overly explicit in authentic contexts. Speakers often implicitly express agreement using nods or *mmm*. In fact, expressions such as *in my opinion*, a typical expression taught in language textbooks as a way of presenting one's view, could even carry the potentially face-threatening implication of 'I know what **your** opinion is, but **mine** is...' (Williams, 1988: 52, emphasis hers).

Thus, it would be productive for us to study naturally-occurring language data rather than commercially available textbooks alone, and preferably data collected in diplomatic negotiations. Needless to say, the confidential nature of diplomacy does not normally allow public access to such data, however. To compensate for this lack of authentic language resources and to help develop everyday skills for further autonomous professional development, a 'learner-as-ethnographer' (Roberts *et al.*, 2001; Tarone & Yule, 1989) approach may be useful. In this approach, you are encouraged to observe verbal and non-verbal expressions of oppositional stance used in a community of diplomats as if you were an ethnographic researcher. By doing so, you expose yourself to the social conventions in operation in the community of practice (Ehrenreich, 2009; Lave & Wenger, 1991; Wenger, 1998). You are then given a chance to jointly engage in a community in which a specific repertoire of linguistic and non-linguistic behaviors, expectations, rights and obligations are shared. Emulating and negotiating such community practices will help you develop socially constructed expertise as you become an increasingly more functional and valued member of that community.

To follow this approach, you are encouraged to first identify an expert diplomat who would function as your model or mentor. You can closely observe his or her behavior, the verbal and non-verbal language of oppositional talk, disagreements in particular and analyze the language in relation to the context in which it is used. It would be productive to focus especially on the relationship between language and context to consider why the diplomat selects certain strategies in that specific context. In doing this, you may ask yourself questions such as these:

- In what contexts does the expert diplomat choose to express oppositional stance? Why? When does the diplomat opt out of disagreements, suppress his or her feelings, or conceal his or her stance? For what purposes and reasons?

- What verbal and non-verbal language strategies of mitigation does the diplomat use in different contexts? How effective do you think they are in the given context? Why?
- How does the diplomat exploit different technologies and future opportunities for negotiations? For example, does the diplomat ever delay expressing disagreement until a subsequent round of negotiation? How does he or she select appropriate media for expressing disagreements and resolving conflicts? (e.g. avoiding email for confidentiality, calling or meeting someone face-to-face to ensure communication of subtleties, selecting email for maintaining records of the thread of conversation)?
- How might the diplomat adjust the selection of strategies according to the cultural and linguistic background of the interactants? For example, when does he or she rely more on rather direct, uncomplicated language forms and strategies? In what cultural contexts are more elaborate verbal and non-verbal expressions and formalities chosen and for what purposes?
- Between whom, with what topics, and on what social occasions may the diplomat see unmitigated disagreements as appropriate, constructive, or even desirable? Why? What might be some positive or negative consequences of unmitigated disagreements?
- In case of stagnant negotiation or communication breakdown, what does the diplomat do and say to deal with the situation? What is his or her repertoire of repair strategies, and how effectively are these used in the context?
- What exactly does the diplomat do to attempt to further improve his or her linguistic and non-linguistic expertise in negotiation?

In addition to expert diplomats, you are invited to observe any immediate peer diplomat or even your international interactants in diplomacy. Exposure to the language of oppositional talk can provide relevant input, potentially facilitating the development of effective strategies (Bardovi-Harlig & Salsbury, 2004). You may also wish to interview any effective diplomats regarding their justifications for and perceptions of their own language choices. This would provide you with an insider (emic) perspective of these well-positioned diplomats, which will most likely help you cultivate your own meta-cognitive strategies for using language and how to develop these further in the community of practice.

Alternatively, if you are working independently and are unable to identify expert diplomats as models, you may analyze the language of agreement and disagreement in electronic language corpora such as the British National Corpus (BNC) and the Michigan Corpus of Academic Spoken English (MICASE) (available free of charge at: http://www.natcorp.ox.ac.uk and http://lw.lsa.umich.edu/eli/micase/index.htm, respectively).

For example, you may search hedging expressions such as *well it seems, well of course,* or *well actually* in a corpus (Malamed, 2010) to investigate how these mitigation devices are used in authentic spoken or written discourse, with whom, and at what level of stakes (see Tottie, 2014 for such a study). This will help you analyze the potential consequences of language choices, including how the hearer responds to the disagreement and how mitigating devices may facilitate the speaker's rapport management. You may also wish to explore through language corpora how certain verbs (e.g. *agree, disagree, concur, oppose, hesitate*) or adverbials (e.g. *wholeheartedly, heartily, with some reservation, reluctantly*) are used in expressing support or opposition.

Furthermore, it would be important to develop meta-cognitive strategies for analyzing your interactant's language and culture as well as for monitoring the effects of your own language choices as you express your stance, especially opposition, in diplomatic negotiations. Because effective communicators often accommodate to each other's level of politeness (Holtgraves, 1997), it would be valuable for you to become aware of your interactant's use of politeness strategies. How do your interactants use language, that is, how formal or informal and direct or indirect do they tend to speak? What type of politeness (positive or negative) do they tend to rely upon? How do they seem to position themselves in negotiating with you? How do your interactants receive your view expressed through your language choice? How well does your language serve your purpose, and are there any points of improvement for future negotiations?

Conclusion

In this chapter, we first considered oppositional talk in relation to the pragmatic notions of *face* and *(im)politeness* as well as the way in which these are constructed locally by interactants in negotiation. We then closely examined three cases of the authentic expression of oppositional stance from business and family contexts, and observed the interrelationship between various contextual factors and the (in)formality, (in)directness, and (im)politeness of the language used in order to develop an explicit understanding of how language and context inform each other. Finally, some meta-cognitive strategies for analyzing the verbal and non-verbal behaviors of expert diplomats, peer diplomats, your interactants and yourself were suggested for further development of English for diplomatic purposes. This chapter intends to encourage an explicit awareness of the role of both mitigating language devices and unmitigated direct disagreement in the process of rapport management. Our choice of language can have direct consequences for our interactions in each local context. Face and (im)politeness constructed through our verbal and non-verbal behavior can negotiate, for example, our social and cultural identities, mutual respect and trust and power construction at the inter-personal level in our everyday interactions and can potentially have an impact on peace-making and the development of amicable international relations in diplomatic contexts.

References

Bardovi-Harlig, K. and Salsbury, T. (2004) The organization of turns in the disagreements of L2 learners: A longitudinal perspective. In D. Boxer and A.D. Cohen (eds) *Studying Speaking to Inform Second Language Learning* (pp. 199–227). Clevedon: Multilingual Matters.

Beebe, L. and Takahashi, T. (1989) Do you have a bag?: Social status and patterned variation in second language acquisition. In S. Gass, C. Madden, D. Preston and L. Selinker (eds) *Variation in Second Language Acquisition: Discourse, Pragmatics, and Communication* (pp. 103–125). Clevedon: Multilingual Matters.

Bjørge, A.K. (2012) Expressing disagreement in ELF business negotiations: Theory and practice. *Applied Linguistics* 33 (4), 406–427.

Bouton, K., Curry, K. and Bouton, L. (2010) Moving beyond 'in my opinion': Teaching the complexities of expressing opinion. In D. Tatsuki and N. Houck (eds) *Pragmatics: Teaching Speech Acts* (pp. 105–123). Alexandria, VA: Teachers of English to Speakers of Other Languages.

Bremner, S. (2013) Politeness and face research. In C.A. Chapelle (ed.) *The Encyclopedia of Applied Linguistics* (pp. 1–6). Oxford: Blackwell Publishing.

British National Corpus (BNC) (2016) See http://www.natcorp.ox.ac.uk (accessed 7 February 2016).

Brown, P. and Levinson, S. (1987) *Politeness: Some Universals in Language Use.* Cambridge: Cambridge University Press.

Cheng, W. and Tsui, A.B.M. (2009) 'ahh ((laugh)) well there is no comparison between the two I think': How do Hong Kong Chinese and native speakers of English disagree with each other? *Journal of Pragmatics* 41 (11), 2365–2380.

DelPrete, D.L. and Box, C. (2014) 'What are you doing?': Exploring mother-adolescent daughter (dis)harmonious discourse. Paper presented at the annual conference of the American Association for Applied Linguistics, Portland, OR.

Dippold, D. (2011) Argumentative discourse in L2 German: A sociocognitive perspective on the development of facework strategies. *The Modern Language Journal* 95 (2), 171–187.

Ehrenreich, S. (2009) English as a lingua franca in multinational corporations – Exploring business communities of practice. In A. Mauranen and E. Ranta (eds) *English as a Lingua Franca: Studies and Findings* (pp. 126–151). Newcastle upon Tyne: Cambridge Scholars Publishing.

Fujimoto, D. (2010) Agreements and disagreements: The small group discussion in a foreign language classroom. In G. Kasper, H.T. Nguyen, D.R. Yoshimi and J.K. Yoshioka (eds) *Pragmatics and Language Learning. Volume 12* (pp. 297–325). Honolulu, HI: University of Hawai'i, National Foreign Language Resource Center.

Fujimoto, D. (2012) Agreements and disagreements: Novice language learners in small group discussion. Unpublished doctoral dissertation, Temple University Japan.

Goffman, E. (1967) *Interaction Ritual: Essays on Face-to-Face Behavior.* New York: Pantheon.

Holtgraves, T. (1997) Yes, but...: Positive politeness in conversation arguments. *Journal of Language and Social Psychology* 16 (2), 222–239.

Houck, N. and Fujii, S. (2013) Working through disagreement in English academic discussions between L1 speakers of Japanese and L1 speakers of English. In T. Greer, D. Tatsuki and C. Roever (eds) *Pragmatics & Language Learning. Volume 13* (pp. 103–132). Honolulu, HI: University of Hawai'i, National Foreign Language Resource Center.

Houck, N. and Fujimori, J. (2010) 'Teacher, you should lose some weight': Advice-giving in English. In D. Tatsuki and N. Houck (eds) *Pragmatics: Teaching Speech Acts* (pp. 89–103). Alexandria, VA: Teachers of English to Speakers of Other Languages.

Ishihara, N. and Cohen, A.D. (2010) *Teaching and Learning Pragmatics: Where Language and Culture Meet.* Harlow: Pearson Education.

Johnson, F. (2006) Agreement and disagreement: A cross-cultural comparison. *BISAL* 1, 41–67.

Kotthoff, H. (1993) Disagreement and concession in disputes: On the context sensitivity of preference structures. *Language in Society* 22 (2), 193–216.

Lave, J. and Wenger, E. (1991) *Situated Learning: Legitimate Peripheral Participation.* Cambridge: Cambridge University Press.

LeBlanc, J. (this volume) Compassionate English communication for diplomatic purposes.

Locher, M.A. (2004) *Power and Politeness in Action: Disagreements in Oral Communication.* Berlin: Mouton de Gruyter.

Locher, M.A. (2012) Situated impoliteness: The interface between relational work and identity construction. In B.L. Davies, M. Haugh and E.A.J. Merrison (eds) *Situated Politeness* (pp. 187–208). London: Bloomsbury Publishing.

Locher, M.A. and Watts, R.J. (2005) Politeness theory and relational work. *Journal of Politeness Research: Language, Behaviour, Culture* 1 (1), 9–33.

Maíz-Arévalo, C. (2014) Expressing disagreement in English as a lingua franca: Whose pragmatic rules? *Intercultural Pragmatics* 11 (2), 199–224.

Malamed, L.H. (2010) Disagreement: How to disagree agreeably. In A. Martínez-Flor and E. Usó-Juan (eds) *Speech Act Performance: Theoretical, Empirical and Methodological Issues* (pp. 199–215). Amsterdam: John Benjamins.

Michigan Corpus of Academic Spoken English (MICASE) (2016) See http://quod. lib.umich.edu/cgi/c/corpus/corpus?page=home;c=micase;cc=micase (accessed 7 February 2016).

Mori, J. (1999) *Negotiating Agreement and Disagreement in Japanese.* Amsterdam: John Benjamins.

Pearson, E. (1986) Agreement/disagreement: An example of results of discourse analysis applied to the oral English classroom. *I.T.L Review of Applied Linguistics* 74, 47–61.

Pomerantz, A. (1984) Agreeing and disagreeing with assessments: Some features of preferred/dispreferred turn shapes. In M. Atkinson and J. Heritage (eds) *Structures of Social Action: Studies in Conversation Analysis* (pp. 57–101). Cambridge: Cambridge University Press.

Riddiford, N. and Newton, J. (2010) *Workplace Talk in Action: An ESOL Resource.* Wellington: School of Linguistics and Applied Language Studies, Victoria University of Wellington.

Roberts, C., Byram, M., Barro, A., Jordan, S. and Street, B. (2001) *Language Learners as Ethnographers.* Clevedon: Multilingual Matters.

Salsbury, T. and Bardovi-Harlig, K. (2001) 'I know what you mean, but I don't think so': Disagreements in L2 English. *Pragmatics and Language Learning, Volume 10* (pp. 131–151). Urbana Champaign, IL: University of Illinois, Division of English as an International Language.

Schegloff, E.A. (2007) The organization of preference/dispreference. In E.A. Schegloff (ed.) *Sequence Organization in Interaction: A Primer in Conversation Analysis* (pp. 58–96). Cambridge: Cambridge University Press.

Schnurr, S. and Chan, A. (2011) Exploring another side of co-leadership: Negotiating professional identities through face-work in disagreements. *Language in Society* 40 (2), 187–209.

Stalpers, J. (1995) The expression of disagreement. In K. Ehlich and J. Wagner (eds) *The Discourse of Business Negotiation. Volume 8: Studies in Anthropological Linguistics* (pp. 275–289). New York: Mouton de Gruyter.

Tarone, E. and Yule, G. (1989) *Focus on the Language Learner.* Oxford: Oxford University Press.

Tottie, G. (2014) On the use of *uh* and *um* in American English. *Functions of Language* 21 (1), 6–29.

Wenger, E. (1998) *Communities of Practice: Learning, Meaning, and Identity.* Cambridge: Cambridge University Press.

Williams, M. (1988) Language taught for meetings and language used in meetings: Is there anything in common? *Applied Linguistics* 9 (1), 45–58.

3 Compassionate English Communication for Diplomatic Purposes

Josette LeBlanc

Introduction

Navigating misunderstandings can be quite a daunting task in one's first language, let alone one's second language. For those with the added pressure of being a professional and culturally sensitive representative of one's country, the importance of being considerate and precise with language, especially when they face an interpersonal challenge, becomes even greater. Although composure may be one quality required of diplomats, this does not mean strong degrees of emotion will not come into play during a diplomatic transaction (Russell, 2004). At any given moment one might enter a dialogue where personal frustration becomes too strong to hide. Perhaps a conversation instigates anger in one of the speakers. What is the next step? Whether you are a consular officer or an ambassador, understanding emotions and their impact on behavior and communication can be a great asset.

Part of this understanding begins with the development of a language and literacy of emotions. The language offered in the following pages will provide diplomats and staff in diplomatic posts with a starting point for developing this literacy via a communicative approach I call Compassionate English Communication (CEC). The basic premise behind the acquisition of this form of literacy is that if we can look at English – or any other language for that matter – through the lens of compassion, one is more likely to arrive at an outcome that serves everyone involved in the conversation. Therefore, via CEC we learn about what it means to be compassionate individuals, and we also learn how to communicate this compassion in English.

While not all diplomats may have compassionate understanding as their final aim, it is nonetheless valuable to make this a viable option for those who hold this outlook. With the growing amount of research that links language use to adaptations in physiological (Petrie et al., 2004; Stanton et al., 2000), emotional (Hart, 2013; Kircanski et al., 2012) and cognitive states (Boroditsky, 2011), this topic becomes even more pertinent to people involved in diplomatic communication. As discussed in Chapter 1 of this volume, language can be a peacemaking tool. Research proves this is indeed plausible, and with this knowledge, diplomatic leaders have a choice: to communicate from a place that perpetuates violence, or communicate from one that promotes peace. Some may view using language as an instrument of peace as a utopian ideal. However, I see this as an opportunity to have a mature discussion about one's linguistic impact on the world, and part of this discussion will continue in this chapter.

What follows are strategies in the form of three language activities that will guide facilitators in helping individuals in diplomatic posts develop compassionate language in English. Prior to the description of these strategies, the chapter begins with an explanation of my definition of CEC, and how it came into being based on my experience and research. After that, facilitators and learners will receive an introduction to the general layout of the activities before arriving at an in-depth, step-by-step description of each activity. Then, the chapter will turn to how compassionate communication relates to persuasion, a skill essential to the field of diplomacy (Kurbalija, 2013). Once the activities have been analyzed, the chapter will conclude with a reflection on the implications of developing CEC within the wider context of diplomacy. Facilitators should consider English as a *lingua franca* from Chapter 4 and World Englishes from Chapter 5 as the communicative contexts for the strategies presented in the activities.

Defining Compassionate English Communication: Experience and Research

Experience: Part 1. Working in the field of TESOL (teaching English to speakers of other languages) teacher education in South Korea, I see a great need for helping Korean teachers of English understand the language of compassion. Not only is this important for the work they will do with their students, but also for their professional development. Through my experience with teachers, I have observed that there are two components to this development: an interpersonal component and a reflective component.

Part of the in-service training in teacher preparation programs involves teaching in front of peers, and after each lesson, teachers must often give and receive feedback. Due to the nature of the training program, this is usually done in their second language, English, which can add more stress to an already tense moment. When I work with teachers, to support a feedback process that is fruitful and less intimidating, prior to the lessons they will teach, I lead awareness sessions based on helping them understand how to provide constructive feedback. These sessions also relate to the reflective aspect of the teaching experience. After each lesson they teach, teachers need to reflect on what happened and think of ways they might change their approach in the future. Awareness sessions help them learn how to reflect from a space of openness rather than from a space where they are being overly self-critical. A way to help them understand these aspects of the interpersonal and reflective components is to bring their attention to the ways in which they may come across as critical of and judgmental toward themselves and others. Not only does this shine a light on their overall understanding, but it also helps them internalize the linguistic form, meaning, and use of how these components are articulated in English. All this is done by helping them see through the lens of Compassionate English Communication (CEC).

Defining Compassionate Communication

Prior to defining how English is integrated into this communicative model (this is discussed in the section titled, Adding 'English' to Compassionate Communication), I will provide an explanation of my approach to Compassionate Communication (I will continue to use the CEC acronym). I define CEC as the ability to reflectively (to the self) and interpersonally (to someone else) communicate with both compassion and empathy (using those as communicative lenses) so that the people involved can arrive at conclusions that connect to everyone's needs. This is done via a process of describing a given scenario, analyzing it via empathic understanding, and finally making a compassionate SMART-Choice request based on the information that has been uncovered (see Figure 3.1).

Description. In order to begin this communicative process, it is helpful to take a step back prior to engaging in empathic analysis and

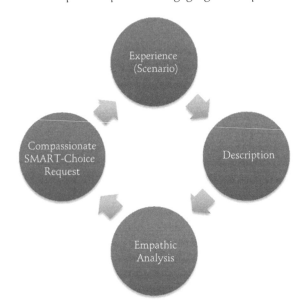

Figure 3.1 Compassionate communication

compassionate SMART-choice requests. One way to do this is to describe without judgment what you observed during a given scenario. By doing this, you give yourself the space you need to be fully present to the moment and mindful of the experience you were or are involved in. Mindfulness, according to the definition of The Greater Good Science Center at the University of California, Berkeley (2014),

> ... involves acceptance, meaning that we pay attention to our thoughts and feelings without judging them—without believing, for instance, that there's a 'right' or 'wrong' way to think or feel in a given moment. When we practice mindfulness, our thoughts tune into what we're sensing in the present moment rather than rehashing the past or imagining the future.

Rather than getting swept away in an emotional reaction, by tuning into the present moment, or by also paying attention to the details of a past scenario, you have a better chance of creating an empathic connection, and as a result, communicating compassionately.

Empathic Analysis. The empathy I refer to in my definition of CEC connects to what Paul Ekman (2003: 180) calls 'cognitive empathy,' that is, the ability to identify what someone is feeling. In relation to the interpersonal communication mentioned above, this cognitive process requires the ability to engage in active listening and empathic analysis. Through active listening, a listener has the task of focusing on listening for the speaker's expressed or hidden feelings and needs. Empathic analysis refers to reflecting on a scenario or experience, and guessing the possible feelings and needs that may have been alive during that moment. Both active listening and empathic analysis can be referred to as empathic understanding. Humanistic psychologist, Carl Rogers explains how this looks in a relationship between a therapist and their client. According to him,

> This means that the therapist senses accurately the feelings and personal meanings that the client is experiencing and communicates this understanding to the client. When functioning best, the therapist is so much inside the private world of the other that he or she can clarify not only the meanings of which the client is aware but even those just below the level of awareness. This kind of sensitive, active listening is exceedingly rare in our lives. We think we listen, but very rarely do we listen with real understanding, true empathy. Yet listening, of this very special kind, is one of the most potent forces for change that I know. (Rogers, 1995: 116)

One can easily substitute the words 'therapist' and 'client' with those of any other human role, such as English teacher or diplomat. What Rogers calls 'personal meanings,' I call 'human needs'. By connecting to the need, a person can offer a deeper level of empathy. Abraham Maslow (1970), the psychologist who brought great attention to the existence and importance of human needs, might say that each feeling is motivated by a need. For example, a feeling of loneliness may be the sign of a need for love (1970: 20), and a sense of discouragement could be related to the need for competence not being satisfied (1970: 21). This recognition of the interrelatedness between feelings and needs is what I define as empathy, and may appear as follows.

Perhaps a client is arguing with an employee at a diplomatic office because a form he sent to the embassy has been misplaced, and now he has to fill it in once again.[1] By privately and silently empathizing, the diplomat may come to the conclusion that this person feels frustrated. By connecting this feeling to the client's possible need for clarity, and by sharing this sense, the diplomat can cause the client to feel even more understood. In this state, the scenario moves from one of defensiveness and aggression, to one of openness and possibility (Rogers, 1980). This final stage of possibility, which I call compassionate SMART-choice request, will be explored in the following section.

As previously mentioned, I also recognize one component of CEC as the ability to communicate to oneself with empathy and compassion, which could be called self-empathy and self-compassion (Neff, 2011; Rosenberg, 2005). I recognize self-empathy as the ability to identify one's own feelings and needs during a given scenario. Since compassion can be defined as 'the feeling that arises in witnessing another's suffering,' which 'motivates a subsequent desire to help' (Goetz *et al.*, 2010), I define self-compassion as observing feelings and needs within one's self (self-empathy), with the intention of wanting to relieve one's own suffering.

According to Kristin Neff's (2011) research, self-compassion has three principal aspects: self-kindness, common humanity, and mindfulness. Neff defines them as follows:

> Self-kindness refers to the tendency to be caring and understanding with oneself rather than being harshly critical or judgmental. Common humanity involves recognizing that all humans are imperfect, fail and make mistakes. Mindfulness involves being aware of one's painful feelings in a clear and balanced manner so that one neither ignores nor obsesses about disliked aspects of oneself or one's life.

Whereas empathy requires that we see the feelings and needs in another, compassion moves us to take action based on those needs. In relation to self-compassion, the act of simply providing empathic understanding may be one of these actions. When we look at our own feelings and needs, we provide ourselves with the compassion necessary to be able to care for another. This may be especially important for charged situations where the natural reaction may be to blame the other person, and even to blame ourselves.

For example, if I feel hurt when someone yells at me, one strategy for making sense of the moment might be to blame myself, 'That client is yelling at me because I'm an idiot. I'm horrible at my job.' From this state of self-blame, I may not have the energy to adequately care for the client. I may just do what I need to do to get him out of the office, thereby coming to a decision that may not have both our best interests in mind. A similar result may occur if I am blaming the other, 'What an idiot! Can't he fill in a simple form?' From here, it may be easy to jump to a conclusion that pushes the client to do something he may not want to do, and as a result cause a state of defensiveness rather than mutual understanding.

A metaphor that is often used to compare the necessity of being compassionate with oneself is one of a parent putting on their oxygen mask before putting on their child's during airline malfunctions. In order to be strong enough to save their child's life, the parent must have enough oxygen. If the masks were put on the other way around, both parent and child might perish. Likewise, perhaps during an interaction with a counterpart, a diplomat feels irritated and recognizes he/she needs understanding. By recognizing this within himself/herself rather than ignoring it, the person creates an opening. This happens as a result of self-compassion's mindfulness factor, or what clinical psychologist, Daniel J. Siegel (2010) calls, mindsight:

> Mindsight is a kind of focused attention that allows us to see the internal workings of our own minds. It helps us to be aware of our mental processes without being swept away by them, enables us to get ourselves off the autopilot of ingrained behaviors and habitual responses, and moves us beyond the reactive emotional loops we all have a tendency to get trapped in. (Siegel, 2010: 2)

In the openness that mindfulness provides as a result of accepting the feelings that exist in the moment, we are given 'the power to recognize restrictive judgments and release our minds from their grip' (Siegel, 2010: Chapter 2, p. 20). For the diplomat, now having the clarity that self-compassion affords, the client or counterpart becomes less an adversary, and more someone who is facing challenges similar to their own.

Compassionate SMART-Choice Request. Because compassion invites us to help, it is the compassion we hold within a challenging reflective or interpersonal dialogue that moves us from simply understanding the feelings and needs to wanting to create a change. This change comes in the form of making requests, or what I call compassionate SMART-choice requests. These requests are akin to the 'desire to help' that compassion encourages since they invite the speaker and the listener to take action. Another reason these requests can be considered compassionate is that they are grounded on a foundation of empathic understanding. According to the *Oxford Learner's Dictionary* (2014), a request involves 'the action of asking for something formally and politely.'

Putting the formality and politeness aside for a moment – this will be explored further in the final activity, *Role-play: Compassionate SMART-Choice Request* – the key point here is that we are asking for something to happen rather than demanding that something happen. This means that whether I am requesting an action of myself or of someone else, the person receiving the request is able to either decline or accept it. This is where the word 'choice' comes into play in the term 'compassionate SMART-choice request'. The acronym SMART (Randall & Thornton, 2001) – specific, measurable, achievable, realistic, time-bound – matters when we look at the elements within a request which will make it first, understandable, and secondly, doable.

A request that is specific outlines a concrete, observable action. A vague request for the diplomat's client may be, 'Would you fill in the form correctly?' The client's interpretation of 'correctly' may be very different from the diplomat's. 'Can you fill in the form from questions 1 to 5?' is much more concrete and observable. It is possible to observe questions 1 to 5 being filled in, but it may be a bit challenging to observe, 'correctly.' The use of 'questions 1 to 5,' also makes the request measurable since we are clear about the amount being requested. To make it even more measurable, we might add a due date. 'Can you fill in the form from questions 1 to 5 by next Friday?' not only becomes measurable and more specific, it also becomes time-bound. When we consider the specific, measurable, and time-bound aspects of a request, we should also reflect on whether or not it is possible for the person to do it. Questions you may ask yourself are: is this within their/my control? Does this person (or do I) have the skills or knowledge to accomplish this request? When taking these questions into consideration, you are closer to making the request achievable and realistic. By then adding a question form to these SMART factors, 'Would you be able to fill in the form from questions 1 to 5 by next Friday?' you not only make the request more understandable and doable, but you also give the person receiving it the choice to either decline or accept it. Choice is vital because whenever we feel pressured to do something, we are not engaging from a place of compassion. This is important to remember whether you are making a request of yourself or someone else. Additionally, when you make a request of yourself, you might inadvertently frame it as a statement rather than a request. We will also examine this in the final activity.

The Observer of CEC. Although it may be obvious, it is worth noting that the Compassionate English Communication (CEC) process – description, empathic analysis, SMART-choice request – will always happen through the lens of the first person, *I*. I bring this up because it reminds us where CEC language begins: from our perspective, and not from someone else's. In order to participate from these lenses, a person needs to see himself or herself as an observer. This will become clearer in the *Introduction of Activity 1: Description versus Evaluation*. Whether we are reflecting on ourselves or if we are trying to communicate with someone, by acknowledging ourselves as the observers of a scenario, we are less likely to judge and blame; as a result, we are better prepared to communicate compassionately. To put this in perspective, and also to summarize CEC, it may be helpful to refer to Table 3.1 below.

Background Research

The steps described in my definition of CEC, as well the English language described further in the chapter, are the basis of the three language activities presented further on. Each step and its elements are an integration of the research and classroom experimentation I have done with other forms of Compassionate Communication (CC), and the reflective practice approach called the Experiential Learning Cycle. CC is a term used in various ways by different educators. Newberg and Waldman (2012) teach 12 steps for speakers and listeners to practice in order to arrive at CC.

The first six steps help the interlocutors get into the mindset of compassion. These include: relaxing, staying present, cultivating inner silence, increasing positivity, reflecting on your deepest values, and accessing a pleasant memory. The next step, observing nonverbal cues, supports the speaker and listener by giving them the chance to notice

Table 3.1 Summary of Compassionate English Communication

Experience (Scenario) as Seen through the Lens of I *(the observer)*

Self (Introspective)	Other (Interpersonal)
Description:	**Description:**
What *I* noticed, saw, or heard in the scenario	What *I* noticed, saw, or heard in the scenario
Empathic Analysis:	**Empathic Analysis:**
What *I* feel and need in relation to the scenario	What *I* think the other may feel and need in relation to the scenario
SMART-Choice Request:	**SMART-Choice Request:**
The action *I* request myself to take	The action *I* request the other to take

what the other is truly thinking and feeling. This provides the foundation for proceeding into the discourse, which includes expressing appreciation, speaking warmly, speaking slowly, speaking briefly, and listening deeply. Although my definition of CEC/CC[2] implicitly relates to some of these steps, namely staying present and listening deeply, and that I acknowledge this mindful approach is very beneficial to individuals in diplomatic posts, my work is closely linked with another framework for CC. This framework, developed by Marshall Rosenberg, is called Nonviolent Communication (NVC), a name often used in tandem with the term CC. NVC encourages users to give and receive messages in ways that promote mutual understanding and compassion. To arrive at this end, Rosenberg (2005: 7) suggests a four-step process (see Table 3.2) we can implement when we listen to or when we want to give a message we think might be hard to hear.

NVC has had the greatest impact on my concept of empathic analysis and compassionate SMART-Choice Request. Via my studies and practice of NVC, I learned that empathy is more than recognizing how we feel; it is about finding the underlying need behind the feeling (Cunningham, 2009; Gill et al., 2009; Rosenberg, 2005). The need is what encourages us to take action, and feelings are the outward expression of our reaction to the needs being met or unmet. It is also via this framework that I recognized the importance of making requests that are choice-based rather than demand-based. When a request is made from an empathic mindset, the listener will feel as if they have a choice, and will not feel as if they are being blamed or punished (Rosenberg, 2005: 85).

However, in my work with teachers, my first intention was not to promote mutual understanding and compassion. My immediate need for the course was to help teachers reflect on the teaching experiences they would encounter. Therefore, when I began teacher training, I started with a framework that focused less on feelings and needs and focused more on systematic inquiry.

Table 3.2 Nonviolent communication

---

1. Observation – Reflect the message back or simply observe the moment by using language that is descriptive rather than evaluative.
2. Feelings – After making the observation, guess the feelings that the other person may be feeling, or identify the feelings that you are feeling.
3. Needs – Identify the possible needs or values that may be behind the other person's feeling, or the needs or values you have in relation to that feeling.
4. Request – Once the first three steps have been articulated, it may be time to make a clear, specific and doable request of the other person, or if it was an internal process, of yourself.

My education in TESOL teacher training includes a rigorous reflective practice founded on the Experiential Learning Cycle (ELC), and so when it was time to present the concept of reflection to English teachers, I also used the ELC. The ELC is a term used to describe the conscious reflective process one takes in order to engage in the inquiry of an experience, and in essence, to learn (Dewey, 1938; Kolb, 1984; Lewin, 1948; Rodgers, 2002a). This cycle (see Figure 3.2 below) offers steps toward this learning process, which can be divided into four parts: experience, description, analysis, and intelligent action or experimentation (Rodgers, 2002b). Description requires a detailed observation of the experience that instigates the reflective inquiry. One must then analyze the experience by considering all the facets discovered in the description. The intention is to try to exhaust all the possible reasons and explanations for the actions and reactions that occurred in that scenario (Rodgers, 2002a: 854). From the view of the ELC, by analyzing the scenario from a variety of perspectives, you will be able to come to an informed decision for your next course of action. Then, from this informed space, it is possible to experiment with an intelligent action plan that will be the foundation of the next experience (Rodgers, 2002a, 2002b). It is intelligent in that it is based on a thoughtful observation and analysis of the experience.

Experience: Part 2. This was the reflective approach I used in the awareness sessions with the interpersonal (giving and receiving feedback)

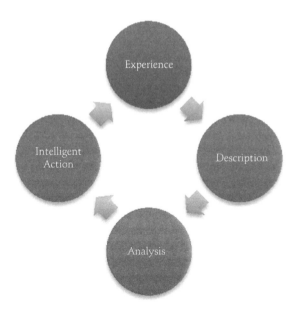

Figure 3.2 Experiential learning cycle

and reflective components described in my definition of CEC. However, I soon realized that the ELC did not tend to an important part of feedback: emotional reactions. Teachers reported feeling uneasy and worried about giving feedback to their peers. They were afraid of creating an unintended conflict due to two main points.

First, because English is their second language, they were worried they would use the wrong words or sentence structures, thereby possibly creating a miscommunication. Secondly, they were not sure what kind of content would create helpful or even appropriate feedback. This is when I began examining how approaches to conflict resolution could be integrated in the reflective feedback process. The approach I relied heavily on was the compassionate communication approach previously mentioned, Nonviolent Communication (NVC).

Quite similar to the ELC, NVC helps users move from one experience to another, informed by a type of communicative process. However, the biggest differences are their interpersonal and introspective emphases. Whereas NVC comes to observation from the perspective of increasing the chance of an open and mutual dialogue, the ELC, especially as defined by Carol Rodgers (2002b), comes to observation from the perspective of reflective inquiry. Rodgers (2002b: 3), whose research is focused on the language teacher's classroom, promotes rich description as a way to 'slow down the teaching/learning process revealing rich and complex details, allowing for appreciation and paving the way for a considered response rather than a less thoughtful reaction.' Within the ELC perspective, this rich description prepares the reflective practitioner to analyze the scenario from a more objective point of view. In relation to NVC, the user has the space to articulate perceived feelings and needs in order to empathize with the person he or she is communicating with. By empathizing, one creates a path whereby a request can be made. Without this empathy, it is unlikely that the request will be understood as a question, or ultimately, as a choice. Instead, it may be heard as a demand (Rosenberg, 2005: 79). On the other hand, since the ELC is more of an introspective model, unlike NVC, the final step involves creating a personal plan for a future change of action. What I noticed about both these final stages (NVC: request; ELC: action plan) was that they required language that was SMART (see the previous definition of *Compassionate SMART-Choice Request*).

By combining both these frameworks, I was able to address most of the needs discovered in the teacher training course. This included both helping the teachers give and receive feedback as well as reflect on their experience with a sense of openness and self-acceptance. Adding language analysis to the mixture is how Compassionate English Communication (CEC) came into being.

Adding 'English' to Compassionate Communication

Because teachers are often concerned about how they come across while giving feedback, it is important to look at the language they will use, and how it might sound either acceptable or harsh to the receiver. What was missing from both the NVC and ELC frameworks was an analysis of how they translated to English learners. This is why I included 'English' in my definition of 'Compassionate Communication' (see Figure 3.3). Awareness sessions include an observation of what certain forms (parts of speech) mean in the specific context of the CEC step we practice. We also examine how the forms are used to construct feedback. Each of the three activities in this chapter is based on one step in CEC (Description, Empathic Analysis, and Compassionate SMART-Choice Request) and comes from my experience in these awareness sessions. Rather than explaining how the parts of speech relate to the CEC steps in this section of the chapter, I introduce a brief language analysis, as well as a deeper explanation of the theory behind each activity.

Compassionate English Communication Activities

Introducing the Activities. The first activity will begin with descriptions of diplomatic contexts. The second activity will ask learners

Figure 3.3 Compassionate English communication

to engage empathic analyses of common dialogues between diplomats and other agents. The final activity will be a role-play based on developing compassionate SMART-Choice requests. I recommend these activities be done in the order they appear in the chapter as each acts as a scaffold for the previous one. Nevertheless, depending on the needs of the facilitator and the learners, each activity can stand on its own as well.

The three activities will have a similar layout, which serves as a guide for the facilitator or learner. Below are the various sections.

- Introduction to the activity – provides information connecting the theoretical background with the form, meaning, and use of the English structures that will arise in connection to the CEC step in question.
- Objective – describes the expected outcome of the basic activity, which should be demonstrated during the closure activity.
- Materials – lists items that will be needed to complete the task.
- Tips for facilitators – informs the facilitator of the preparation needed prior to the beginning the activity.
- Language – informs the facilitator of the type of language they can expect to see emerge from the activity.
- Pre-task – provides linguistic or contextual support to the learner.
- Basic task – explains the tasks central to achieving the goal of the activity. Suggestions based on how to approach the tasks depending on language proficiency, contextual layout, group size, interpersonal relationships, and teaching approach are also provided in this section.
- Expansion tasks – provides options for extending the basic task in the event that deeper exploration is needed. These expansion tasks can also stand on their own.
- Closure tasks – gives learners the chance to reflect on the implications of what they have learned. Depending on how you want to conclude the exploration of the concept, this can be done after either the basic and expansion tasks.

How long each activity takes to accomplish will depend on the facilitator's teaching style, the learners' language proficiency, and the learners' previous background with this concept. It is possible to do the basic task in approximately 50 minutes.

Additionally, since these activities ask learners to examine their personal experiences, it will be important for the facilitator to foster a safe environment. This should be a space where learners are able to explore the emotions without a fear of being ridiculed or judged. Prior to beginning the activities, the facilitator should consider the dynamics that exist between the learners, between the facilitator and the learners, as well as between the learners and the content with which they are about to engage. If the facilitator senses a strong disconnection in any of these realms, they may want to consider finding ways to repair or address the situation so that learners can gain most from the activities.

Introduction of Activity 1: Description versus Evaluation

In the following activity, learners will practice their observation or descriptive skills. As mentioned in the definition of Compassionate English Communication (CEC), it is descriptiveness that makes it possible to create a space of openness. However, if the observation is clouded with language that is evaluative or judgmental, instead of being open to a conversation, the listener may become defensive. The same can be said for the times when we are reflecting on ourselves. By being able to consider our reaction through the lens of description, we are less likely to instigate a situation that could be uncomfortable for all parties involved. Below (see Table 3.3) are examples of evaluative language, with a short explanation of the

Table 3.3 Distinguishing evaluations from descriptions

Forms of language that promote evaluation	Evaluation	Description
Adjectives used to describe an interpretation of someone's character or ability; use of the verb *to be* in this case also creates an interpretation	• You are annoying. • I'm horrible at finishing paperwork on time.	• I felt annoyed when you told me that I would have to stay late in the office for the third time this week. • Last Friday and last Thursday I didn't give my paperwork to the director the day after it was due.
Adverbs of frequency (always, never, seldom, frequently, etc.) to describe behavior	• I'm always late. I never make it to a meeting on time.	• During the last three meetings this week, I arrived 20 minutes after the scheduled time.
Present tense used to describe general behavior	• He doesn't listen well. He talks too much.	• When I was talking to him yesterday, I tried to say something two or three times, but he kept talking.
Comparatives and superlatives	• Mary is much kinder than John. • Mary is the best...	• Each time I meet Mary for a meeting, she offers to buy me coffee because I traveled a long distance to meet her. But when I meet John, he doesn't offer or mention the distance I drove.

grammatical form that creates the potential evaluation, and the alternative description.

Looking at the first example in Table 3.3, one can easily see how the first evaluative statement, '*You are annoying*', could create distance, and how its counterpart, the descriptive statement, 'When you told me that I would have to stay late in the office for the third time this week, I felt annoyed', provides even the slightest bit more space for communication. The adjective 'annoying' used with the 'be' verb implies that 'annoying' is embedded in the person's character, while the descriptive statement points to a specific scenario when the listener felt annoyed by the action. The first places ownership on the listener, while the second seems to place ownership on the speaker. Each of the forms in Table 3.3 can be analyzed via this perspective.

Another way to check in with ourselves to see if we are using language that is evaluative rather than descriptive, is to listen for our use of the second person 'you' or the third person 'he, she, they' instead of the first person 'I'. As Gordon Thomas (2014) noted in his research on effective relationships between parents and their children, combined with active listening (listening with empathy), the 'I' message reduces the sense of blame and shame in the listener. It tells the receiver the speaker feels a certain way, and that although the reaction is related to the interaction, it comes from within the speaker. Communicated with a tone that conveys a genuine intention to inform and not blame, as well as culturally dependent body language that encourages openness (Randall & Thornton, 2001: 87–88), the idea is that it is easier to receive an 'I' message than a 'you' message. More can be found on this topic in Chapter 6.

When we engage in CEC, it is important to find the language to describe what we see rather than the judgmental thoughts that may be showing up. However, what constitutes an evaluation may be ambiguous at times. For example, when a woman smiles, it seems plausible to think she is happy. Or if we see a person with a certain skin color, we may jump to a conclusion about where they are from. The intention of the *Description versus Evaluation* activity is to help us see through the lens of what is, rather than the lens of our personal history. The activity may uncover assumptions, (Rodgers, 2002b: 7–8), and moralistic judgments (Rosenberg, 2005: 5–18) we hold that block us from connecting and communicating effectively with another person, or even ourselves. It is important to keep in mind that the description is the first step to the rest of the conversation. As the educator Patricia Carini (2000: 4) advocates, description gives us the skills to see a person's, 'uniqueness, complexity, and integrity.' It is this lens we will try to develop in the following activity.

Description of Activity 1 – Description versus evaluation

Objective. By the end of this activity, learners will be able to explain the difference between a description and an evaluation. In verbal or written form, learners will also be able to make an observation by describing elements in a picture.

Materials. Picture(s) of people in an ambiguous situation (i.e. it might be hard to define what is really happening in the picture: see Example 3.1).

Tips for facilitators

- Different types of media can be used for this activity (i.e. video, listening and reading texts, realia…).
- *Language.* In addition to being aware of the language presented in Table 3.3, facilitators should be prepared to address the language that emerges from the pictures or media they bring to class. Below are some examples of the language forms that may emerge.

Language for the basic task

- Present continuous for the in-class picture description.
- Vocabulary and collocations to describe: actions, facial and body features, objects in a room, colors, as well as any language connected to possible interpretations such as emotions, relationships, culture, and social and professional positions.

Language for the expansion tasks

- Past tense for the reflective description of a personal experience.
- Question and answer forms.

Basic task

(1) Using the picture (see Example 3.1) as a prompt (or choose your own), elicit from the learners what they notice. Because this is an awareness raising activity, it is important that the facilitator does not give the learners hints. The experiential impact of this activity comes from the ambiguity (Rodgers, 2002b: 7). Use questions such as: what do you see in the picture? Or, what do you notice in the picture?
   - Depending on what skill you want the learners to practice, ask them to individually write, or verbally share with a partner what they notice.

Example 3.1 Picture of a scenario

- Depending on the learners' proficiency, you may need to assist them in finding the language they want. This is where it will be beneficial to predict before the lesson the possible language that may emerge (see suggestions in the 'Language' section above).
(2) If the learners wrote their thoughts, ask them to share with a partner, and then ask volunteers to share with the class. If they already shared with a partner, again, ask volunteers to share with the class.
(3) At this stage, some learners will be describing what they see and some will be developing stories about the people in the picture. These different perspectives are valuable. While they are sharing their ideas, write them on the board in point form, dividing them into two columns. One will be for descriptions, and the other for evaluations, but do not label the columns yet. Some expected responses might look such as the ones in Example 3.2.

  In some cases, learners may only describe what they see. It may take time for them to start making evaluations. Take the time you need so that at least two evaluations are made.
(4) Once something has been written in both columns, ask the learners to share (in pairs or with the whole class) what they think the difference is between both columns. When they have given you answers close to what you are looking for, write down description and evaluation at the top of the corresponding columns.
  - Depending on the level of comfort among members of the group, as well as the language proficiency of the learners, another approach is to ask everyone in the class how they know that the woman is

The woman is holding a document.	The woman is angry because the man made a mistake.
The man is wearing a gray suit.	The man is annoyed at the woman.
The woman has beige skin.	The woman is American.

Example 3.2 Description versus evaluation board work

angry because the man made a mistake. This should uncover the idea that they might not really know.

(5) Ask them to try again, with a different picture or source, this time only focusing on the descriptive aspect of what they see, and not what they imagine.
- Depending on your approach and the learners in the classroom, you may give them the chance to ask you for the language words they want to know, or you can give them a list of vocabulary they need to match with the corresponding parts in the picture.

Expansion Task 1. To give learners an opportunity to internalize the language and the concept they learned above, the activity can be expanded so that they share a scenario from their past which they thought was challenging, confusing, or even exciting.

(1) Give learners individual time to think of such a scenario. Time may be given to write about or draw this moment. Giving them this opportunity will help them develop the image in their mind and prepare them for the next stage.
(2) In small groups (3–4), one person will describe their scenario while the others listen. When this is done, the rest of the group must now ask the speaker questions to help them uncover details they may have missed. The questions should lead the speaker toward describing, and not evaluating. For example:
- *Description prompting questions:* What time of the day was it? Was this the first time you met this person? What did he tell you after that?
- *Evaluation prompting questions:* Why do you think he said that? What are some reasons for his (or your) reaction? If you had not been in a hurry, would the circumstances have been different?

In order for the learners to successfully accomplish this task, they may need to spend time with various question forms, and also time learning more about which questions lend themselves to eliciting answers similar to the prompts in Table 3.3.

Expansion Task 2. Make a list of statements such as the ones in both the evaluation and description sections in Table 3.3, or elicit statements that the learners are curious about. This could be a challenging statement they have heard or said. For example, 'My supervisor always tells me about meetings at the last minute.'

(1) Individually or in groups, ask the learners to analyze all these statements against the prompts in Table 3.3. Using the criteria they need to determine if the statements are evaluations or descriptions.
(2) If they believe a statement is an evaluation, they must change this statement using descriptive language.

Closure Task. Have a short discussion or ask learners to write about the implications of this activity on their experiences in the field of diplomacy. Here are some questions you may ask:
• What struck you about this activity?
• How will making the distinction between description and evaluation influence you in your work as a diplomat?

Introduction to Activity 2 – Empathic Analysis

The following activity will help learners understand the language that can be used when engaging in the second part of CEC: empathic analysis. As mentioned in the definition of CEC, this involves being able to look at a scenario introspectively and interpersonally via the lens of feelings and needs. However, prior to providing examples of English feelings and needs vocabulary, it is important to look at the cultural challenges and benefits of learning emotion words. After this, we will take a closer look at resources for the language of feelings and needs, as well as what grammatical structures should be used to express them.

Cultural Challenges and Benefits. Taking into consideration that English is the most commonly used language between speakers of other languages (see Chapter 5) (Crystal, 1997; Friedrich, 2007; McKay, 2002), it could be said that developing skills to communicate compassionately in English may increase diplomatic understanding between different cultural groups. However, as the research of Pavlenko (2005) and Wierzbicka (1986) shows, there is a high risk of miscommunication when it comes to translating emotion words between languages. Certain words such as 'shame', or 'disgust' can be seen as language specific rather than universal (Wierzbicka, 1986, 1999). This means that even though two cultures share a similar emotion word, the sense that it evokes will depend on your cultural and social upbringing. Therefore, it cannot be assumed that when second language (L2) learners use the word 'disgust' in English that they mean precisely the same thing a first language (L1) user of English would when they use the same word. It is very important for the facilitator of the following activity to keep this in mind.

Another important point for the facilitator to keep in mind is that although English is the language used, and if learners engage in the following activity, they will learn new vocabulary as well as English communicative strategies. It is the awareness gleaned from the activity that will affect the way they react in an interaction. This awareness and understanding goes beyond the English language. As shown elsewhere in research in interpersonal communication,

> Safety, connection, meaning, respect, caring, etc. are qualities which are universally cherished even though the words for their expression and the means for their fulfillment vary drastically in different cultures and for different individuals. (Gill *et al.*, 2009: 153)

With the knowledge that, at the core, each person from every culture shares the same basic emotions (Ekman, 2003), we can begin to create a platform for dialogue toward understanding.

Table 3.4 Feelings when needs are not met and when they are met

Feelings when needs are not met			*Feelings when needs are met*		
ANGRY	**SAD**	Overwhelmed	**COMFORTABLE**	**HAPPY**	**INTERESTED**
Angry	*Depressed*	Scared	*Calm*	Adventurous	Absorbed
Annoyed	*Disappointed*	Shocked	*Comfortable*	Affectionate	*Curious*
Disgusted	*Hopeless*	Stressed	*Confident*	*Alive*	Energetic
Irritated	*Hurt*	*Surprised*	Empowered	*Amused*	*Enthusiastic*
ASHAMED	*Sad*	*Suspicious*	*Free*	*Cheerful*	Focused
Ashamed	*Unhappy*	Tense	*Peaceful*	*Content*	Inspired
Deflated	*Upset*	*Uncertain*	*Relaxed*	*Delighted*	*Interested*
Embarrassed	**SCARED &**	*Worried*	Relieved	*Excited*	
Guilty	**ANXIOUS**	**TIRED**	*Satisfied*	Hopeful	
Regretful	*Afraid*	*Heavy*	*Secure*	*Happy*	
CAREFUL	*Alarmed*	*Tired*	Trusting	Joyful	
Careful	*Anxious*	*Bored*	**GRATEFUL**	Loving	
Doubtful	*Concerned*	Withdrawn	*Glad*	Playful	
Guarded	*Confused*	**JEALOUS**	*Grateful*	*Proud*	
Hesitant	Fearful	Envious	*Pleased*		
Resistant	Frightened	*Jealous*	Thankful		
Shy	Hesitant				
Unwilling	*Impatient*				
Vulnerable	*Nervous*				

Language of Feelings and Needs. Part of this understanding comes with developing a literacy of feelings and needs, which is the aim of this *Empathic Analysis* activity. The feelings (Table 3.4) and needs (Table 3.5) lists were created with the English learner in mind. The italicized words can be found in the Oxford 3000, a list of English vocabulary considered to be the most important to learn, selected by linguists and language teachers from the *Oxford Learner's Dictionary* (2014). By learning the italicized words, learners will not only develop their feelings and needs literacy, they will also learn words valuable to their basic development as English communicators. The underlined words indicate that the word is either found in a different form in the Oxford 3000 (e.g. the adjective 'relieved' in the feelings list can be found as the noun 'relief'; the noun 'fairness' in the needs list can be found as the adjective 'fair'). Some of the underlined words do not appear in the Oxford 3000, but have been added to the feelings (e.g. empowered, vulnerable, etc...) and needs (e.g. compassion, honoring agreements, etc...) lists because I believe they are important to learn in order to understand the full spectrum of human feelings and needs.

In relation to sentence structure, it is important to consider the difference between expressing, 'I feel...' versus, 'I am...' when describing how one feels. As Siegel (2010, Introduction, p. 3) explains, 'Similar as those two statements may seem, there is actually a profound difference between them. "I am sad" is a kind of self-definition, and a very limiting one. "I feel sad" suggests the ability to recognize and acknowledge a feeling,

Table 3.5 Human needs

CONNECTION	MEANING AND	Growth	BEAUTY	Justice
Belonging	UNDERSTANDING	Independence	Beauty	Good health
Community	Acknowledgment	Integrity	Creativity	Honesty
Competence	Acceptance	Learning	Expression	Honoring
Compassion	Appreciation	Meaning	Fun	agreements
Connection	Authenticity	Peace of mind	Humor	Openness
Contribution	Autonomy	Privacy	Inspiration	Order
Dependability	Celebration	Reciprocity	Joy	Relief
Empathy	Challenge	Self-reliance	Love	Rest
Encouragement	Choice	Shared Reality	Mourning	Safety
Friendship	Clarity	Solitude	Peace	Security
Harmony	Comfort	To be seen for your	SAFETY	Shelter
Kindness	Compassion	intentions	Clean air	Trust
Recognition	Consideration	To be heard	Ease	Clean water
Respect	Courage	Understanding	Fairness	
Support	Empathy		Food	
	Freedom			

without being consumed by it.' For this reason, I recommend that the facilitator encourage the use of, 'I feel... because I need...' For example, if I am in a meeting that is taking longer than I planned, I may say to myself, 'I feel irritated because I need freedom.' When trying to analyze what someone else may be feeling and needing, I may say, 'Maybe he feels irritated because he needs freedom.' We add 'maybe' because we can never be sure what another person needs or feels unless we ask them. In this case you could use the structure, 'Are you feeling irritated because you would like/you need freedom?'

These sentence structures may seem unnatural, and may be a bit convoluted when we consider their communicative use. However, the intention behind these structures is more about developing an awareness of the connections between feelings and needs. Once learners have acquired the language, they have the choice to use it in a way they feel would most likely convey their sense of authentic empathy.

Description of Activity 2 – Empathic analysis

Objective. By the end of this activity, learners will be able to identify, in written and verbal forms, the possible feelings and needs present during a given scenario.

Materials. Blank pieces of paper for each group; feelings and needs list for each group; feelings and needs cards

Tips for facilitators. Choose feelings and needs words that are the most important for your learners. Consider their cultural background and linguistic understanding mentioned in the introduction of this activity prior to beginning.

Language. For the pre-task, basic task, and closure task, facilitators can refer to Tables 3.4 and 3.5, choosing the vocabulary they feel meets the needs of the learners. Since these lists are quite extensive, facilitators are only meant to use them as a guide. They should also refer to the sentence structures mentioned in the introduction to this activity.

Pre-task. To achieve the objective of this activity, learners will need a basic understanding of feelings and needs vocabulary. Here are a few strategies for helping learners understand and remember the vocabulary.

Pre-task 1. *Learners encounter and try to clarify the feelings and needs vocabulary*

Choice 1: Show pictures of people that would elicit feeling words. Show them to the learners and see what they come up with. Another option is to mime the feelings. Write their answers on the board.

Choice 2: Facilitators may want to choose feelings and needs they believe will be appropriate based on their learners' language proficiency and language needs. In order to help learners clarify the feelings and needs vocabulary, the facilitators can give them an opportunity to look for the definition in a dictionary, guess the meaning from context (texts or photographs), or discuss the meaning as a class.

Pre-task 2. *Learners try to remember the feelings and needs vocabulary*

Once the meaning has been clarified, there are a few activities that can be done to help learners remember the vocabulary.

A.   Feelings Charade: Prepare a deck of 'feelings' flashcards. Each learner must pick a card and mimic it to the best of their ability. The others must guess the feeling.

B.   Needs Gauging: Make a list of statements familiar to your learners. For example:
    a1. You're late again!
    b1. I can't believe I just said that.
    c1. I have a stack of paperwork to do and I haven't even started.

Using a list of needs such as the one in Table 3.5, learners must guess what needs might be behind such (a1, b1, c1) statements. For example:

    a2. They might have a need for *honoring agreements* or *understanding.*
    b2. They might have a need for *competence* with the way they express themselves in front of others, or *compassion* for the vulnerability they feel at the moment.
    c2. They might have a need for *ease* or *support.*

Basic task. The basic task will give learners the opportunity to internalize the vocabulary from the pre-activities.

(1) Elicit from the learners various social scenarios within their work that may bring them discomfort. This should not be a scenario that would trigger intensely charged emotions such as the death of a colleague, or a precarious legal matter. In comparison, ask the learners to share a milder scenario. Some examples may be: 'my supervisor always tells me about meetings at the last minute;' or 'residents sometimes come to the office without the appropriate documents and yell at me.'
    •   Cluster learners in groups of 3 or 4, and ask them to brainstorm a list of such scenarios. Once they are done, ask them to share their list with the class while you write them on the board.
(2) Each group should choose a different scenario. You can also assign the scenarios you think would be appropriate for each group. Ideally there should be at least four different scenarios in the class. Each scenario will rotate to each group, giving everyone the chance to work with a few different scenarios.
(3) Using their scenario as the heading, ask the groups to draw the following table (Example 3.3), or provide a blank table for them to fill in.

Scenario:			
Me		**Other**	
Feelings	**Needs**	**Feelings**	**Needs**

Example 3.3 What's happening inside you and me right now?

Before doing the task on their own, students should have the opportunity to engage with the whole class through working on one scenario (Example 3.4).

The task is to first empathize with themselves, 'Me', by identifying their feelings, and then the needs connected to those feelings. Remind them to refer to their feelings and needs lists. You can encourage them to use the sentence structure, 'I feel _____ because I need _____'.

- Then they should do the same for the other person involved in the scenario. In this part of the activity, they can use the structure 'Maybe he/she feels _____ because he/she needs _____.'
  - Note: For both the self-empathy and empathy for the other, give the learners enough time so they have a chance to really get a sense of the feelings and needs. For example, if we look at the feelings and needs elicited for the supervisor (Example 3.4), the learners may want to discuss how they came to that conclusion. Maybe the supervisor has a very full schedule (feeling: overwhelmed) and does not have the time to tell his team ahead of time of every meeting. He needs support and would appreciate this from his team. Or perhaps the supervisor is confident in her decision to not tell the team about the meeting. Maybe her need for trust in the team is being fulfilled, and therefore does not see a reason to tell people ahead of time.

Scenario: My supervisor always tells me about meetings at the last minute.			
Me: Diplomat		**Other: Supervisor**	
Feelings	**Needs**	**Feelings**	**Needs**
1. frustrated	shared reality	3. overwhelmed	support
2. calm	ease	4. confident	trust

Example 3.4 Whole class practice

(4)   After the whole class practice, each group works on their own table. They should at least have one set of feelings and needs for both 'Me' and 'Other.' Depending on time, you can ask them to fill in more spaces, but remember the other groups need to work on each scenario as well.

(5)   Rotate the scenario tables so each group has a new one. They do the same task they did previously. Continue rotating until you notice they have addressed several of the possible feelings and needs.

Closure Task. Have a short discussion or ask learners to write about the implications of this activity on their experiences in the field of diplomacy. Here are some questions you may ask:

* What reaction did you have when you were trying to find a need for yourself?
* What reaction did you have when you were trying to find a need for the other person?
* How will looking through the lens of feelings and needs change the way you interact with others?

Another approach is to ask the learners to identify the feelings they felt while doing the activity, and also to identify the needs that were met or not meet during the activity. Ask the learners to use the feelings and needs lists, as well as the suggested sentence structure.

Introduction to Activity 3 – Role-play: Compassionate SMART-Choice Request

The following activity will help learners move from identifying feelings and needs to being able to make SMART-choice requests, which is the final step in Compassionate English Communication (CEC). As described in the introduction to this chapter, it must encourage a sense of choice, rather than obligation. Moreover, in order for a request to be SMART, the language must be specific, measurable, achievable, relevant, and time-bound. Please refer to that explanation prior to beginning.

In this activity, we will examine the difference between what constitutes a request versus a demand. In the simplest sense, if the questioner is able to accept a 'no' to a request, then a request has been made. To help learners realize the difference between requests in the CEC sense of the word, it is important to shed light on the difference between language forms that encourage a sense of choice as opposed to forms that give very little choice, if any, to the listener. Much of this sense will depend on the delivery (intention and tone) of the user, but the forms below also stand on their own in relation to these interpretations. For example, the imperative form is used in order to give a command, and *would you* or *could you* + *infinitive* are forms often used as to signal a polite request. Table 3.6 describes how these forms are defined and used.

The concept of politeness should be framed in the context of English as a *lingua franca* discussed in Chapter 4, and the different cultural perspectives

Table 3.6 Requests or demands?

	Meaning	*Forms*
No choice	1. Imperative form implying there is no choice. This is a clear demand.	• *Prepare these documents by 5pm!*
	2. Implying obligation and necessity.	• *You **must** prepare these documents by 5pm.* • *You **have to** prepare these documents by 5pm.* • *You **need to** prepare these documents by 5pm.*
	3. Giving strong advice while implying that something bad will happen if it isn't followed.	• *You **had better** prepare these documents by 5pm.*
Mild choice determined by the speaker	4. Giving mild advice.	• *You **should** prepare these documents by 5pm.*
Choice is determined by the speaker	5. Giving permission.	• *You **can** prepare these documents by 5pm.*
	6. Giving permission – formal and polite.	• *You **may** prepare these documents by 5pm.*
Choice is determined by the listener	7. Request questions – formal and polite.	• ***Could you** prepare these documents by 5pm?* • ***Would you be willing to** prepare these documents by 5pm?* • ***Would you be able to** prepare these documents by 5pm?* • ***How do you feel about** preparing these documents by 5pm?* • ***Would you mind** preparing these documents by 5pm?*

of politeness referred to in Chapter 2. The notion of 'directness' and 'indirectness' examined in Chapter 6 should also be considered prior to engaging in this activity. By being mindful of these points, the facilitator can be sensitive to the unique interpretations of politeness each learner brings.

In relation to the SMART aspect, one sentence structure that could help learners identify if it meets the criteria would be: *By 5pm today* (adaptable time) *I will* fill in these documents *so that* I can finish my work and also meet the deadline. The template looks like this:

(Time bound - ie: Next week, Every Friday..)_____ I will (specific, relevant, achievable, measurable action)_____ so that (specific, relevant, achievable, measurable result)_____.

This is especially useful for the reflective quality of this part of CEC. For requests, we also need to ask if it's SMART. Looking at the request questions in Table 3.6, we notice that they are time-bound and somewhat specific. Perhaps they have already discussed the details (measurability) of the documents, thereby not making it necessary to repeat again. We may also want to assume that they negotiated the relevance and achievability. Otherwise, the request may look like this, 'Would you be able to prepare these documents by 5pm today so that you are able to finish your current responsibilities and meet the deadline?' It may be helpful for the facilitator to show the contrast before beginning in order to highlight how parts of SMART requests may also be expressed at the other stages in the conversation prior to making the actual request.

Description of Activity 3 – Role-play: Compassionate SMART-Choice request

Objectives.

- By the end of this activity, learners will be able to identify what forms are requests, and what forms are demands or close to demands.
- By the end of this activity, learners will be able to make SMART-Choice requests.
- By the end of this activity, learners will be able to name the feelings they felt as the person making the request or demand, and also as the person receiving the request or demand.

Materials. Copies of Table 3.6; role cards; blank pieces of paper for each group; feelings and needs list and/or cards used in Activity 2 (for support during the closure task)

Language. For the pre-task and basic task, facilitators can refer to Table 3.6 as well as the SMART-choice request sentence templates. For the closure task, facilitators can refer to Tables 3.4 and 3.5 from the previous activity.

Pre-task. Prior to the role-play activity, it will be important to clarify the difference between the various forms. The facilitator may want to spend some class time with the different modals and auxiliaries, and then take some time with the question forms. Once the learners have a basic understanding of these forms and their meaning, it is time to put them to use in the role-play.

Basic task.

(1) Using the elicited scenarios from Activity 2, create role cards with individual scenarios. Give a stack of role cards to each pair (see Example 3.5).

(2) Give pairs time to describe what the scenario might look like for them. This brings them back to the work done in Activity 1 and will help them connect to the scene. Additionally, prompt them to consider the analysis they did in Activity 2 to help them get a sense of the feelings and needs that may have been at play for both characters. This will give the learners a greater sense of where the request might come from.

(3) Provide an example of how the scenario might play out based on the different forms from Table 3.6. For example, if they are practicing the imperative form for Role-play 1, the subordinate diplomat might tell the supervising diplomat, 'Tell me about the meetings two days before!' If they do Role-play 2, the supervising diplomat might tell the subordinate diplomat, 'Be at the meeting in 10 minutes.' If they are practicing the polite request forms, Role-play 1 might sound like this, 'Would you be able to tell me about the meeting a day in advance?' and for Role-play 2, 'Could you be at the meeting in 10 minutes?'

(4) Give pairs the opportunity to role-play the various forms. See the Closure Task for more details.

Scenario: *My supervisor always tells me about meetings at the last minute.*

Characters: Supervising diplomat and subordinate diplomat

Role-play 1: Supervising diplomat makes a request or demand of the subordinate diplomat.

Role-play 2: Subordinate diplomat makes a request or demand of the supervising diplomat.

*Switch characters

Example 3.5 Sample role card

Forms	Feelings		Needs	
	Saying the form	Hearing the form	Saying the form	Hearing the form
1.	Upset, confident...	Scared, annoyed...	Understanding	...
5.	Calm, confident...	Unsure, confused...	...	...

Example 3.6 Sample of Activity 3 closure task

Closure Task. This closure task is a bit different from the previous closure tasks, as learners should do it during the basic task. After each role-play, learners should write down how they felt saying and hearing the statement or the question (see Example 3.6). Encourage learners to use the feelings and needs lists (Tables 3.4 and 3.5) introduced in Activity 2.

Compassionate Communication in Relation to Persuasion

After engaging in the CEC activities, one may wonder how and if it differs from persuasion. James Price Dillard (2010), academic expert on persuasive influence, defines persuasion, 'as the use of symbols (sometimes accompanied by images) by one social actor for the purpose of changing or maintaining another social actor's opinion or behavior.' This is similar to what Dr Petru Dumitriu (2013), Permanent Observer of the Council of Europe to the United Nations Office, describes as 'persuasion by repetition' in the book, *Persuasion, the Essence of Diplomacy*: 'Persuasion implies that someone assimilates knowledge by being exposed to new information. Repetition of the messages containing the new information will modify learning, thus having a persuasive impact as well' (Dumitriu, 2013: 100). Is this not also what the CEC model does? After listening to someone express themselves, I describe what the speaker said or did, and reflect back on the feelings and needs I noticed. Then, finally, I take this new information and make a request thereby aiming to modify the learning. In a sense, I make requests until you change your perspective.

The difference is that although change may occur via the use of CEC, when it is used for interpersonal communication, the true purpose is to create a compassionate connection. Rosenberg's (2005) perspective on the objective of Nonviolent Communication (NVC) directly relates to my definition of the purpose of CEC and is worth mentioning here:

> If our objective is only to change people and their behavior or to get our way, then NVC is not an appropriate tool. The process is designed for

those of us who would like others to change and respond, but only if they choose to do so willingly and compassionately. (Rosenberg, 2005: 81)

The CEC framework works toward mutual and self understanding, and is closer to the process of persuasion that Joe Borg (2013), European Commissioner Fisheries and Maritime Affairs, exemplifies in his chapter, Cornerstones of Persuasion: Inclusion and Empathy. Here, he explains the negotiation process he led as Malta's Minister of Foreign Affairs in relation to Malta's addition to the European Union. The way he brought empathy to the negotiation table was to make sure that all the stakeholders had a voice and that they felt their perspective had been honestly taken into account. He credits the success of the referendum, and a 'convincing "yes"' (Borg, 2013: 116), to including the public in the negotiation process. He also credits it to the stakeholders believing that he and his committee were sincere in their desire to listen to the stakeholders' needs.

I am sure that genuine, honest persuasion cannot be rhetoric, cannot be show, and cannot be theatrics. It has to be something that you genuinely believe in, and people sense this. I can say from my experience that whenever you try to put on a show, people can pay you lip service. Whenever, you try to impress them with fantastic words they might be impressed for a moment, but then they will call your bluff when the true test comes. (Borg, 2013: 117)

When people sense they have been empathized with, then persuasion becomes more than simply changing behavior; it becomes an act of deepening understanding and awareness. If it were simply about changing someone's behavior, then persuasion could be likened to coercion. This brings us back to the essence of making a compassionate SMART-choice request via CEC, 'Choosing to request rather than demand does not mean we give up when someone says "no" to our request. It does mean that we don't engage in persuasion until we have empathized with what's preventing the other from saying "yes"' (Rosenberg, 2005: 81).

Conclusion

Although learning Compassionate English Communication is a lifelong process, both diplomats and language facilitators, having engaged in these three activities, now have a stronger understanding of what it means to be compassionate in a communicative sense. This involves being able to describe rather than evaluate, to empathically analyze the self and other, and also to make SMART-choice requests instead of demands. When considering the implications of developing this language and its connected awareness, facilitators and learners may find it both helpful and inspiring to look to one of the greatest diplomats of our time, Nelson Mandela. In his May 10, 2004 address to the South African parliament to mark 10 years of democracy, Mandela expressed the value of being able to accept others:

> Historical enemies succeeded in negotiating a peaceful transition from apartheid to democracy exactly because we were prepared to accept the inherent capacity for goodness in the other. (2012: 57)

The ability to accept even in the unlikeliest of circumstances comes with being able to see the other as human, which is the essence of empathy and compassion. Via empathy and compassion, we can see the goodness, or in other words, the same human qualities we all share. From this space, understanding develops. This is what Mandela speaks to. The language offered in the above activities is a starting point for such understanding. The awareness of this language will help diplomats bring compassionate intention to the negotiation table and to other professional interactions. Being able to do this in English will open their spectrum of communication across various cultures, and create a space where international relations are then based on mutuality. It seems that only positive implications can come from adopting such communication skills.

Notes

(1) I realize that diplomatic work can be much more complex than dealing with paperwork. My intention throughout the chapter is to provide a simplified scenario that is easily transferable to other contexts. The scenarios will thus focus on clerical work.

(2) Although used for different reasons, the terms Compassionate Communication (CC) and Compassionate English Communication (CEC) are related. Different parts of the chapter will address this.

References

Borg, J. (2013) Cornerstones of persuasion: Inclusion and empathy. In J. Kurbalija (ed.) *Persuasion, the Essence of Diplomacy* (pp. 109–119). Geneva and Malta: DiploFoundation and Mediterranean Academy of Diplomatic Studies.

Boroditsky, L. (2011) How languages shape thought. *Scientific American* 2, 62–65.

Carini, P. (2000) *From Another Angle: Children's Strengths and School Standards: The Prospect Center's Descriptive Review of the Child*. New York: Teachers College Press.

Crystal, D. (1997) *English as a Global Language*. Cambridge: Cambridge University Press.

Cunningham, J. (2009) *Compassionate Communication: Empathy's Awakening*. Booklet presented at the Nonviolent Communication in Education workshop, Seoul, South Korea.

Dewey, J. (1938) *Experience and Education*. New York: Collier Books.

Dillard, J.P. (2010) Persuasion. In C.R. Berger, M.E. Roloff and D.R. Ewoldsen (eds) *The Handbook of Communication Science* (pp. 203–218). Thousand Oaks, CA: SAGE Publications, Inc.

Dumitriu, P. (2013) Persuasion: Bad practices and … others. In J. Kurbalija (ed.) *Persuasion, the Essence of Diplomacy* (pp. 97–105). Geneva and Malta: DiploFoundation and Mediterranean Academy of Diplomatic Studies.

Ekman, P. (2003) *Emotions Revealed*. New York: Holt Paperbacks.

Friedrich, P. (2007) *Language, Negotiation and Peace: The Use of English in Conflict Resolution*. London: Continuum.

Gill, R., Leu, L. and Morin, J. (2009) *NVC Toolkit for Facilitators*. Lexington, KY: Freedom Project.

Goetz, J.L., Keltner, D. and Simon-Thomas, E. (2010) Compassion: An evolutionary analysis and empirical review. *Psychological Bulletin* 136 (3), 351–374.

Hart, W. (2013) Unlocking past emotion: Verb use affects mood and happiness. *Psychological Science* 24, 19–26.

Kircanski, K., Lieberman, M.D. and Craske, M.G. (2012) Feelings into words: Contributions of language to exposure therapy. *Psychological Science* 23, 1086–1091.

Kolb, D. (1984) *Experiential Learning Experience as a Source of Learning and Development*. Englewood Cliffs, NJ: Prentice Hall.

Kurbalija, J. (ed.) (2013) *Persuasion, the Essence of Diplomacy*. Geneva and Malta: DiploFoundation and Mediterranean Academy of Diplomatic Studies.

Lewin, G.W. (ed.) (1948) *Resolving Social Conflicts: Selected Papers on Group Dynamics by Kurt Lewin*. New York: Harper & Row.

Mandela, N. (2012) *Notes to the Future: Words of Wisdom*. New York: Atria Books.

Maslow, A.H. (1970) *Motivation and Personality*. New York: Harper & Row.

McKay, S.L. (2002) *Teaching English as an International Language*. Oxford: Oxford University Press.

Mindfulness. In The Greater Good Science Center at the University of California, Berkeley. See http://greatergood.berkeley.edu/topic/mindfulness/definition#why_ practice (accessed 11 October 2014).

Neff, K. (2011) Self-compassion for caregivers [Web log post to *Psychology Today*]. See http://www.psychologytoday.com/blog/the-power-self-compassion/201105/self-compassion-caregivers

Newberg, A. and Waldman, M.R. (2012) *Words Change Your Brain: 12 Conversational Strategies to Build Trust, Resolve Conflict, and Increase Intimacy*. New York: Hudson Street Press.

The Oxford 3000™ from the *Oxford Advanced Learner's Dictionary*. See http://www.oxfordlearnersdictionaries.com/wordlist/english/oxford3000/ox3k_A-B/ (accessed 15 November 2014).

Pavlenko, A. (2005) *Emotions and Multilingualism*. Cambridge: Cambridge University Press.

Petrie, K.G., Fontanilla, I., Thomas, M.G., Booth R.J. and Pennebaker, J.W. (2004) Effect of written emotional expression on immune function in patients with human immunodeficiency virus infection: Randomized trial. *Psychosomatic Medicine* 66 (2), 272–275.

Randall, M. and Thornton, B. (2001) *Advising and Supporting Teachers*. Cambridge: Cambridge University Press.

Rodgers, C. (2002a) Defining reflection: Another look at John Dewey and reflective thinking. *Teachers College Record* 104 (4), 842–866.

Rodgers, C. (2002b) Seeing student learning: Teacher change and the role of reflection. *Harvard Educational Review* 72 (2), 230–253.

Rogers, C.R. (1980) *A Way of Being*. New York: Houghton Mifflin Company.

Rosenberg, M.B. (2005) *Nonviolent Communication: A Language of Life*. Encinitas, CA: PuddleDancer Press.

Russell, W.E. (2004) 'Control yourself, Sir!': A call for research into emotion cultures in diplomacy. In H. Slavik (ed.) *Intercultural Communication and Diplomacy* (pp. 391–402). Geneva: DiploFoundation.

Siegel, D.J. (2010) *Mindsight: The New Science of Personal Transformation* [Kobo version]. See http://www.kobobooks.com

Stanton, A.L., Danoff-Burg, S., Cameron, C.L., Bishop, M., Collins, C.A., Kirk, S.B., Sworowski, L.A. and Twillman, R. (2000) Emotionally expressive coping predicts psychological and physical adjustment to breast cancer. *Journal of Consulting and Clinical Psychology* 68 (5), 875–882.

Thomas, G. (2011) Origins of the Gordon Model. See http://www.gordontraining.com (accessed 15 November 2014).

Wierzbicka, A. (1986) Human emotions: Universal or culture-specific? *American Anthropologist* 88 (3), 584–594.

Wierzbicka, A. (1999) *Emotions across Languages and Cultures*. Cambridge: Cambridge University Press.

4 English as a *lingua franca* in East and Southeast Asia: Implications for Diplomatic and Intercultural Communication

Andy Kirkpatrick, Sophiaan Subhan and Ian Walkinshaw

Summary

Ten nations make up the Association of Southeast Asian Nations (ASEAN)[1] and they officially adopted the ASEAN Charter in 2009. While Article 2 of the Charter urges 'respect for the different languages of the peoples of ASEAN,' Article 34 makes English the sole official working language. It states, simply, that, 'the working language of ASEAN shall be English.'

In this chapter we shall consider the implications of the role of English as the sole working language of ASEAN for diplomacy and communication among the peoples of ASEAN. Using data drawn from the Asian Corpus of English (ACE), a million-word corpus of naturally occurring spoken English as used as a *lingua franca* between Asian multilinguals, we shall investigate how Asians use English to discuss topics of mutual interest and importance. After some reflections on excerpts of such naturally occurring utterances, suggestions for classroom application of the insight afforded by these are offered. The chapter will conclude with proposals for necessary communication skill sets for diplomats and other professionals who wish to communicate successfully through English with Asian multilinguals. These communication skills are likely to be particularly important for people whose first language is a native variety of English, as they need to learn how English can be adapted to suit different cultures.

Introduction

In this chapter we shall look at how speakers of English as a *lingua franca* (ELF) use the language in naturally occurring contexts, including informal collegial interactions, discussions among consular officials and courtroom exchanges. We have chosen these different settings to show how context can determine language use, in particular the use, or non-use, of communicative strategies designed to ensure successful communication. We conclude with some recommendations for people who are likely to be engaged in ELF interactions in the future.

The data we use is all taken from the Asian Corpus of English (ACE), which we describe in a later section, and the participants are overwhelmingly Asian multilinguals for whom English is an additional language. These Asian multilinguals are nationals of one of the countries that comprise the Association of Southeast Asian Nations (ASEAN). There are also participants from Hong Kong. Before presenting and analyzing the data we begin by briefly summarizing recent research into ELF and explaining why we are using ELF data drawn from ACE and ASEAN.

Recent Research into ELF

In discussing ELF 'we must be careful not to categorize ELF as a specific, and stable variety of English' (Kirkpatrick, 2012: 132). ELF is more usefully seen as describing a function of language rather than a specific variety of it. ELF is dynamic and ELF speakers are constantly negotiating meaning (Canagarajah, 2013). The increase in the use of ELF has led to a corresponding increase in interest in it, with the realization that ELF is now the international *lingua franca*. By way of illustration, some 1 billion Asian multilinguals currently use ELF; and it has been estimated that there are 400 million Chinese currently using or learning English (Bolton & Graddol, 2012). This number alone outstrips the total number of native speakers of English in today's world. Given the extent to which ELF is currently employed, it is crucial that it becomes a focus of linguistic research (Mauranen, 2006). Examples of research projects so far implemented include the Vienna Oxford International Corpus of English (VOICE) collected and analyzed by Barbara Seidlhofer and her team at the University of Vienna (https://www.univie.ac.at/voice/). VOICE comprises a corpus of naturally occurring English as used as a *lingua franca* by speakers of English as an additional language. As Seidlhofer points out, it is essential that ELF is conceptualized as having been appropriated by non-native users 'who become acknowledged as agents in the processes of how that language spreads, develops, varies and changes' (2010: 362) rather than being 'owned' by native speakers of the language. She continues that ELF research seeks to uncover 'new rules of engagement' in intercultural encounters (2010: 364) and that users of English in ELF contexts 'make use of their multifaceted plurilingual repertoires in a fashion motivated by communicative purpose and the interpersonal dynamics of the interaction' (2010: 363).

Inspired by VOICE, which is largely Europe-focused, Kirkpatrick and his team have compiled the Asian Corpus of English (ACE), comprising some 1 million words of naturally occurring English as used as a spoken *lingua franca*. The participants are overwhelmingly Asian multilinguals from the 10 nations of ASEAN along with nationals from China (including Hong Kong), Japan and Korea. Eight data collection teams from across East and Southeast Asia were responsible for collecting and transcribing the data. The corpus, comprising complete speech events covering a wide range of interactions, topics and settings, is freely accessible from the website (http://corpus.ied.edu.hk/ace/). The need for an Asian corpus of English as a *lingua franca* was stimulated by the signing in 2009 of the official Charter of the Association of Southeast Asian Nations (ASEAN), which made English the sole official working language of the group. The ASEAN group, which was originally founded in 1967 and comprised five founding member states, currently comprises 10 Southeast Asian nations. The countries of ASEAN are characterized by 'political, cultural and historical diversity' (Severino, 2005: 15), being host to more than 1000 languages. While the ASEAN Charter also seeks to encourage respect for the different cultures, languages and religions of the peoples of ASEAN (Kirkpatrick, 2010: 7), it is not clear how this respect is to be nurtured given the official status of English as the sole working language. As Friedrich and Gomes de Matos (2012) have pointed out, the recognized need for a *lingua franca* should not 'clash with the desire to build community and preserve local language and culture' (2012: 23). Ways of promoting English as the *lingua franca* of ASEAN while maintaining local languages will be proposed later in the chapter.

A major use of a *lingua franca* over thousands of years has been in diplomacy. A key task of all diplomats is to be able to use language(s) in ways that do not inflame, but which seek peaceful solutions to problems and disputes. In multilateral diplomacy where speakers of many different first languages are present, it is impractical to expect that all participants speak each other's languages. One solution is to use interpreters and translators, but this can be expensive: the annual translation and interpreting bill for the European Union is in excess of US$ 1billion. Another is to use a common language. Historically many languages have been used as diplomatic *lingua francas* from Aramaic and Persian through to Arabic, Malay and French (Ostler, 2010). Today, however, the most commonly used diplomatic *lingua franca* is English. ELF might seem an ideal conduit for diplomatic communication, given that previous research into the communicative strategies adopted by ELF speakers has indicated a common desire for cooperation to facilitate successful communication. However, as we shall later show, cooperation is not always the goal.

The editors of a review of recent trends in ELF research conclude that these trends 'evidence the supportive and cooperative nature of interactions in ELF where meaning negotiation takes place at different levels' (Archibald *et al.*, 2011: 3). House has spoken of the 'solidarity of non-native ELF speakers' (2003: 569). Findings pointing to the cooperative nature of ELF interactions have also been reported by Firth (1996) and Meierkord (2012). Firth identified strategies such as the 'let it pass' principle, whereby speakers, instead of seeking immediate clarification when they did not understand what a speaker was saying, would let it pass, hoping, often correctly, that the meaning would become clear later. Meierkord's findings indicate that 'the conversations are characterized by their participants' desire to render the interactions normal and to achieve communicative success' (2012: 15). In a study of the communication strategies of Asian ELF speakers, Kirkpatrick (2010: 141) identified 15 communicative strategies adopted by ELF speakers to ensure successful communication. While some of these are likely to be common to all speakers in similar communicative situations, some may be specific to ELF interactions. For example, he noted a combination of 'speaker paraphrase' and 'participant prompting,' as in Excerpt 1 below (2010: 136–7). (S1 is a Singaporean female, L1 is a Laotian female and M1 is a Burmese female.) The participants are all qualified English teachers attending a professional development course in Singapore. The Singaporean is asking the Laotian what sort of support the Laos government provides to poor students. The figures in square brackets indicate the number of times the Singaporean student paraphrases her original question in order to help the Lao listener understand it.

Excerpt 1

S1: ...do the children you know in er in your country those who come from very poor families are they given financial assistance?

L1: ehm

SI: are they in terms of money? [1]

LI: ehm

SI: I mean does the government support them? [2] OK is there like you know those children who are very poor and their parents cannot afford to send them to school? [3] Does the government actually given them assistance? [4]

M1: yeah, the government will assist. I think so your government will assist.

(two second silence)

SI: example, you know like buying uniform for them or textbooks or paying for their school fees? [5]

L1: I think they don't do like that yes, only the family and parents can afford

SI: can afford

L1: yes afford them er for example in the countryside some students cannot learn because it's hardly for them to go to school

In this example the Singaporean patiently paraphrases her question five times, without displaying irritation or impatience. After the fourth paraphrase, the Burmese participant enters the conversation and offers a prompt – a possible answer, which she hopes will help the Laotian finally understand the original question. But when this clearly does not help – there is a two-second silence – the Singaporean paraphrases her question for the fifth time and the Laotian finally understands it. It is important to stress that the context here is itself supportive, given that all three participants are attending the same professional development course and are genuinely interested in the topic. Even though the Laotian participant's English proficiency is not as high as the other two participants, they treat each other as equals, as evidenced by the lack of a display of any irritation or impatience. The often cooperative and supportive nature of ELF talk is an important advantage for interactants with differing levels of proficiency.

That said, however, ELF talk may also reflect speakers' own cultural schemata as well as issues arising from variation in linguistic proficiency. In a study of speech practices of Chinese, Indian and Korean teaching assistants in the United States, Yule (1990) found that the more fluent Indian speakers, when providing street directions for the Chinese and Korean hearers to follow (as part of a guided task), assumed a 'speaker knows best' attitude, ascribing discrepancies or misunderstandings to their interlocutors' lack of proficiency. They assumed that the receiver was 'in some sense less competent than the sender since his opinions or descriptions are rarely given much attention' (1990: 57) and that this was the cause of their interactive difficulties. Consequently, they tended not to solve the set tasks successfully. However, when the less fluent Chinese and Korean speakers were in the dominant position of giving directions to the Indian participants, the tasks were completed more successfully. Yule concluded that giving fluent speakers experience in less dominant roles within a dyad 'may turn out to be a much more effective lesson for students in developing their communication skills than simply allowing them to practice their fluency by giving presentations or speeches when they are in complete control of the information process' (1990: 61). This would seem to offer excellent advice for the training of those engaged in *lingua franca* communication. Indeed, the ACE data reveal a similar phenomenon: the Singaporean speaker in Excerpt 1 demonstrates great sensitivity in dealing with her less proficient interactant, presumably as she sees herself as an equal in the discussion with a genuine interest in the opinions and knowledge of the other participants. This need for fluent speakers of English to be trained by assuming the less dominant roles in interactions may be of particular importance to 'native speakers' whose first language is English: studies conducted in Hong Kong showed that local employees had the most communicative difficulties 'when they needed to interact with inner circle speakers of English as a first language' (Nickerson, 2010: 511).

The data collected in ACE provide an excellent source of teaching materials for those who need to engage in negotiations and discussions using English as a *lingua franca*. For example, one could display the transcript of Excerpt 1 to the students utterance by utterance, first giving them the opportunity to suggest what responses they might have made had they been in the Singaporean speaker's position. The students' suggestions and responses can then be compared with the Singaporean's actual responses. The teacher could also point out that the Laotian interactant was clearly having trouble understanding the Singaporean's question and elicit students' suggestions about how the other participant in the interaction could help to resolve the issue. In this way the teacher could elicit or introduce the strategy of 'participant paraphrase,' as practiced by the speaker from Myanmar. Role play based on similar contexts could also be developed with students being required to play both the role of the more fluent participant as well as the less fluent participant and evaluating how the different roles influenced their experience of the interaction. They could also list the strategies they adopted and evaluate their relative success. In later sections we provide further practical suggestions for facilitators of English for diplomatic purposes to help their students develop competencies for working in English as a *lingua franca*.

The research indicating that ELF speakers cooperatively strive for communicative success has largely been based on interactions where the stakes are not high. As Yule noted above, however, in task-based exchanges (particularly high-stakes ones) there can be a tendency for the more proficient speakers to blame the less proficient ones for problems encountered in completing the task. Recent research also illustrates that ELF communication is not always smooth and communicatively successful. For example, Jenks' study on ELF talk in online chat rooms led him to conclude 'ELF interactants are not inherently mutually supportive and do not always seek to build consensus; on the contrary, they highlight problems or troubles in communication through laughter, joking, and ridicule' (Jenks, 2012: 386). Walkinshaw and Kirkpatrick (2014) identify the use of mock impoliteness and contradictions or counterclaims that appear to threaten directly the face of the relevant interactant(s). Similar confrontational strategies are illustrated in some of the data we discuss below.

Ensuring successful communication when the speakers come from a variety of linguistic and cultural backgrounds is no easy task. 'ELF cannot be seen as a culturally reduced or identity neutral medium of communication' (Archibald *et al.*, 2011: 4). It has long been established that speakers may transfer their own pragmatic and cultural norms from their first language when speaking in a second language and that these may be interpreted against first language or first culture norms (Baker, 2011; Gumperz, 1982; Klimczak-Pawlak, 2014). For example, a person who transfers Chinese request-making norms when making requests in English, or who transfers patterns of Chinese argument when putting forward an opinion may be classified by native speakers of English as someone who 'beats around the bush' or who never gets to the point. This is because a common rhetorical strategy in Chinese is to provide reasons for a request before making it, much as supporting arguments are often presented before making the main point (Kirkpatrick, 1995; see Kirkpatrick & Xu, 2012: 125 ff. for several examples of this). In the 1970s, one of the authors (Kirkpatrick) conducted a study into the communication problems that were besetting what was then known as the Royal Hong Kong Police. At that time, the majority of the senior officers had been seconded from the United Kingdom and the junior ranks were mostly Cantonese. Few of the senior officers had experience of Chinese cultures or knew any Chinese languages. It became clear that a major problem in communication – aside from the obvious one of few expatriate officers being proficient in Chinese – was caused by the Chinese police transferring Chinese rhetorical styles into their English; and that these rhetorical styles were being interpreted and evaluated by the senior officers as if they had been uttered by British speakers of English (see also Young, 1994). So, as indicated above, Chinese police wanting to make a request tended to preface their request with the reasons for it. A typical example occurred when a Chinese police constable requesting a period of leave began his request by saying that his mother was ill, that he had to take her to hospital and so forth. The English officer became irritated, wanting the constable to come to the point and make his request explicitly, e.g. 'Can I have some leave on Thursday please sir?' Making a direct request in this way of a senior officer would have been extremely face-threatening to the Chinese, not least because the direct request could have been met with a direct 'No'. Taking a more indirect approach by prefacing the request with reasons is a far less threatening strategy, respecting, as it does, the relative status of the parties involved. If the request is to be refused for any reason the senior officer can indicate this before the request is actually made by giving a reason why no leave is being granted at the moment. This allows the requestor, the police constable in this case, to withdraw from the interaction with his face intact. Conversely, if the leave can be granted, the senior officer can grant the request before it is explicitly made, thereby enjoying the face-boost of appearing thoughtful and sensitive. Consequently, materials and role plays were developed to show how Chinese rhetorical norms could be transferred into the English of the Chinese police, and how these norms could be interpreted and responded to in this type of cross-cultural communication.

Thus, when English is used as a tool for diplomacy and conflict resolution, it is imperative that interactants of all linguistic origins are conscious of how English is used as a *lingua franca*. Specifically, interactants need to be sensitive to the fact that speakers' own cultures may be reflected in the way they use English and the impact this has on utterance production and rhetoric, as well as rights and obligations vis-à-vis turn-taking, topic control and possession of the floor. As mentioned previously, it is also worth remembering that the majority of users of English in today's world are non-native speakers using English as a *lingua franca*. Multilinguals in Asia have shaped English to reflect their own cultures, such that it is now possible to talk about the distinct Englishes of India, Pakistan, Bangladesh, Sri Lanka, Nepal, Malaysia, Singapore, Brunei and the Philippines, whose speakers have taken ownership of English, shaping and adapting it to suit their own values and needs. By contrast, 'native' English speakers are a minority, so the onus is on them to become familiar with how English has been adapted by other groups, how Englishes encode the cultural values of their speakers and the implications of this for intercultural communication. Part of this consciousness-raising is awareness that so-called 'native' varieties of English can be difficult for speakers of other varieties to comprehend, not due to linguistic deficit but to issues of speaker idiomaticity and intelligibility (Seidlhofer, 2009). Englishes spoken by educated speakers from Hong Kong and Singapore are actually more internationally intelligible (e.g. Kirkpatrick *et al.*, 2008; Smith & Rafiqzad, 1979). A further point is that ELF can be a channel of revolution and resistance to the 'linguistic imperialism' propounded by Phillipson (1992). To this end, Whitehead (2011) argues, it is essential that the ELT profession develops accountable professional standards. The profession also needs to ensure that its practitioners receive training in the use of ELF, some suggestions for which have already been made and to which we return in the implications section of the chapter. We now provide a brief overview of the official role of English in ASEAN and the ASEAN or Asian way.

ELF in ASEAN and the Asian Way

ASEAN aims to promote the so-called ASEAN way, which can be encapsulated in two Malay concepts, *musyawarah* (dialogue) and *muafakat* (consensus) (Curley & Thomas, 2007). The ASEAN way underlines the importance of consensus building and group consultation, not only between the respective nations but also between governments and the private sector (Wu, 2011). Wu notes that 'While ASEAN as a collective may know what it wants, these consultations help the group ascertain how to get there.' Of course, consensus building is crucial to all diplomatic activity. However, as we show below, it seems to have particular significance for the ASEAN way.

Given that, as we noted above, ASEAN represents rich linguistic, cultural and religious diversity, maintaining dialogue and reaching consensus is likely to provide challenges. This is a major reason for the drawing up of the ASEAN Charter, which aims to define 'a more cohesive structure with specific rules of engagement for member countries,' including 'enforceable obligations' (Kumar & Siddique, 2008: 75). At the same time, ASEAN's slogan is 'unity in diversity,' a popular catchphrase among diverse nations or communities. For example, it is also the slogan for Indonesia, and the European Union. Quite how the adoption of English as the sole working language will promote unity in diversity is not made clear, since the promotion of a single language (as is the case with English in ASEAN and with the promotion of Bahasa Indonesia as the national *lingua franca* of Indonesia) usually serves to undermine linguistic and cultural diversity.

While seeking consensus and facilitating dialogue are key aims in all diplomacy, diplomatic discussions can be tense and high stakes are often involved. As a minister in the Cambodian government reported when discussing the role of English in ASEAN (Clayton, 2006: 230–231):

> If we don't know English, how can we participate? We need to know English so that we can defend our interests. You know, ASEAN is not some kissy-kissy brotherhood. The countries are fiercely competitive, and a strong knowledge of English will help us protect our interests.

In such contexts, while seeking consensus and facilitating dialogue remain important aims, discussions may be hard-edged and passionate. The patience shown by the Singaporean speaker in (1) above is unlikely to be replicated when the stakes are high and participants are trying to win arguments or, at the very least, ensure that their arguments and points of view are understood, if not accepted. The Cambodian minister cited above also understood that the role of English in ASEAN had little connection with a native speaking variety of English, saying, 'You know, when we use English we don't think about the United States or England. We only think about the need to communicate' (Clayton, 2006: 233).

In this section of the chapter we have briefly reviewed recent research into ELF and shown ELF speakers need to develop a range of communicative strategies to ensure successful communication between speakers from a variety of linguistic and cultural backgrounds. It is thus important that those who engage in ELF communication are trained not to judge ELF speakers' against their own cultural norms, in order to avoid misleading stereotyping and serious misunderstandings. We have also reviewed research that shows that multilingual ELF users tend to be supportive in seeking a collegial and collaborative atmosphere in which successful communication is the goal, while warning that, when the stakes are high and individual or national interests are at stake, discussions are likely to become more hard-edged. We have also given a brief review of the role of English in ASEAN. In the next section of the chapter we illustrate the use of ELF in a variety of settings, employing data from the ACE corpus.

ELF use in ASEAN

We here explore how English is used as a *lingua franca* in ASEAN. In the first excerpts we attempt to identify concrete evidence in the ACE corpus for an ASEAN or Asian way. The participants in these excerpts are consular staff from Bruneian, Malaysian and Indonesian embassies who are undertaking a professional development course at the University of Brunei. They are discussing how they might handle complaints or problems connected with the issuing or non-issuing of visas. In these excerpts there are three participants. S4 is a Bruneian female, S5 a Malaysian male and S6 an Indonesian female.

In Excerpt 2 below, the Bruneian female makes explicit reference to an Asian way. This is picked up by the Indonesian female who says, as an example of the Asian way, that she dislikes refusing requests. The notation conventions are provided in the appendix.

Excerpt 2
S4: <soft> no problem </soft> SO that was about VISA as well you know=
S6: =yeah (1) <soft> visa (as) </soft>
S5: mhm: mhm
S6: but (1)
S4: but is THERE is there particular asian way to say it (.) <soft> what they want us to say </soft> hh e:r (.) <1> you go with </1>
S6: <1> THE THING is </1> i (.) i've never (.) like refuse any asian: (.) <soft> countries you know </soft> when they come to us to for visa (.) maybe other countries but not asians so far so (.) that's why when in case of nigerian yes i (.) <2> once </2>
S4: <2> mhm </2>

This notion of an 'Asian way' is further developed in Excerpt 3. It is worth noting that the 'Asian way' is also directly contrasted with 'western culture,' when the Malaysian male says 'they will totally follow the procedure'.

Excerpt 3

S4: =so that's that's asian </L1mal> lah </L1mal> you know =
S6: = yeah yeah =
S4: = <L1mal> ah </L1mal>
S5: <1> but sometimes i suspect (.) yeah</1>
S6: <1> we don't we don't be like </1> <2> it's it's nice</2>
S4: <2> <L1mal> ah </L1mal> </2>
S6: to refuse (.) you know =
S4: = yeah
S6: people when they come and ask you for a favor or something like that =
S4: = <3> and then </3>
S5: <3> th- </3>
S4: especially (.) you know <4> with phone calls </4> like that
S6: <4> yeah and <un> x <un> </4>
S6: <5> yeah especially if you know them </5>
S5: <5> i think i think in the western (.) </5> i think in the western culture they will (1) totally follow the (.)
S6: yeah
S5: the procedure right if (.) tomorrow means tomorrow if you cannot means cannot =
S4: = yeah
S6: <6> <soft> i don't know </soft> </6>
S5: <6> erm </6> but because we: you know being asian we want to: (.) we we don't like to hurt others
S6: yeah
S5: and er <7> @@@ </7>
S6: <7> @@@ </7> hh we like to be nice @@@@

Excerpts 2 and 3 are interesting in that they illustrate that an 'Asian way' has real meaning for the participants and that they are conscious of a possible tension between following the Asian way and strictly correct procedure. The excerpts show that achieving consensus is at the forefront of their thinking and influences their decisions and actions.

Crucially, the context for the excerpts above is collegial; the stakes are not high and the participants are discussing a topic of mutual interest. Excerpt 4 is also taken from a context where the participants are working together toward a common goal. They are discussing the finer points of debating. S2 and S4 are Bruneian males, S5 is a Pakistani male, S6 is a Cambodian male and S7 is a Malaysian female. It is worth noting that, even though the Cambodian speaker (S6) says the least in this excerpt, his three contributions ('yeah, same place,' 'I mean it's you mean it's the you mean to interact face to face,' and 'caseline') are all picked up by other participants. We have underlined his contributions to make them easier to identify.

Excerpt 4

S2: =exactly

S5: and they (.) not facing each other (.) and you don't er (.) you are <1>not </1>

S2: <1>er</1> so: it's not in existence of (.) er what do you call that?

S4: it's like so (.) virtual interaction?

S7: but we can't say they're not at the same place or same time (.) sometimes they are at the same time=

S2: =yeah

S5: y-y-you usually not at the same place and same time @@@

S2: i mean (.) i-it is possible.

S4: =then

S2: so if it's possible it's still possible then w-w-we cannot include that (.) yeah

S6: yeah (.) same place

S4: then we just skip the (.) <5> same place at the same time </5>

S7: <5> <un> xx </un> the same </5> virtual mediums

S4: yeah just just erm (.) focus on virtual interaction

S2: that's it

S4: that erm (.) which not include paralinguistic right?

S7: mhm (.) does not include paralinguistic

S2: so how would you write this. how would you say this.

S4: virtual interaction in FORM of linguistic.

S5: <soft>having the linguistic features</soft>

S4: and not paralinguistic @@@@ (18) okay.

S2: do we need to have a specific goal? (.) like erm (.) what is the interaction used for like to create BONDS or (.) okay if it's to create BONDS then face to face interaction is obviously better right?

S4: yeah (.) we need to focus on that as well=

S7: =yeah

S6: i mean (.) it's er (.) y-y-you mean it's the (.) you mean to (.) interact f-face to face.

S2: okay so we have (.) definitions down? (.) what else (.) what else do we have

S4: we have some points as well

S6: caseline

S2: okay. so (.) let's think of a caseline. i already have mine. (1) you guys wanna come up with something?

These examples can all be used in the classroom to generate discussion into whether there really is an ASEAN way and, if so, in which contexts it is likely to be realized and in which contexts collegiality might be sacrificed in order to advance an interactional goal. Students could also be provided with a range of contexts and be asked to judge whether these are likely to be high stakes or low stakes and the implications of this for how the interaction develops. As will be illustrated in the next excerpts, in some contexts a desire for consensus and collegiality is discarded in favor of pressing home one's argument while rebutting those of interlocutors.

The final extracts from the ACE corpus come not from diplomacy but from the courtroom. We include these to show that the context influences the language used by ELF speakers, just as it influences the language of all speakers. The courtroom data provide examples of ELF speakers who, contrary to Firth's (1996) findings, do not let a matter pass in the hope all will become clear later. Direct, confrontational questioning and bald-on-record disagreement are common currency in these exchanges, where winning the argument supersedes the desire for interactional comity. The first courtroom excerpts are drawn from a dispute over the boundaries of a property. The participants are L1 speakers of Cantonese. The setting here determines the use of language, and the 'Asian way' is clearly not applicable to this context. In Excerpt 5 below, S5 demands to know S2's point, employing a direct and confrontational line of questioning with few mitigating devices or softeners.

Excerpt 5

S2: that is the distance from the top of the retaining wall to the surface of the berm
S5: then what's your point?
S2: okay
S5: what's the point?
S2: now okay my point is with that figure in mind...

A few lines later S5 continues:

S5: sorry I can't catch your point
S2: okay
S5: really
S1: it is
S5: I can't catch your point if I project

So in the space of a few turns, S5 repeats four times that he cannot catch the point that S2 is trying to make. This represents a direct threat to S2's face. The next set of excerpts of courtroom data offer further examples of contradictions that threaten an interlocutor's face:

Excerpt 6

S3: yes I agree this therefore this portion was classified to the low 7355
S2: no I think maybe you have misunderstood my question what I'm saying is your answer to me earlier…

Excerpt 7

S2: but the boundary was here right
S3: yes
S2: so what makes you think that this portion would be used by the owner of 7355?

Excerpt 8

S2: would you agree with me that you have not taken into account the evolution history of the lot 7355?
S3: no I do not agree.

In Excerpt 6, S2 interrupts S3's utterance to assert that S3 has misunderstood S2's question, and frames S3 as failing to fully comprehend the content of the exchange – a potential threat to S3's face as a competent actor in a professional milieu. S2 then reinforces the face-threat by pointedly prefacing his clarification with 'what I'm saying is,' implicitly reiterating his belief that S3 has not understood what S2 is saying. In Excerpt 7, S2's use of 'so what makes you think' could be evaluated as questioning the validity of a point made earlier by S3. Again S3's face as a competent professional is threatened. And in Excerpt 8, S3 counters by directly disagreeing with S2's assertion, without offering redress of any kind. In the next samples of courtroom dialogue we further illustrate how the situational context and the objectives of the exchange override any desire for cooperation or consensus.

Excerpt 9

S1: …based on the plan and this photo the material was in fact part of the original approved=
S2: =no=
S1: =building structure
S2: no it is not
S1: it you
S2: that is
S1: are sure
S2: of yes it is erm the er er erm (.) of the (.) part of the (.) canopy (.)
S1: why (.) are you so sure? have you talked to the person (.) or company (.) who or which constructed this structure?
S2: hm:
S1: you didn't.

S2: no
S1: why were you so sure?
S2: hm: (28)

In Excerpt 9, the two participants disagree without regard for one another's face-needs. S1's assertion that 'the material was in fact part of the original approved building structure' is directly contradicted by S2, who says 'no it is not'. A few turns later S2 asserts that the material was part of the canopy rather than the original structure. S1's rejoinder 'why are you so sure' appears to undermine the quality of S2's statement, particularly as, not having received a satisfactory response, he repeats it in the following turn.

In sum, face-work and rapport management are not a priority in the courtroom exchanges outlined above. Indeed, undermining interlocutors' face appears to be a common practice, perhaps as a function of the interactional objectives in that milieu: to advance one's arguments while discrediting those of one's opponents. We therefore suggest that facilitators of diplomatic communication ensure their students understand the importance of situational/institutional context, relative power and status of the participants, and the potential influence of these on the type of linguistic and rhetorical forms adopted. Clearly, the default 'Asian Way' schema may be overruled by interactional factors, particularly when the stakes are high.

Discussion and Conclusion

In this chapter we have shown that, while ELF speakers do tend to cooperate in their desire to ensure successful communication and, in so doing, focus on the message of the communication rather than the form (Archibald *et al.*, 2011), this does not mean that all ELF communication is cooperative. The situational context and the interactional objectives determine the type of language employed. We illustrated this with extracts taken from the ACE corpus. We showed that the notion of an 'Asian way' appears valid, with the consular officials in Excerpts 2 and 3 making explicit reference to this and contrasting it with the procedures adopted by 'western culture'. We demonstrated that, when engaged in a group task, the ELF speakers were cooperative and made efforts to comprehend the contributions of less proficient interactants. However, we then showed that when confrontation is expected (e.g. the courtroom case), then oppositional disagreements could be voiced with little regard for interlocutor face concerns or overall group rapport. These exchanges also illustrated that speakers focused on message rather than form; non-standard forms or mispronunciations did not disrupt the conversational flow or occasion any misunderstanding. Finally, the excerpts from courtroom exchanges also demonstrate how the setting and context determine language use: these exchanges were characterized by direct contradictions and disagreements, all threatening the recipients' face.

What lessons can be drawn from the examples that might aid successful communication in ELF interactions?

The first is that training in ELF communication is essential for all potential ELF users, including speakers of English as a first language. It is not enough to teach some ill-defined notion of English when the English will be required to secure conflict resolution between people of differing linguistic and cultural backgrounds. People will need to learn how ELF is used and the importance of focusing on the message being conveyed rather than on the linguistic form. At the same time, people will need training in recognizing how the cultural values and pragmatic norms of ELF speakers may be reflected in their use of English. They need training to avoid stereotyping ELF speakers by evaluating their use of English against their own cultural or linguistic norms and thus making inaccurate assumptions about the speaker's personality or intelligence. By the same token, they need to be aware that their own cultural values and pragmatic norms are not necessarily shared. What seems normal to them may seem inappropriate or even offensive to others. In short, people engaged in ELF communication need emotional intelligence and sensitivity to alternative ways of speaking and doing (Kirkpatrick & Sussex, 2012).

In the specific context of ASEAN, the promotion of English as the sole working language has provided further impetus for education systems and curricula to make English the first language, other than the national language, to be learned in schools. English is a compulsory subject in all the region's primary schools except Indonesia. This means that English, in the great majority of cases, has replaced local languages in the primary curriculum. The case for a *'lingua franca* approach' to the teaching of English in ASEAN has been proposed (Kirkpatrick, 2012) from which the following two principles are taken: (1) to ensure that the English curriculum is ASEAN- or Asian-centric and incorporates knowledge of the cultures and religions of the countries of ASEAN; and (2) the teaching of English should be delayed until children have fluency and literacy in their mother tongue and the national language (these are often different languages in multilingual ASEAN). This would ensure children develop a sense of self-worth and confidence in their own cultures before being required to learn English. An ASEAN-centered English curriculum would then ensure they became familiar with the languages and cultures of the region.

Such measures might help ASEAN marry the apparently contradictory policies of making English the sole working language while ensuring respect for the many languages, cultures and religions of ASEAN. Citizens confident in the value of their own languages and cultures, knowledgeable about regional languages and cultures and who are trained as ELF speakers are more likely to be able to maintain dialogue and reach consensus in diplomacy and conflict resolution than those who have been taught that English is the language of native-speaking 'others' over which they have no ownership and whose too-early introduction to English has undermined their confidence in their own cultures and languages. At the same time, all who are required to negotiate using ELF need specific training in the use of ELF. This is particularly important for those who use English for diplomatic purposes in ASEAN's richly multicultural and linguistically diverse milieu, where the Englishes used by the Asian multilinguals concerned are likely to have been shaped by local languages, cultures, and values.

Note

(1) The five founding member nations of ASEAN were Indonesia, Malaysia, the Philippines, Singapore and Thailand. Brunei, Cambodia, Laos, Myanmar and Vietnam have since joined.

References

Archibald, A., Cogo, A. and Jenkins, J. (eds) (2011) *Latest Trends in ELF Research*. Newcastle: Cambridge Scholars Publishing.

Baker, W. (2011) Culture and identity through ELF in Asia: Fact or fiction? In A. Archibald, A. Cogo and J. Jenkins (eds) *Latest Trends in ELF Research* (pp. 35–51). Newcastle: Cambridge Scholars Publishing.

Bolton, K. and Graddol, D. (2012) English in China today. *English Today* 28 (3), 3–9.

Canagarajah, A.S. (2013) *Translingual Practice: Global Englishes and Cosmopolitan Relations*. New York and Abingdon: Routledge.

Clayton, T. (2006) *Language Choice in a Nation Under Transition: English Language Spread in Cambodia*. Boston, MA: Springer.

Curley, M. and Thomas, N. (2007) Advancing East Asian regionalism: An introduction. In M. Curley and N. Thomas (eds) *Advancing East Asian regionalism* (pp. 1–25). London: Routledge.

Firth, A. (1996) The discursive accomplishment of normality: On 'lingua franca' English and conversation analysis. *Journal of Pragmatics* 26, 237–259.

Friedrich, P. and Gomes de Matos, F. (2012) Toward a nonkilling linguistics. In P. Friedrich (ed.) *Nonkilling Linguistics: Practical Applications* (pp. 17–38). Hawaii: Center for Global Nonkilling.

Gumperz, J.J. (1982) *Discourse Strategies. Volume 1*. Cambridge: Cambridge University Press.

House, J. (2003) English as a lingua franca: A threat to multilingualism? *Journal of Sociolinguistics* 7 (4), 556–578.

Jenks, C. (2012) Doing being reprehensive: Some interactional features of English as a lingua franca in a chat room. *Applied Linguistics* 33 (4), 386–405.

Kirkpatrick, A. (1995) Chinese rhetoric: Methods of argument. *Multilingua* 14 (3), 271–295.

Kirkpatrick, A. (2010) *English as a Lingua Franca in ASEAN: A Multilingual Model.* Hong Kong: Hong Kong University Press.

Kirkpatrick, A. (2012) English as an Asian lingua franca: The lingua franca approach and implications for language education policy. *Journal of English as a Lingua Franca* 1 (1), 121–140.

Kirkpatrick, A and Sussex, R. (2012) A postscript and a prolegomenon. In A. Kirkpatrick and R. Sussex (eds) *English as an International in Asia: Implications for Language Education* (pp. 223–232). Dordrecht: Springer.

Kirkpatrick, A. and Xu, Z. (2012) *Chinese Rhetoric and Writing: An Introduction for Language Teachers.* Anderson, SC: Parlor Press. http://wac.colostate.edu/books/kirkpatrick_xu/

Kirkpatrick, A., Deterding, D. and Wong, J. (2008) The international intelligibility of Hong Kong English. *World Englishes* 29 (3–4), 359–377.

Klimczak-Pawlak, A. (2014) *Towards the Pragmatic Core of English for European Communication.* Dordrecht: Springer.

Kumar, S. and Siddique, S. (2008) *Southeast Asia: The Diversity Dilemma.* Singapore: Select Books.

Mauranen, A. (2006) A rich domain of ELF: The ELFA corpus of academic discourse. *Nordic Journal of English Studies* 5 (2), 145–159.

Meierkord, C. (2012) *Interactions Across Englishes.* Cambridge: Cambridge University Press.

Nickerson, C. (2010) The Englishes of business. In A. Kirkpatrick (ed.) *The Routledge Handbook of World Englishes* (pp. 506–519). London: Routledge.

Ostler, N. (2010) *The Last Lingua Franca.* London: Penguin.

Phillipson, R. (1992) *Linguistic Imperialism.* Oxford: Oxford University Press.

Seidlhofer, B. (2009) Accommodation and the idiom principle in English as a lingua franca. *Journal of Intercultural Pragmatics* 6 (2), 195–215.

Seidlhofer, B. (2010) Lingua franca English: The European context. In A. Kirkpatrick (ed.) *The Routledge Handbook of World Englishes* (pp. 355–371). London: Routledge.

Severino, R. (ed.) (2005) *Framing the ASEAN Charter.* Singapore: Institute of Southeast Asian Studies.

Smith, L. and Rafiqzad, K. (1979) English for cross-cultural communication: The issue of intelligibility. *TESOL Quarterly* 13, 371–380.

Walkinshaw, I. and Kirkpatrick, A. (2014) Mutual face preservation among Asian speakers of English as a lingua franca. *Journal of English as a Lingua Franca* 3 (2), 267–289.

Whitehead, D. (2011) English language in fragile states: Justifying action, promoting success and combating hegemony. In H. Coleman (ed.) *Dreams and Realities: Developing Countries and the English Language* (pp. 333–369). London: The British Council.

Wu, D. (2011) ASEAN's third way? (2011) *The Diplomat.* See http://thediplomat.com/2011/11/aseans-third-way/ (retrieved November 2011).

Young, L.W. (1994) *Cross-Talk and Culture in Sino-American Communication.* Cambridge: Cambridge University Press.

Yule, G. (1990) Interactive conflict resolution in English. *World Englishes* 9 (1), 53–62.

Appendix

Notation Conventions

ACE has adopted the transcription conventions of VOICE in order to ensure researchers can easily compare the two corpora. Overlapping utterances are marked with numbered tags, e.g. <1>…</1>. Laughter is indicated through @@@, each symbol approximating a syllable. A short pause is indicated by a period flanked by brackets, e.g. (.) and a longer one by the length of the pause in seconds flanked by brackets, e.g. (2). {xx} signifies unintelligible speech, and capitals indicates a raised voice. An equal sign (=) at the end of one utterance and the beginning of another indicates a join. A colon inserted after a vowel indicates lengthening (e.g. o:h). To preserve confidentiality all names and places mentioned are replaced with [First name 1], [Place 2] etc.

5 World Englishes and Peace Linguistics: Their Contribution to English for Diplomatic Purposes

Patricia Friedrich

Introduction

World Englishes is an academic orientation and a way of seeing linguistic relationships that acknowledges the existence of great variation across linguistic expressions in the English language. These variations are historically and culturally motivated and are also, as a matter of course, to be expected in a language that has grown to be used by a very large portion of the world's population for a very large number of functions.

To acknowledge the reality, contribution, and role of World Englishes is to in a way endorse a view of the world according to which difference is treated as inclusive diversity and where one's position in the world of languages is also seen in relative rather than absolute terms. That is, World Englishes scholars and students are more interested in describing and analyzing Englishes as they happen in the world and as they are manifested within different cultures than in prescribing extrinsic rules. Once aspects of the dynamics of English use and need are known, one can use the information to create better pedagogical practices, language policies, etc.

In this chapter, I will first present some basic tenets of World Englishes to then bring it together with Peace Linguistics to highlight the importance of the acknowledgment of Englishes in diplomatic communications. I will also briefly document how Peace Linguistics elements, aligned to World Englishes perspectives, further enhance the job of those working toward an equally peace-fostering diplomacy. The chapter will close with activities that teachers of Diplomatic Englishes can present in the classroom or that learners of Diplomatic English can attempt on their own. The ultimate goal is that, when engaged in diplomatic negotiations, users of Diplomatic Englishes remember that language also needs to be negotiated, that the form of our words matters, and that one's view and use of English is relative to their place in the world, linguistic background and linguistic repertoire. Accessing these aspects of linguistic communications can help those engaged in acts of diplomacy get the best of their interactions, as they pursue greater peace and understanding and their best interests along with the interests of their counterparts.

World Englishes

The last few decades of the 20th century brought greater awareness that English, much like it happens to all natural, living languages, is not a static and monoform unit; rather, it changes and adapts depending on the environment, the cultures, and the language users that make use of it in different parts of the world. Given this awareness, it has become necessary to refer to English in the plural Englishes, as a way to acknowledge the great diversity in grammatical, vocabulary, structural and cultural underpinnings of the different varieties used in different realms of life.

Languages are constantly changing, and throughout history, we have seen such process of change lead to both the formation of new languages (e.g. Latin gave origin to Portuguese, Spanish, Italian, French and Romanian) and the disappearance of the original language (which now, in the case of Latin, has the status of a dead language since it does not change anymore). English is constantly changing too, but what complicates predictions regarding its maintenance as 'one language' or its possible fragmentation in multiple languages – after all, we are already calling it 'Englishes' – is the presence of global and virtual forms of communication and media on a scale never experienced before.

Historically, geographical isolation has meant the development of local norms that not always coincide with the norms of other varieties, thus in time generating enough changes for intelligibility to be partially or fully compromised. Of course the classification into languages is more a political and social phenomenon than a linguistic one, but once intelligibility falls significantly, the more reason there is for an understanding of varieties as new languages. However, contemporarily, geographical distance has been somewhat neutralized by virtual communications, which erase physical boundaries. The future of English is harder to predict because of that. However, for the foreseeable future, it seems reasonable to expect that English will continue to serve its role as an important language of international communication, a fact which makes World Englishes information and awareness all the more necessary.

Relying especially on the lead provided by the seminal work of Braj Kachru (1983 and after), we have gradually studied and profiled different varieties of English with an eye on increasing understanding and facilitating communication, teaching and policy-making. Notice we, in World Englishes, have privileged the term language 'variety,' and we tend to avoid the term 'dialect' because the later at times has a hierarchical connotation that subordinates it to 'standard' language. This later term is more an abstract ideal than anything else, and while we must go beyond just replacing linguistic terms to truly revise our beliefs, introducing language that is already inclusive in its form already hints at a positive intention.

In the realm of World Englishes, there exists less judgment of the correctness of a variety and more consideration of its functional range. That is, we are constantly asking ourselves what purposes and functions a given variety fulfills in the real world. In that sense it is important to observe, analyze and find the uses that a language variety has and can have without the prejudice of *a priori* prescriptive judgments. In their intrinsic logic, all languages are rule-governed, so it is more a matter of understanding what the rules are and what purposes they serve than issuing normative 'should-bes.'

Expecting to find users of language around the world that employ the very same static varieties all the time, means almost always being met with disappointment. In turn, successful communication may at times require great flexibility and an expectation of differences, followed by good strategies to understand and make oneself understood despite variation. As explained by Kachru and Nelson (2001: 13):

> It is now generally recognized that, for purposes of rational analysis, descriptive characterizations of language provide the most positive opportunities for cogent insight into the way language actually works, as opposed to prescriptive declarations of the way one or another group or individual wishes language to work.

Thus, having a degree of acceptance and openness toward understanding the linguistic perspective of different users will go a long way in unveiling the dynamics of language itself as it *is* and not as one expects it *ought to be*.

According to Kachru's own framework, we often place the countries of the world within three Concentric Circles – the Inner, Outer and Expanding Circles of English. The Inner Circle is represented by those countries where English originated (i.e. Britain and the first wave of colonial countries, where English was established as a first language, for example, the United States, Canada, Australia and New Zealand). There are many intranational functions played by English in these countries, since its official or *de facto* official status means roles in institutions such as the government, education and the law. The Outer Circle is comprised of those countries where English arrived via colonization and was established as a second or additional language, for example, India, Malaysia, Nigeria and Kenya. These countries have other official or *de facto* official languages alongside English, but often the users are not so-called native-speakers of the language (although some may be). Just like the Inner Circle: countries in the Outer Circle offer opportunities for intranational use, for example, in education, the law and communication across different linguistic groups. Finally, the Expanding Circle is formed by the other countries in the world, those for which most of the functions performed by English involve communication of an international nature. Even when English is used within the country, it is more likely for communication with international travelers, businesspeople, diplomatic workers, etc., or in foreign language education. This circle is called 'Expanding' because the movement of expansion has not yet stopped, with new users and new uses coming into being every day.

A World Englishes framework has made us further aware that when it comes to linguistic rules, not all environments will look to the Inner Circle, and especially the US and Britain for adequate models of language. Even within the Inner Circle, one will find that grammar, phonology, and syntax rules are not always those originating in American and British environments, but that Australia and New Zealand, for example, also have many locally generated rules. In time, the same happened to the colonial contexts of the Outer Circle, where local grammars, vocabulary, and patterns of pronunciation have developed. While the countries in the Expanding Circle tend to look for models especially in the Inner Circle, they too are loci for creativity and innovation. With all this diversity come greater possibilities of linguistic expression, but when communication across countries and across the Circles is at stake, greater chances of clashes and misunderstandings due to varying codes also exist.

Instead of trying to come up with universalizing rules of what language 'should' be, a World Englishes framework usually advocates that language be looked at contextually and be understood given its historical and social contexts in ways that are not limiting. Rather, WE offers us a focus on uses that are fostering of greater participation of individuals and their communities in their own linguistic destinies, spreading awareness to the fact that living languages are always changing and adapting to the environments where they occur. For that reason, World Englishes is a very empowering framework: it puts the focus back on those who use the language for a variety of functional roles, regardless of their status as native-speakers, users of English as a second or foreign language, or any other such labels. This is an important consideration here because many of the interactions that go on everyday around the world in business, diplomacy, and education do not involve so-called native speakers at all. These users, along with anyone else who uses English, need to come to terms with variation where it occurs: in social situations, boardrooms, meeting rooms, classrooms, etc.

Peace Linguistics

Peace Linguistics is primarily associated with Brazilian linguist Francisco Gomes de Matos, featured in Chapters 1 and 8 of this volume. According to his view peace is:

A profound process of humanization, a system of humanizing oneself and others, or in less abstract terms, a system of becoming humanizers, that is, persons imbued with such values as compassion, dignity, human rights, justice, peace, solidarity, (cross) cultural understanding and who apply such ideals in everyday (inter) actions. (Gomes de Matos, 2005: 2)

It follows that given the elements of this process, language must figure prominently as a catalyst for peace. Through language we can convey compassion, solidarity, and uphold another's dignity. Respect for linguistic human rights can guarantee that individuals have access to the linguistic resources they need. Cross-cultural understanding can be pursued by envisioning the kind of language that speaks more directly to a person's belief and value system. And justice many times depends on our speaking up when faced with injustice. Peace linguists and educators believe that we can learn the steps to use language in ways that are more conducive to peace and understanding, and it is clear that diplomacy must play a decisive role in (linguistic) peace processes.

Peace linguistics can be incorporated to the language curriculum at many levels. The most straightforward is a revision of vocabulary, but more can be done. Examples include (see Chapter 1) the following:

- The use of humanizing language;
- The design of strategies to deal with differences constructively;
- An emphasis on language that fosters peace rather than language used with a strategic agenda in mind;
- A focus on agreement rather than disagreement and controversy;
- The avoiding of pompous language, which typically brings up reservations, walls, and resistance.

Table 5.1 Examples of variation in vocabulary across Englishes

- He wants to buy a *smoking*. (Brazil, tuxedo)
- Did you bring the equipments? (India, plural form)
- She interviewed the outgone president. (Nigeria, former)
- Drive carefully, especially when you get to the stopstreet.[1] (South Africa, intersection with a stop sign).
- This sounds to me like a *furphy*[2] (Australia, a rumor or false report)
- Let's *prepone*[3] the meeting. (India, opposite of postpone)

Englishes, Peace and Diplomacy

This view of language and English as a diverse ecosystem of varieties which users resort to when they interact in different realms of life has many implications for diplomacy and for international negotiations because this is one such realm of use that tends to bring together users of language of the most diverse backgrounds, linguistic expectations, and cultural orientations.

It is to be expected that within the realm of diplomacy, interactions will often and likely take place between and among users of English from the three circles, and since English is a common choice for diplomatic negotiations, it is reasonable to expect that different Englishes can be at play at any given point in time. Being exposed to different Englishes increases one's chances of understanding them, and such familiarity also puts rules and linguistic 'laws' in perspective. Many users of language start seeing uses that they once thought of as 'wrong' as simply 'different.' This change in perspective is very important when it comes to accepting that language, despite being English, will at times be unfamiliar and to creating an environment of cooperation in face of differences, be they linguistic or otherwise.

One's position in the world is then relativized, and an understanding develops that more important than a binary separation between native and non-native speakers is a consideration of how one's familiarity or not with a variety influences one's intelligibility and response to language and of how ideas of purpose and audience work within different realms of use.

Table 5.2 Examples of pronunciation difference across Englishes

---

- Non-rhotic varieties common in English from England (the deletion of 'r' in word-final and before consonant environments, and elongation of preceding vowel, for example car /ca:/ or port /pɔːt/.
- Diphthongs in Australian English include for example /əu/ in words such as 'coat' and 'boat' where in American English the pronunciation would be /ou/.
- Addition of a final /i/ in Brazilian English when the word ends in a stop (i.e. consonants such as /k/ or /g/). For example, like /laiki/ or take /teiki/.
- Open vowel in Jamaican English in words such as man /mon/ and loss of diphthong in such words as way /we:/ and day /de:/.

If in diplomacy negotiations are the driving force when it comes to the content of interactions, studying World Englishes leads one to understand that negotiations regarding the form, the language itself, are also taking place all the time even when we are unaware of them. These negotiations will be mediated by the linguistic and cultural background of the participants involved, the purpose of the particular situation of communication and the message being communicated (among other elements). Awareness that elements of the negotiation will have to be bargained at the moment the interaction takes place will help the participants prepare for possible misunderstandings and utilize the necessary strategies to overcome them.

In addition, while everyone might be using 'the same' diplomatic language, for example French or English, the deep rhetorical beliefs about *how* to use them can vary greatly, adding to the complexity of using Englishes in context. For example, when it comes to politeness, a participant, given his or her cultural beliefs, might go 'straight to the point' assuming that saving time is a sign of consideration. They might, as a result, present a thesis statement addressing the purpose of conversation (or a solution, a plan, a demand) right away, taking the other participants by surprise if they believe meaningful interactions should be prefaced by a period of 'getting to know' your interlocutor. On the other hand, a member of another sociolinguistic group might believe that showing respect and consideration is more readily achieved through an initial period of small talk or ice-breaking and thus spend considerable time trying to foster that, to the impatience of the other party/parties.

This is just one of the many differences that can come to add to and influence the diversity of pronunciation, vocabulary, syntax and grammar that can exist in situations of communication involving participants from diverse backgrounds. When something as important as diplomatic understanding is at stake, it is worth discovering which linguistic practices can minimize conflict and misunderstanding in these situations.

Table 5.3 Some differences in cultural/rhetorical belief that influence language/ English use:

- High-context (i.e. people of this orientation typically place great importance on interpersonal relationships) and low-context (i.e. people of this orientation typically place great emphasis on straightforwardness of message (Hall, 1976)). Those that value high-context tend to be more verbose while they also avoid overly direct statements.
- Directness or indirectness (Tannen, 1994, for example). Those that value directness tend to state their purpose at the beginning of their communications and pay less attention to 'breaking the ice-or engaging in small talk'. Those that value indirectness often 'read between the lines' and imply what they mean.
- An inclination for individualism or collectivism (Hofstede, 2001). Collectivism means the valuing of the social collective well-being over the individual. High collectivism tends to correlate with high-context.
- A preference for inductive or deductive modes of presentation of information. To check for individual preferences one may observe whether they present a thesis first followed by a number of arguments and evidence if necessary or whether that person would rather lead the interlocutor through their whole logical reasoning before presenting at the end a resulting conclusion.
- The degree of power distance in their environment (i.e. more hierarchical or flatter, Hofstede, 2001). If one believes the separation that exists between them and their hierarchical superiors is very great, they will use language in ways that signal that recognition. Likewise, if one believes that the environment in which they operate is hierarchically flatter, they will use language accordingly.
- A view on whether conflict should be avoided or actively dealt with.

International English, English as a *lingua franca*, and World Englishes

In this chapter, English as a *lingua franca* (ELF) refers to the function that English performs in many international and intranational contexts when the participants of communication use English because it is the language that they have in common (regardless of the many different relationships they can have with the language itself – native speaker, user of English as a second or additional language, etc.[4]). That is, English performs the function *'lingua franca'* in these contexts: it provides a common language that enables communication to take place among people that without that linguistic commonality would be unable to fully communicate verbally. Given this understanding of *lingua franca* as a function, we can claim that diplomatic communication offers ample opportunities for such function to be performed. The term 'International English' would potentially refer to a universalized variety of English to be used in situations of *lingua franca* communication (the term *lingua franca* itself has been often used to refer to this international variety, especially one forming in the European context – see Jenkins, 2007 for example).

However, an appreciation of World Englishes, in my view obviates the need to use these other terms, except for *lingua franca* in the sense described above, because the plurality of a language that expands is in the very nature of that expansion, and achieving some sort of overarching universal is unlikely given the diversity of people who use the language and the uses they make of them. Instead, what we see in situations of communication where individuals originally from a number of backgrounds come together is that they must develop the necessary strategies to negotiate language in the context it occurs. In that sense, the kind of negotiation that will likely take place between a Japanese, a Brazilian, and an American will be one, in the case of that interaction, and another when that same Brazilian finds him/herself negotiating English meaning with an Argentine and a Belgian in another instance. These will be different Englishes, requiring different strategies depending on such elements as familiarity with the varieties being used, degree of intelligibility, previous knowledge of the interlocutors, etc.

Because of the above, the realm of diplomacy offers a fertile terrain for the function 'English as a *lingua franca*' to be performed. Yet users of English for diplomatic purposes need to develop awareness of, respect for, and the right strategies to deal with the many Englishes they may encounter in their career. Judging these Englishes in terms of more 'right' or more 'wrong' will do little to make communication happen smoothly. Instead, one can analyze what aspects of another's English are less familiar and more obscure to them, and what strategies will make the conversation/communication more productive.

An ability then to bring together and utilize different linguistic and sociolinguistic elements to achieve better communication can greatly benefit the user of diplomatic English; a solid understanding of the dynamics of World Englishes is a wonderful addition to this knowledge quest. In that spirit, I offer the suggestions for activities below.

World Englishes awareness activities

Activity 1 – Invite students to learn more about their linguistic networks. Ask them to list items that contribute to their linguistic repertoire, for example, the place where they were born, languages they speak/use, their occupation, hobbies or special activities they engage in. Reassure them that they can choose the items they feel comfortable about sharing. Once they have listed these items, explain that each of these groups represents a speech community, with its own practices and language, and that our idiolect (i.e. our individual variety) is a result of all these influences and therefore no two people have the same linguistic fingerprint. Pair up the students and ask them to create a diagram with the intersection of their linguistic experience. It might look something like this:

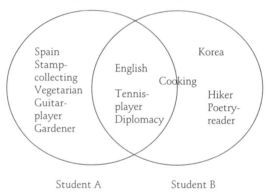

Spain
Stamp-
collecting
Vegetarian
Guitar-
player
Gardener

English

Cooking

Tennis-
player
Diplomacy

Korea

Hiker
Poetry-
reader

Student A   Student B

Have the students share with the class what they think the impact of being a part of these networks might have on their linguistic repertoire. For example, someone who reads poetry frequently might have a specialized language understanding, while someone who is a gardener might know the names of many species that for non-gardeners are simply 'plant', 'flower,' or 'tree.' Because the two participants in this mock interaction are tennis players, they likely share some linguistic items relating to that activity. The same is true of their involvement in diplomacy and their English knowledge. Remind students that they can always look for commonalities in networks to help establish communication and understanding. These commonalities can also provide topics for conversation during social interactions within their professional practice.

Activity 2 – Draw an image of the Three Concentric Circles either on the board or in a handout. Write a list of countries with different relationships with English and ask students to place them in the different areas of the image. If you are working alone, you can research the profile of each of the countries and decide where they fit better. As mentioned above, the model of the Concentric Circles of English was first created by Braj Kachru (see 1983, for example). For example,

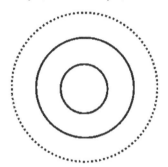

Malaysia/Brazil/Argentina/France/New Zealand/Philippines/South Korea/Japan/United States/England/Singapore/India/China/Jamaica

Note 1: South Africa is traditionally placed in the Inner Circle, but of the environments in that area, that country is arguably the most challenging to be placed neatly in one circle alone, with arguments being possible for parts of it to be placed in the Outer and Expanding Circles too.

Key to the answers: Brazil, Argentina, France, South Korea, Japan and China are usually placed in the Expanding Circle. India, Malaysia, Philippines, Singapore, and Jamaica are usually placed in the Outer Circle. New Zealand, United States, and England are often placed in the Inner Circle.

Activity 3 – Have students read newspapers in English from different countries in the Inner and Outer Circles (you can also include Expanding Circle countries although the number of newspapers will likely be smaller). Have them identify uses of English with which they are unfamiliar. These can refer to matters of usage, vocabulary, grammar rules or any other aspect of English form. Make a list of these occurrences. Have the students rephrase the sentences or expressions using their own varieties (if they can infer the meaning from the context, they can do that – if not, they can consult a dictionary of International English, a thesaurus, or another resource). As a follow up, ask students for strategies that they could have used in context if those expressions had been used face-to-face with them and they did not know the meaning.

Activity 4 – Select five to six audio samples from users of English around the world. Inform the students of the general context and subject matter of each sample. Create two or three probing questions and present them to the students before they listen to each segment. Have them answer the questions while they listen. Ask that they take note of any expressions that they can understand but whose meaning might be obscure. Have the students discuss their answers in pairs. Once that is done, clarify any lingering questions. Discuss with the students strategies for clarifying any parts they did not understand were those passages to be uttered to them in real life.

Note 2: Strategies can include asking for clarification (e.g. 'What did you mean by _____?'), repeating (e.g. 'You haven't had access to the report?'), or paraphrasing to check the meaning (e.g. 'Do you mean that we should wait to finish the project?').

Note 3: If the audio sample also contains video (a TV interview, for example), you can experiment with allowing the students to just listen first and then listen and watch the video at the same time. Since they will likely understand the passage better when they also look at the video, you can discuss the strategies they used (i.e. looking at facial expression, hand gestures, body language, lip-reading) to make up for partial understanding of the actual words/sentences/utterances.

Activity 5 – Identify commonly used expressions in Diplomatic English. Distribute sentences containing such expressions to pairs of students. Ask that they identify features of different rhetorical beliefs as shown in Table 5.3 (e.g. directness or great power distance). Ask that the students come up with alternatives for diverging contexts. For example, if the utterance, 'Good morning, Sir. I am honored with your presence here. Did you have an enjoyable flight? Are you happy with the fine weather we are having, Sir? Shall we start our meeting momentarily?' appeals more to indirectness and a significant degree of power distance, the alternative, 'Hello. It's nice to see you. Let's start the meeting in five minutes?' would appeal to flatter hierarchical lines and to directness. Ask students which version they prefer. Do they favor one for all situations? Would they choose differently depending on the situation? On the status of their interlocutor? On the basis of the number of times they met before?

Note 4: Students can then discuss with which groups and in which contexts each variant would be more appropriate and likely more welcome.

Activity 6 – Create a class list of locally generated terms in Englishes from around the world. You can start with the elements from Table 5.1. Notice that this list should contain elements that are for the most part different from the more common uses outside of these regions. Discuss strategies to unveil the meaning of these expressions should they happen in real-life communications. Suggest synonyms or ways to express these same ideas in the students' own varieties of English.

Activity 7 – Introduce students to or remind them of terms often used to describe people's relationships with language. Some terms you can use are as follows:

- Native-speaker
- Second-language writer
- User of English as an additional language
- User of English as a foreign language
- Non-native speaker
- First language
- Non-native speaker
- Mother tongue

Ask students what ideas they have about these expressions and challenge them to question the assumptions about them and their usefulness and accuracy. For example, can a person be more comfortable writing in a language that is not 'native' to them than in their native language? Can a person choose to keep a 'second language accent' to signal their membership in a group of their peers? What happens when a user of English as a foreign language moves to a country of the Inner Circle? How do they use language then? How do their beliefs about English and their users affect their professional activities? The idea is to have them challenge common, limiting assumptions about how people use language and about language ownership. At the end of the activity, ask students to narrate what this has to do with Diplomatic English(es).

Activity 8 – As with the previous activity, this one asks students to question commonly used terms and to discuss how they aid or limit the employment of language for a wide range of communication purposes. Some possible terms are as follows:

- variation
- mistake
- error
- intelligibility
- proficiency
- negotiation
- grammatically correct
- attitudes toward language
- linguistic innovation
- accent

Ask students how they feel about each of the terms. Invite them to explain the relevance, irrelevance or relative usefulness in light of a World Englishes framework and of their own experience and expectation regarding Diplomatic English(es).

Activity 9 – Once the students have had a significant amount of time to consider how a World Englishes approach can potentially enhance their language use, pair them up and give them cards with examples of situations of communication that they are likely to encounter in their professional interactions. The cards can be as vague or as specific as the needs of the students demand. For example, a card could read,

> You and your negotiating partner have agreed on the general terms of a student exchange program, but some disagreement remains as to what fields of knowledge should be included in the deal. Start a conversation where you explain to one another why you are suggesting a set of particular fields of expertise for this program.

Before the students start, elicit from the whole group vocabulary items that might be useful. Note any disagreement on terms, especially if the group has participants from different linguistic backgrounds. Have the class observe the conversation and take note of any elements (linguistic, rhetorical pattern, attitude) that could cause conflict in real life situations. Engage in whole-group discussion after each pair role-plays.

Activity 10 – The journal *World Englishes* contains a variety of articles tackling a range of aspects of English use and change from around the world. It would be instructional to have the students read select articles – on aspects such as the use of English in different realms of life, characteristics of new varieties, or the linguistic profile of different countries. In class, students can describe what they read and present short expositions on one of the following:

(1) What was to you the most surprising aspect of English use in this context and why? (e.g. English has official status and many uses in education in this part of the world)
(2) What aspect of English use in this context, if any, would likely be the most challenging if you were to interact there? (e.g. the pronunciation of vowels is quite different from that in my variety, and that could make understanding more difficult)
(3) What aspect of English use by these users most closely resembles your own experience with English? (e.g. English is mostly used for international communication and that is the case in my linguistic community as well)
(4) What aspects of English use by these users could you utilize to create community and situations of understanding and positive interaction? (e.g. users of English in this context seem to value their collectivity, so we can use that to build community)

Activity 11 – (This activity is adapted from ideas in Friedrich & Gomes de Matos, see first chapter and 2009). To a large degree, language users have become desensitized to the language of violence in our everyday life. From the titles of movies to how we name animals (e.g. killer bees and killer whale), we have often normalized violence in language. This activity invites learners to think of areas of expression and expressions themselves that are not fostering of a vocabulary of peace. Students are also invited to think of often-used words and phrases that carry a degree of violence. Students can be asked to simply brainstorm items or to think of particular categories to investigate. For example, what are some titles of movies that contain a vocabulary of violence? How about idiomatic expressions? How about more peaceful counterparts? Are there more or fewer peace-promoting names, expressions or titles in day-to-day life?

Note 5: A few examples to share - 'to be stabbed in the back' meaning to be betrayed; 'to make a killing in the stock market' meaning to make a lot of money; 'to wage war on the middle class' meaning to make the conditions of living hard on that group; 'a war of words' meaning a discussion. Chances are students will find expressions that foster peace, but likely they will unfortunately be fewer.

After these steps, students should be challenged to think of phrases and expressions they can use in their professional practice to enhance peaceful interactions. They can make a list to share with the class to become part of their linguistic repertoire.

Notes

(1) See entry in the Oxford *Dictionary*.
(2) See the Australian National Dictionary Centre and its reports.
(3) See The Christian Science Monitor article (Preponed Meetings and Other Time Travels by *Ruth Walker, 2 May, 2008*).
(4) In this chapter, as it happens elsewhere in my scholarship, I do not place much emphasis on these categories traditionally used to describe one's relationship with a language (e.g. native speaker) because it is my understanding that these demarcations are becoming less and less representative of the many complex relationships that people can have with languages in such a globalized world.)

References

Friedrich, P. and Gomes de Matos, F. (2009) Toward a nonkilling linguistics. *Toward a Nonkilling Paradigm*. Honolulu: Center for Global Nonkilling.

Gomes de Matos, F. (2005) Using peaceful language: From principles to practice. In *UNESCO-EOLLS Online Encyclopedia*.

Hall, E.T. (1976) *Beyond Culture*. Garden City, NY: Anchor Books.

Hofstede, G. (2001) *Culture's Consequences: Comparing Values, Behaviors, Institutions, and Organizations Across Nations*. Thousand Oaks, CA: Sage.

Jenkins, J. (2007) *English as a Lingua Franca: Attitude and Identity*. New York: Oxford University Press.

Kachru, B. (1983) *The Indianization of English: The English Language in India*. Oxford: Oxford University Press.
Kachru, B. and Nelson, C. (2001) World Englishes. In A. Burns and C. Coffin (eds) *Analysing English in a Global Context*. London: Routledge.
Tannen, D. (1994) *Talking from 9 to 5*. New York: Avon Books

6 Negotiating in English

Danton Ford and Paul Kim Luksetich

Introduction

ELT/ESP

In recent years, the field of ELT has developed far beyond simply teaching English conversation, reading, writing and listening. Global professionals who want to improve their English often need training in a certain area or field of English usage. This need has given rise to one popular approach to teaching ESL known as English for Specific Purposes (ESP). ESP is most visible within the field of international business where there is a focus on learning specific business English skills such as presenting, conducting meetings, negotiating, business writing and other general correspondence, or for specific professions such as aviation, finance, logistics, etc. The market is fraught with books catering to this need for specific English communication skills for various business purposes or occupations.

A number of ESL publishing companies offer books on the market targeting business professionals. Several business-specific books in areas such as negotiation, meetings, socializing, and presentations are available. These books present both know-how of business communication skills and their application along with specific phrases and vocabulary needed for various situations. Such books have become essential for classes on business English.

English for Diplomatic Purposes

On the other hand, resources for diplomats who need to polish their skills in English for the purpose of diplomatic work are practically non-existent. It is generally accepted that English primarily serves as the *lingua franca* (see Friedrich, this volume) among non-native speakers and this is certainly true in the area of diplomacy. As stated by Barbara Seidlhofer (2005: 339), '…it cannot be denied that English functions as the global *lingua* franca.'

Nowhere is clear communication more important than in the field of international diplomacy, where agreements and relations between countries can depend on the understanding or misunderstanding of how messages are conveyed. Sometimes even the usage of a single word becomes crucial. In her book *Hard Choices*, former Secretary of State Hillary Clinton

(2014: 258) stated that, 'It is easy to get lost in the semantics but words constitute much of a diplomat's work.'

Accordingly, diplomats need access to materials and resources and training that can help them improve and develop their English communication skills. This chapter is one attempt at addressing this need, specifically in the area of diplomatic negotiation, by providing effective English language used in negotiations along with sample dialogs and exercises. Through these dialogs and exercises, the reader will learn expressions used at every stage of the negotiation process (introductions, openings, stating positions, proposals/counter-proposals, difficult situations, and closings).

Diplomatic Negotiations

Diplomatic negotiations typically occur in three stages: pre-negotiations, formula stage and details stage. Pre-negotiations take place through correspondence between embassies and/or intermediaries, and are usually not face-to-face. The main purpose of this stage is to confirm that parties are willing and ready to meet and talk. Key issues that are dealt with during this stage are agreement on the need to negotiate, overall objectives, agenda and consensus on the negotiation process and timing. This stage is likely to be completed through a series of telephone calls or emails between two or more parties.

During the formula stage, negotiations are conducted face-to-face. At this stage negotiators agree in broad terms on the overall configuration and form of negotiations. Parties seek to clarify general principles to be followed as well as overall framework and formulas. The type of communication expected would be that of asking open ended questions with general, as opposed to specific, answers to assist in mapping out each party's expectations.

The final stage is the core of the negotiation process, often termed the details stage. This is where all the specifics are agreed upon and filled in. These details include: actual numbers and specific dates, definitions, actions, implementation, verification mechanisms, etc. Here persuasive language is used with conditional statements, and parties to the negotiation begin to draw up initial draft agreements.

This chapter will focus primarily on the formula and details stages of the diplomatic negotiation process. It should also be noted that these two stages could easily overlap during the negotiation process. Commonly used English expressions and phrases for the two stages will be introduced, explained and presented in context. These examples are intended to give diplomats the most appropriate language choices during different parts of the negotiation process with their counterparts. Furthermore, all expressions will be presented in order of most to least formal.

Cross-Cultural Communication Issues

Certain sections of this chapter will also give consideration to two communication styles, namely low-context and high-context. These are important because they influence language choices made during certain stages of the negotiation process, especially when it comes to stating positions. Readers will be informed of which English negotiation expressions conform to which of the two communication styles. High- and low-context communication styles were first identified by Edward Hall. In his book *Beyond Culture* (1976: 79) he described the two styles as follows:

> [...] a high context (HC) communication or message is one in which most of the information is either in the physical context or is internalized in the person, while very little is in the coded, explicit, transmitted part of the message. A low-context (LC) communication is just the opposite; i.e., the mass of information is vested in the explicit code.

Given the tendency toward non-verbal and implicit messages, high-context communication is often characterized by indirectness and non-verbal cues with the primary goal of maintaining harmony and good relations with others. Therefore, high-context expressions often have a softer tone, lack definitiveness and can come across as vague (depending on the interlocutor). Countries/cultures with a high-context tendency in communication include Japan, Korea, China, Vietnam and many Arab and African countries (see Neiuliep, 2012: 63).

Low-context communication on the other hand is characterized by a more assertive and often direct way of communicating. Messages are intended to be explicit and without ambiguity. The primary goal of low-context communication is to ensure there are no misunderstandings and everything that is said is clear. Consequently, expressions are likely to be brief and to the point. However, less preoccupation with rapport can result. Countries/regions with a low-context tendency in communication include Switzerland, Germany, Scandinavia, the United States, France, and the United Kingdom.

In consideration of this difference in direct and indirect styles of delivering messages, before entering a negotiation, interlocutors should ask themselves the following questions suggested by Christopher Moore and Peter Woodrow in their book *Handbook of Global and Multicultural Negotiation* (2010: 54) in order to ensure effective communication:

- *Are you or your counterpart direct or indirect in communication?*
- *Are you or your counterpart explicit or implicit as to content or meaning?*
- *Are you from high- or low-context cultures?*
- *How permissible is the expression of emotions, and in what context?*

- *To what extent is communication nonverbal or verbal?*
- *What do 'yes' and 'no' mean in this context?*

Contemplating and answering these questions before entering into a negotiation will help partners in a negotiation be better prepared to communicate effectively and deal with any potential problems that might arise due to different communication styles. Note, however, that interlocutors tend to fall within a continuum, with high-context orientation at one end and low-context at the other and should not necessarily be categorized strictly as one or the other.

Consider as well that while acknowledging that cultural factors can influence a negotiation, many senior-level diplomats indicate that ultimately a logical presentation of ideas supersedes communication styles prescribed by culture. For additional cross-cultural communication considerations in English see Chapter 4 in this volume.

Translation

We would be remiss if we did not acknowledge the obvious fact that during many diplomatic negotiations interpreters are employed to aid in the facilitation of communication. With this said, through studies and interviews it has been proven that there are several disadvantages to using translators. First of all, there is the simple exchange of words between one language and another. Many words in one language may have a subtle difference in meaning in another and thus may cause misunderstandings in translation. Secondly, being fluent in a language does not necessarily mean you are fluent in the culture(s) of the places where that language is used. Moreover, culture, which is intimately linked to language, often does not translate well if at all. The following example illustrates this point. Burr (1998: 395, cited in Baranyai, 2011: 8) explains that:

> The different way of thinking, and the different means of expression that characterize the various cultures can also influence the negotiations. When Chairman Mao drew a parallel between Secretary of State Henry Kissinger and the busy swallows who are preparing for the storm, the American politician didn't quite understand the metaphor and the Chinese leader had to explain his meaning.

Lastly, using a translator obviously increases the communication time. Since the act of negotiating successfully often requires proper timing, utilizing an interpreter could be an obstacle. For these reasons, those who engage in international negotiations would benefit greatly from a working level of proficiency in English regardless of whether or not they choose to employ a competent interpreter.

In light of the aforementioned considerations of ESP language teaching, a paucity of diplomatic English resources, cross-cultural issues and use of translators, the following sections will present specific language and examples for the purpose of diplomatic negotiations in English.

Opening Negotiations

Building rapport

When one thinks of negotiations, one tends to focus on persuasion and facts as being crucial components to a successful outcome. While persuasion and facts are undoubtedly important aspects of the negotiation process, the willingness of your counterparts to listen to these facts and be persuaded is just as vital as the information you have to share. Therefore, it is important to build rapport with the party with which you are negotiating. This is the beginning of diplomacy.

Establishing rapport during negotiations is not unlike any other relationship building process, except the objectives are often much different than one of a purely social nature. Building rapport is like 'preparing the soil before planting the seed.' (Runion & Windingland, 2012: xx). By the same token, it is in this soil that the negotiation seed will be planted, and your first impressions may determine whether the plant bears fruit or not.

To assist in opening dialogues for successful negotiations, this section will introduce useful and diplomacy-appropriate expressions for relationship building as well as applicable situations where these expressions would be used. As mentioned in the introduction, we recognize that not every negotiation will be the same, given differences in culture and context. The goal of this section is to provide generally accepted language to promote building rapport.

Cultural considerations

The introductions, expressions and protocol provided below are primarily based on principles used in English-speaking Western countries for making introductions. It should be noted that these principles may not be applicable in all situations or countries where cultural differences may dictate alternative protocol. Even though English may be the common language between diplomats from different countries, the cultural norms of the respective countries involved are still likely to influence interactions. For instance, in many countries only professional titles or titles of honor will be used instead of names when negotiating participants make their introductions. This is quite common in Middle Eastern countries such as Saudi Arabia. According to Lucille Redmond (2009), 'If you are dealing with a government minister, the correct form is "Excellency," and with members of the large royal family - who are often involved in high-level business - "Your Highness" or "Your Royal Highness," depending on the branch of the family.' (2009: 46).

In other countries, such as those in East Asia, it may be expected that interlocutors use only last names with appropriate titles. Take, for instance, the practice that in Korea one would refer to the division director as 'Director Lee' rather than the Western title of 'Ms Lee' (or simply by her first name). Accordingly, it is important to understand the appropriate protocol for introductions before one meets diplomats from other countries.

A: Introducing yourself

Introductions	Allow me to introduce myself.
	Let me introduce myself.
	My name is....
	Hello, my name is...
	I'm...

Sample dialogue

Situational setting: All party members to the negotiation have gathered in Wellington, New Zealand before the official meeting has started.

- Typically the 'host' or 'chair' will give a short opening statement which will include a self-introduction
- (S)he may then invite everyone around the negotiation table to introduce themselves

Harold Jones: 'I'd like to welcome everyone here. **Allow me to introduce myself. I am** Harold Jones, Minister of Trade and I am happy to start this discussion regarding our two countries' free trade agreement. Why don't we take a minute to introduce ourselves? Let's start with our guests from the Republic of Korea. Mr Lee, could you begin?'

Jeong Hoon Lee: 'Thank you Minister Jones. **My name is** Jeong Hoon Lee, and I am the 1st Vice Minister of Trade for Korea. **It's a pleasure meeting everyone**(See B).'

B: Introducing others

Introducing Others	May I introduce you/everyone to...
	Let me introduce you/everyone to...
	I'd like to introduce (you/everyone to)...
	This is...he/she's my...
Standard Introduction Responses	It's a pleasure/honor meeting you/everyone.
	Pleased to meet you/everyone.
	It's nice to meet you/everyone.

Sample dialogue (continued)

Jeong Hoon Lee: '**Let me now introduce everyone to** Director-General Moon. Director-General, could you say a few words about yourself?'

Jin Sup Moon: 'Thank you Vice-Minister Lee. **My name is** Jin Sup Moon and I am the Director-General for International Trade Policy. **Pleased to meet everyone.**'

The above dialogues demonstrate clear, simple, and brief ways to make an introduction. They are easy to understand by first providing the speaker's intention, name, and title. By utilizing this language, one is able to begin the process of building rapport in situations where one is meeting counterparts for the first time.

C: Standard pleasantries-questions

Hosting the	I /We trust your flight (in) was pleasant.
Negotiation	How are the/your accommodations?
	How are you finding (insert your city/country) so far?

D: Standard pleasantries-responses

Guest to the	Thank you for preparing this event/meeting/conference/etc., you
Negotiation	have made me/us feel very welcomed/comfortable.
	I/We have found (city/country) to be wonderful.
	My/Our trip in was very nice.

Sample dialogue (continued)

Harold Jones: '**It's a pleasure to meet both of you**, Vice-Minister Lee and Director-General Moon. **I trust your flight in was pleasant**. I know spending 13 hours on a plane can be tiring.'

Jeong Hoon Lee: 'Thank you for your concern Minister Jones. **Our trip in was very nice. Thank you also for preparing this meeting, you have made us both feel very welcomed and comfortable.**'

In the preceding dialogues, we can see an exchange of pleasantries and further rapport building with small talk. Typically at this point all parties should be familiar with names and titles and be relatively comfortable enough to smoothly transition into the formal negotiation process.

Self and Group Introduction Language Activity

Directions

Self-Introductions

(1)   The facilitator will hand out various business cards (excluding his/her own or those of the participants) to class members.
(2)   Each member studies his/her business card for two to three minutes with the purpose of assuming the role of the individual represented on the card.
(3)   Group members will then introduce themselves to each other and engage in some small talk utilizing the above expressions.
(4)   After participants have introduced themselves to three to four people, gather trainees as one group for the purpose of giving a brief report about who they met (name, title, organization, etc.).

Group-Introductions

(1)   After participants have had a chance to practice a self-introduction the facilitator will collect the cards and again randomly redistribute them for a group introduction activity.
(2)   Participants will get into delegations of three members and will designate one of the group members as the 'head' of the delegation.
(3)   Each delegation then meets with another group of three with the goal of (a) introducing him/herself and (b) introducing others.
(4)   Upon completion of the activity, ask participants to give a brief report about some of the people they met (name, title, organization, etc.).

Stating Objectives and Agenda

As mentioned in the introduction, objectives and agenda for a negotiation will already have been agreed upon during the pre-negotiation stage. Objectives and agenda in a formal negotiation are almost never decided upon unilaterally. All parties to a negotiation will have a say in determining the agenda. The typical wisdom is that any party that determines the agenda in a negotiation has a significant advantage over others since that party will then control the issues to be discussed and the order in which to discuss them.

Therefore, parties will want to prevent one side from bringing an agenda to the table that has not been agreed upon. After self-introductions and small talk, the formula stage is likely to open with reconfirming objectives and agenda that have already been agreed on. In some cases, there may also be a sudden change to the agenda that will need to be dealt with at the table.

A. Objectives

Reconfirming Objectives	Shall we begin by reconfirming our main purpose for this negotiation? (state objective)
	Let's reconfirm our main purpose for this negotiation. (state objective)
	We expect to come to an agreement on...
	We're hoping to achieve...
	As we all know, we are here to...

Sample 1: Reconfirming objectives

A. **Shall we begin by reconfirming our main purpose for this negotiation?** We are here to establish a mutually beneficial exchange program.

B: Yes, that's our understanding as well.

Sample 2: Reconfirming objectives

A: **We expect to come to an agreement on** joint legislation to combat the problem of cross-border drug trafficking.

B: That's what we want as well.

Sample 3: Reconfirming objectives

A: **As we all know we are here to** agree on terms for future technology sharing

B: Yes, that is correct.

B. Agenda

Reconfirming Agenda	If I may, I would like to reconfirm the agenda for today's meeting.
	Shall we confirm the agenda before we start?
	Let's run through the agenda once before we start.
	We've already identified three issues to discuss...
	As you know we have agreed on the following three agenda items.

Sample 1: Reconfirming agenda

A: **Let's run through the agenda once before we start**. First on the list is transport. Next is time frame, and last is cost sharing.

B: That's our understanding as well.

Sample 2: Reconfirming agenda

A: **We've already identified three issues to discuss**; first length of the conference, budget breakdown, and number of speakers.

B: Yes, that's correct.

Sample 3: Reconfirming agenda

A: As you know we have agreed on the following three agenda items: time period, number of PKO troops, and locations of deployment.
B: Yes, that's right.

As the previous language and dialogues show, it is essential to reconfirm already agreed upon objectives and agenda items set forth in the pre-negotiation stage. It is also worth noting the use of the words 'we', 'our', and 'let's' which foster a sense of teamwork among all parties that they are there to work together to come to an agreement as opposed to conveying an atmosphere of contention.

C. Changes to the agenda

Adding/Removing or Re-ordering the Agenda	We would like to propose the omission of an item from the agenda.
	Could we reconsider the order of the items on the agenda?
	We would like to make an addition to the agenda.
	We would like to change the order of the agenda items.
	There is one item we need to remove from the agenda.
	We need to add ... to the agenda.

Sample 1: Changes to the agenda

A: We would like to make an addition to the agenda.
B: Ok, what would you like to add?

Sample 2: Changes to the agenda

A: There is one item we need to remove from the agenda.
B: What item would you like to remove?

Sample 3: Changes to the agenda

A: Could we reconsider the order of the items on the agenda?
B: What order would you like to see the agenda set at?

These examples are notably different in level of directness. The first and third dialogues are more indirect by using the words 'would like to' and 'could we' whereas the second is more direct and assertive with the use of the word 'need'. Many factors will determine when to be direct or indirect including culture, relationship, context, level of importance the agenda item has, and others.

Stating Objectives and Agenda Language Activity

Directions

With a partner, use the prompt information below to utilize the language learned in order to (1) state the objective of the negotiation, (2) review agenda items, and (3) add additional items.

Scenario 1

Person A	Person B
Objective: Agricultural Trade Agreement	**Objective**: Agricultural Trade Agreement
Agenda Items:	Agenda Items:
(1) Lowering tariffs on agricultural products	(1) Lowering tariffs on agricultural products
(2) Rice imports	(2) Rice imports
(3) Animal products	(3) Animal products
(4) Agree to additional item	(4) *Add*: customs inspection procedures

Scenario 2

Person A	Person B
Objective: Cross border natural gas pipeline agreement	**Objective**: Cross border natural gas pipeline agreement
Agenda Items:	Agenda Items:
(1) Pipeline capacity	(1) Pipeline capacity
(2) Location	(2) Location
(3) Cost sharing	(3) Cost sharing
(4) *Add*: Environmental impact	(4) Agree to additional item

Scenario 3

Person A	Person B
Objective: Cyber-security Cooperation	**Objective**: Cyber-security Cooperation
Agenda Items:	Agenda Items:
(1) Information and technology sharing	(1) Information and technology sharing
(2) Jurisdiction	(2) Jurisdiction
(3) Penalties	(3) Penalties
*Agree to change	*Change order*: Reorganize item order to 2,3,1

Stating Positions and Asking Questions

In every negotiation, parties must be clear in defining their positions. The language used during this process is critically important in determining the outcome. Thus, this section will center on introducing expressions for both stating your position as well as clarifying your counterpart's specific objectives. Because there is no 'one size fits all' approach to stating your position, (that is one expression may be appropriate in some negotiation contexts while not appropriate in others), these expressions are divided into direct and indirect styles of communication in accordance with the high-and low-context cultural tendencies previously mentioned in the introduction.

Positions

The logical first step to any negotiation is for each party (or parties) to clearly state their position. A position is simply the desired outcome a party is looking to achieve through the negotiation process. Below is a small sample of phrases commonly used to express a position.

A. Expressing positions

Position	Direct	Indirect
Expressing Needs*	We expect...	It is important for us to...
	We must have...	We wish to have...
	We need...	We're hoping to...
	We want...	We would like...
Saying 'no'	We're unable to...	We're afraid that's not possible.
	That will not be acceptable / possible.	It will be difficult for us to...
	We will not...	We're not sure that we can...
	We can't...	It's not easy for us to agree to
	That won't do /We won't....	that.

* To avoid being perceived as giving orders or commands to your counterpart(s), use 'need,' 'must,' and 'have to' only in reference to *yourself (see examples below)*. This can be done by changing the word 'You' to either 'We' or 'I.'

No	Yes
You need to give us more time.	**We** need more time.
You must...	**We** must...
You have to...	**We** have to...

It should be noted that using the indirect language in stating positions may not be effective when speaking to a low-context interlocutor. On the other hand, while a speaker should be sensitive and aware of whom s/he is speaking with and in what setting, as previously mentioned, a logical presentation of ideas should be the top priority when communicating in diplomatic negotiations.

Sample 1: Stating position (indirect):

A: **It is important for us to see** a solid commitment to flood relief in the form of both monetary and personnel support by all delegates present within two weeks of the end of this conference.

B: **It will be difficult for** our delegation to commit to the actions you speak of within that time frame.

Sample 2: Stating position (direct):

A: **We expect** a firm agreement on lifting sanctions by your party no later than the first of next month.

B: Until the council passes the resolution **we're unable to** agree to lifting sanctions.

Asking Questions

Another crucial element in the negotiation process is to confirm what another party has said or to check their understanding of what you have said in order to avoid any confusion or misunderstandings. In English (as in any other language) it is important to phrase your questions as clearly as possible so they are not misconstrued. The following are expressions in question form that serve different purposes to ensure clear and simple communication between all parties.

Note: Expressions can be modified to suit your particular situation.

B. Questions 1

Checking Questions (to make sure people understand)	• Do you understand what I mean? • Do you see what I mean? • Are you with me? • Does this/that make sense? • Do you see my point?
Development Questions (to elicit more information)	• Would you elaborate on that a little? • Could you say a little bit more about that? • Can you give us an example (of)...?
Seeking Clarification	• If I understand you correctly, you think that... • I'm not sure I understand what you're saying. • I'm not sure I understand what you mean by that. Are you saying...? • I don't quite follow you; do you mean (that)...? • Why do you feel (that)...is important? • What exactly do you mean by...? • Do you mean that...? • Are you saying that...?

Sample 1: Checking for understanding.

A: If we are able to agree to the lowering of tariffs, then the burden on both our exporters and your importers will be reduced. **Do you see what I mean?**

Sample 2: Asking a development question.

B: **Do you mean that** if tariffs are reduced, your exporters will lower prices? **Could you give us a** specific **example** of this?

Sample 3: Asking for clarification.

A: **We would like to see** a solid commitment to flood relief in the form of both monetary and personnel support by all delegates present within two weeks of the end of this conference.

B: **I'm not sure I understand what you mean by that. Are you saying that** you want us to make a commitment in two weeks or to have delivered aid within two weeks?

C. Questions 2

Open-ended Questions (encourage more information sharing)	• What...? • How....? • Why...?
Close-ended Questions (focus on more details)	• Would you expand on that, please? • Could you clarify that a little more?* • Can you give me some more details on that?* • Can you explain that in more detail?* • Can you go over that one more time?* • Can you be more specific?* • Do you plan to...? • Are you going to...? • Is there...? • Did you...?
Factual Questions	When will we begin...? Who will lead the team? How long will... take? What is the...? Where will the... take place?

Even though these questions fall under the category as close-ended, one should expect to get more than a 'yes/no' response.

Sample 4: Encouraging information sharing.

A: **How** does your ministry plan to address the water shortage?

B: We have an agreement with neighboring countries to exchange water reserves for electricity.

Sample 5: Getting into details.

A: **Did you** confirm the date of shipping as the fourth of next month?

B: Yes, that is the confirmed date.

Sample 6: Fact seeking.

A: **When will we begin** breaking ground on the tunnel connecting our two countries?

B: After the agreements have been finalized by the financing team. By the way, **who will lead the team** from your side?

These expressions are designed to help ensure clarity of communication and reduce the potential for misunderstandings. When negotiating or during any other official meeting, it is best to resist the temptation to pretend that you understand everything that is being said if you do not. Giving the impression you understand what is being said when you do not creates multiple problems for all parties involved and may even jeopardize the entire negotiation process. Always ask questions if your counterpart speaks too fast, uses words you do not know, or is otherwise unclear and difficult to understand. Remember that good negotiators are expected to ask many questions. Studies show that one out of every five statements by a negotiator is a question (see *Negotiation Essentials*, 2012). Therefore, develop the habit of asking questions.

Stating Positions and Asking Questions Language Activity

Directions

With a partner, use the previously learned expressions

(1) Person A states a position: (e.g. We would like to see a 10% increase in fuel aid.)
(2) Person B asks a question regarding partner's position statement: (e.g. Is that in addition to the 500 tons of already agreed upon natural gas and petroleum?)
(3) Person A answers the question: (e.g. Yes, 10% in addition to the 500 tons.)

Practice 1

Person A	Person B
Position:	Question: clarification
(1) 5% reduction in tariffs on agricultural products	(1) Clarify if A's position includes alcohol and tobacco
(2) Answer question	

Practice 2

Person A	Person B
Question: factual	Answer: (1: direct, 2: indirect)
(1) Ask B for distance of proposed cross border pipeline	(1) 1,500 kilometers (direct expression)
(2) Ask B the cost percentage breakdown for the pipeline	(2) 60/40 (indirect expression)

Practice 3

Person A	Person B
Position:	Question: development
(1) Minimum 15 year sentence for cyber-crime against the government	(1) Use development question to get an example from A
(2) Examples: sedition, defamation, libel, sabotage	

Presupposition in questions

Look at the following questions:

- Do you agree with that?
- Does it make more sense to drop this clause?
- Will it be just as good?
- Should we ...?
- Can we agree to ...?

The above are general and open-ended questions BUT by negating the auxiliary verb, you can bring an element of presupposition into the sentence. This implies that the person you are speaking to SHOULD be doing whatever is stated in the question.

Original question	Presupposition question	Meaning
Do you agree with that?	**Don't** you agree with that?	Implies your counterpart *should* agree with you.
Does it make more sense to drop this clause?	**Doesn't** it make more sense to drop this clause?	Implies it does make *more* sense.
Will it be just as good to increase regulations on both domestic and foreign securities?	**Wouldn't** it be just as good to increase regulations on both domestic and foreign securities?	Implies that it is *just as* good.

Original question	Presupposition question	Meaning
Should we look at the visa approvals this way?	**Shouldn't** we look at the visa approvals this way?	Implies doing it this way is *correct*.
Can we agree to make concessions on the issue of deadlines?	**Can't** we agree to make concessions on the issue of deadlines?	Implies that you're *willing* to make concessions and so *should* your counterpart.

It is often recommended during negotiations that one not use the negative forms of verbs because this engenders negative feelings. However, using the negative form is how presupposition questions work. Keep in mind, as useful as these expressions can be, they must be used with discretion. Be sure to put every effort in reading and judging your counterpart's reception of presupposition questions. Overusing these types of questions can give the impression of being pushy and overbearing which leads to the opposite result.

Presupposition Activity

Directions: With a partner, use presupposition language to communicate the following.

(1)   You want to table an issue and move on to the next issue.

_____
_____
_____
_____

(2)   You want your counterpart to reconsider your suggestion to finish early for the day.

_____
_____
_____
_____

(3)   You want your counterpart to look at a problem from another point of view.

_____
_____
_____
_____

(4)   You want your counterpart to agree to an extension on the deadline by one week.

_____
_____
_____
_____

(5) You think it would be better to link two issues together.

----

(6) You think there is room for flexibility by both sides on the current issue being discussed.

Proposals, Counter-Proposals, and Concessions

At both the formula and details stages, parties to a negotiation will make proposals to each other in hopes of closing gaps and differences in order to reach a satisfactory agreement. This section will look at language choices that will be commonly used to both make and respond to proposals. Another part of the proposal and counterproposal process will be the making of concessions. Concessions are what negotiators are willing to give to the other side during a negotiation in an effort to motivate counterparts to give them what they want. Effective ways to make concessions will also be explained in this section.

Presenting/offering a proposal

When you make proposals during a negotiation, word choice can determine how your counterpart will receive your proposal. Forceful or demanding proposals are unlikely to be received well by the other party to the negotiation. Therefore, the language of proposals should focus on giving the other party a chance to decide if it is acceptable or not and then respond accordingly.

A. Proposals

Presenting/ Offering a Proposal	• Would/Could you accept...?
	• Would it be possible...?
	• We propose...
	• We suggest...
	• How do you feel about...?
	• How about...?
	• Why don't we...?

Responding to a proposal

When you respond to a proposal, whether in the affirmative or the negative, some words that are best avoided are 'reasonable,' 'unreasonable' and 'fair', 'unfair'. These words are highly subjective and can cause misunderstandings. For example, saying that a proposal is 'unfair' or 'unreasonable' may indirectly imply that your counterpart who made the proposal is also unfair or unreasonable. Therefore, the most common and more neutral way to respond to a proposal is by stating that it is either 'acceptable' or 'unacceptable' (see Jim Hennig, 2008: 93–94).

Moreover, avoid using expressions such as 'seems acceptable', 'might be acceptable,' if you intend to give a definitive answer. Using words such as 'seems' and 'might' weaken your response by making it vague and ambiguous. However, if your intention is to show your openness to considering a given proposal without committing to it, you may choose to use such words. In this case, however, there will usually be a condition or other additions to the proposal that you would like to make. Thus, noncommittal words such as 'seems' or 'might' or other similarly vague words may be necessary at times. Here are some examples.

B. Responses to proposals

Responding to a Proposal Definitively	We find that acceptable.
	That would be acceptable.
	That's acceptable.
	That would not be acceptable.
	We won't be able to accept that.
	We cannot accept that.
	That's not acceptable.
Responding to a Proposal Non-definitively	We could be open to that.
	We might consider that.
	That might be acceptable.
	That seems acceptable.
	We would find it difficult to accept that.
	I'm not sure we could accept that.
	I don't think we could accept that.

Two communication techniques should be mentioned here as they are directly related to responding to a proposal in the negative. First, management consultant Phil Baguley (2000: 112) recommends that if you are going to turn down a proposal or disagree with a suggestion made by a counterpart, you give the reasons why you cannot accept first. Then at the end of your sentence you can state that you disagree or cannot accept. This is quite contrary to the way English is usually expected to work. Typically,

English speakers would state that they disagree first and then proceed to explain why (although when communicating bad news usually explanation comes first for most speakers).

On the other hand, it is well known that as soon as you state, 'I cannot agree', 'I cannot accept it', or 'I don't like that idea', your counterpart will have a negative reaction to these statements. The result is that the other party is less likely to listen to what is coming next, which are the reasons why the proposal is unacceptable. Because the reasons are the most important part of the sentence, your counterpart needs to be aware of and fully understand them. Therefore, by stating reasons first, you are more likely to engage your counterpart to listen and fully understand why you are disagreeing.

Here is an example to illustrate this point:

> '**I disagree** because that idea doesn't address the main issue and will be difficult to implement.'

Reverse the order by giving your reasons for disagreeing first and then stating that you disagree.

> 'That idea doesn't address the main issue and will be difficult to implement, therefore **I cannot agree**.'

Whenever possible try to reverse the order by giving reasons first and then stating that you disagree or cannot accept a proposal.

The second technique to consider when disagreeing is to disagree with positions, suggestions and proposals rather than people. It is quite easy to say, 'I disagree with you...' or 'I disagree with your proposal.' However, it is more effective to replace the words 'you' and 'your' with the word, 'that.' For example, 'I disagree with **that** proposal/suggestion/idea.' This change in one word makes a significant difference in how the listener hears what you are saying. You make the proposal or suggestion the target of your disagreement instead of the person who stated it. For additional disagreement techniques see Chapter 2 in this volume. The following dialogues demonstrate how this looks in practice.

Sample: Offering a proposal and responding

A: **We propose** an agreement where both sides share an equal responsibility for funding.

B: **We find that acceptable.** (Definitive)

A: **We suggest** increasing humanitarian assistance over the course of six months.

B: Due to the overall ineffectiveness of the assistance that we have seen as well as problems with transparency and monitoring **we won't be able to accept that.** (Definitive, giving reasons first.)

A: **How about** a 10% increase on capping emissions by the end of next year?

B: **We find that acceptable.** *(Definitive)*

A: **Would it be possible to** decrease humanitarian assistance and start to focus more on development assistance?

B: Given the current domestic problems facing the country, **I don't think we would be open to that idea at this time.** (Non-definitive, *giving reasons first*) (Using 'that idea' instead of 'your idea')

A: **How do you feel about** extending the agreement for a few more years?

B: **That might be acceptable.** *(Non-definitive)*

A: **Would/Could you accept** more frequent inspections of nuclear facilities?

B: We feel there are some sovereignty issues here that need to be addressed first, and therefore **would find it difficult to accept that proposal.** *(Non-definitive, giving reasons first)* (Using 'that proposal' instead of 'your proposal')

Making concessions

Concessions are what we are willing to give to the other side, usually in return for something we would like in the deal. Most negotiators would advocate as a general rule that concessions should not be given unilaterally. That is, anytime you offer something to the other side, make sure you get something in return. In other words, avoid unilateral concessions except for only the most difficult negotiation situations where you face a deadlock or otherwise find it impossible to make progress.

Concessions are usually characterized by expressions such as, 'If you... then we will...' or 'We would be able to... if you are willing to...' When stating concessions it is best to have the counterpart act or commit first in the concession statement rather than the other way around. In other words, you ask them to play their card first. Compare the following two concession statements:

(A) '**We will** accept an increase in agricultural imports **if you** can guarantee lower tariffs on our luxury items.'

(B) '**If you** can guarantee lower tariffs on our luxury items, **we will** accept an increase in agricultural imports.'

Which statement of concession appears more effective? Statement B does because it places the responsibility on the other party to agree to make a concession first by simply reversing the order of the two clauses of the concession statement. It is usually preferable to word your concessions with the counterpart acting first.

C. Concessions 1

Concessions & Conditions	• If you are willing to...we will be able to... • On condition that we agree on...then we could... • If you could...we could ... • On the condition that you... • If you... then we can accept... • As/so long as...we could agree to...

Sample: Concessions & Conditions

A: **If you** give us 10% of the profits you make from the drilling, we can accept up to 5 platforms being built in that area. *(counterpart acting first)*

A: **If you could** increase your investment by 20% over the next year, **we could** guarantee more market access. *(counterpart acting first)*

A: **On the condition that we agree on** a 6-month timeline, **then we could** commit up to 500 troops to this operation. *(counterpart acting first)*

Necessary conditions

When negotiating in English, utilization of the word 'necessary' is another effective way to state conditions. The following are some 'necessary conditions' expressions.

D. Concessions 2

Expression	Example
in order for...it is necessary for...	**In order for** us to agree to the contract it is **necessary for** us to have full confidence in intellectual property rights.
in order to...it is necessary to...	**In order to** increase trade volume it is **necessary to** have job security for our factory workers.
...is a necessary condition for...	Increased investment **is a necessary condition for** decreasing carbon emissions.
...is necessary for...	Employer provided insurance **is necessary for** employee retention.

It should be noted that the concession process (outlined in this section) of a negotiation is usually quite detailed in a bilateral setting. However, it is important to recognize when multilateral agreements are made participating countries are more likely to vote in favor of the agreements if the language of concessions used is more ambiguous. Thus, concessions or other actions are likely to be written as general principles to follow rather than as detailed expectations. This allows each country to interpret the clauses of the agreements in accordance with their interests. The 2010 Nagoya Protocol, which addressed conservation and sustainable use of biodiversity, is often viewed as a good example of the use of ambiguous language in a multilateral agreement.

Proposals, Counter-proposals and Concessions Language Activity

Directions
(1) Make 'flash cards' with the expressions provided in the tables below.
(2) Separate participants into Group A (proposing group) and Group B (accepting/rejecting group).
(3) Group A utilizes the 'Presenting/Offering Proposals' expressions while group B uses the 'Responding to Proposals Definitively/Non-definitively' expressions.
(4) Both groups will also get cards with the 'Concessions & Conditions' expressions.
(5) Have participants lay the cards face-up in front of them.
(6) Participants will have to pick up a card and use the expression on that card in order to make a statement during the negotiation.
(7) Once a card is used, it is turned over and cannot be used again.
(8) The goal of the exercise is for a team to use up all their cards first:
    (a) For example, a participant picks up the card '**We suggest**' and states, '**We suggest** that all parties equally share in the cost of the construction.'
    (b) Participant then turns that card over.
(9) After the completion of one round (i.e. all cards have been used) have both groups switch roles and conduct the activity again.

Suggested topics for this activity: Free Trade Agreement (FTA), Green Initiatives Memorandum of Understanding (MOU), Anti-Drug Trafficking Joint Legislation, Combating Cross-border Human Trafficking, etc.

Group A

Presenting/Offering a Proposal	
	• We propose...
	• We suggest...
	• How about...?
	• Would it be possible...?
	• How do you feel about...?
	• Would/Could you accept...?

Concessions & Conditions	• If you... then we can accept...
	• If you could...we could ...
	• If you are willing to...we will be able to...
	• On condition that we agree on...then we could...
	• On the condition that you...
	• As/so long as...we could agree to...
	• In order for...it is necessary for...
	• In order to...it is necessary to...
	• ...is a necessary condition for...
	• ...is necessary for...

Group B

Responding to a Proposal Definitively	• That would be acceptable.
	• That's acceptable.
	• We find that acceptable.
	• That would not be acceptable.
	• That's not acceptable.
	• We cannot accept that.
	• We won't be able to accept that.
Responding to a Proposal Non-definitively	• That seems acceptable.
	• That might be acceptable.
	• We would be open to that.
	• We might consider that.
	• I'm not sure we could accept that.
	• I don't think we could accept that.
	• We would find it difficult to accept that.
Concessions & Conditions	• If you... then we can accept...
	• If you could...we could ...
	• If you are willing to...we will be able to...
	• On condition that we agree on...then we could...
	• On the condition that you...
	• As/so long as...we could agree to...
	• In order for...it is necessary for...
	• In order to...it is necessary to...
	• ...is a necessary condition for...
	• ...is necessary for...

Interruptions vs. Interjections (Stopping vs. Inserting)

A natural part of negotiation is inputting your ideas. However, the language you use to accomplish this is crucial to the negotiation process. Two ways people often add to a speaker's discussion are through interruption or interjection. What is the difference between the two? One should look at an interruption as an act of completely stopping a speaker and taking control of the discussion. On the other hand, an interjection should be viewed as inserting a brief statement, question, etc. momentarily without taking over the conversation. Keep in mind that an interruption is often viewed more negatively than an interjection. Even though the two words have very slight and subtle differences, the manner in which you insert your own opinion, information, or ask a question can determine the willingness of others to listen to you. Keep in mind the fact that cultural differences may dictate whether an interruption is viewed positively or negatively (see Chapter 7 of this volume).

The following expressions are useful when an interruption occurs; they give the speaker ways to politely interject.

A. Interruptions and interjections

Stopping an Interruption	• May I just finish?
	• Please, let me (him/her) finish.
	• If I could just finish.
	• We can't all speak at once. One at a time, please. [Name], you were saying...?
	• I haven't finished what I was saying.
Exploiting an Interruption	• Perhaps we should talk more about...
	• Let's think about this new point.
	• You have a point there, let's explore it further...
Continuing After an Interruption	• To get back to what I was saying...
	• As I was saying...
Commenting on an Interruption	• That's a good point.
	• I see what you mean.
Asking to Interject	• Pardon me, if you could just give me a second to offer my opinion here...
	• If I could say something here for a second, please.
	• I'd like to make a point here if I could.
	• Excuse me, may I add something here?
	• Could I just comment on that?
	• Can I come in here?

Sample 1: Stopping an interruption and continuing after.

A: ...and because they did not honor the treaty we need to increase the severity of sanctions...

B: Now wait a minute! I don't believe this is an appropriate time to talk about...

A: **If I could just finish** what I was saying I think everyone will understand more clearly. Thank you. **As I was saying...**

Sample 2: Asking for permission to interject and exploiting an interruption.

A: ...and because they did not honor the treaty we need to increase the severity of sanctions...
B: **If I could say something here for a second, please.** (pause)
A: Go ahead.
B: We have reliable sources that say that it wasn't the opposition forces that are responsible for that incident.
A: **Ok. Perhaps we should talk more about this.** Could you elaborate on that a little more?

Sample 3: Asking for permission to interject.

A: And that is where we propose to...
B: **Excuse me, may I add something here?**
A: Well, I guess, go ahead.
B: I agree with everything you've said up to this point, however, there does seem to be...

The expressions presented above can be effective. However, in some cultures and situations it may be taboo to interrupt those of higher rank or standing among the group (see Chapters 2 and 7 in this volume). Therefore, it is advisable to interrupt and/or interject with discretion and to understand your counterpart's social and cultural norms regarding this.

Interruptions and Interjections Language Activity

Directions

In pairs, take turns reading each script to your partner. As one person is reading, the other must try to interrupt at least three times using the expressions for 'Asking to Interject'. It is the duty of the script reader to manage the interruption with the 'Interruptions and Interjections' expressions. Afterwards, brief as a group as to what was and was not effective in dealing with the interruptions.

Script 1

I am deeply concerned about the possible impact that the proposed oil-drilling project is likely to have on the environment. There is a growing recognition of the increased risk of oil spills in this region. As we all know, the Arctic has a harsh environment: its remoteness, extreme weather, lack of infrastructure, and environmental stress due to climate change all pose serious challenges for the offshore industry. Protection of the environment should be a top priority for the international community. I feel that a careful approach is needed to any offshore drilling proposal.

We are all aware that with the melting of the Arctic sea ice, the region presents unique opportunities for socio-economic development to many nearby countries and beyond. However, we must not forget that the Arctic is also home to many endangered species.

Script 2

We face a challenging issue because the nature of the matter is multifaceted. Many ideas have been presented by all concerned parties with regard to the development and protection of the Arctic region. Climate change in the Arctic region has provided new opportunities for regional development, yet this development could also pose problems for the environment. For some, these changes may bring positive transformations to their lives. For others, any changes could detract from quality of life. I believe it is the job of this council to use its best judgment in weighing the decision to allow development in the Arctic. I personally feel that we can come to a win-win decision on development for all parties involved.

Dealing with Difficult Situations

Conflict resolution

While going through the three stages of diplomatic negotiations, you should expect to encounter differences in some shape or form. Some of these differences could be minor and do not necessarily require a lot of diplomatic maneuvering. On the other hand, some differences may be quite significant and grow to become conflicts. Keep in mind that language often shapes and determines the outcomes of these conflicts. In this section we will explore three aspects of conflict resolution: (1) Avoiding volatile situations (2) Defusing volatile situations and (3) Getting back to common ground.

Avoiding volatile situations

Despite differences in positions and opinions, negotiations can become difficult simply because of the language used. It is crucial, for example, that participants who are not native English speakers (and those who are as well) be sensitive to both the words they use and how they use them. First, it is important to understand how we express our opinions regarding a person or issue. One way to give an opinion is to make a value judgment or evaluation. This is a common error in negotiations and can lead to volatile situations (see Chapter 3 in this volume). Use the following tips and expressions to avoid creating disharmony at the negotiation table.

Evaluation vs. observation

Evaluation: Judging what happened. *Evaluations* draw a conclusion about or judge what a person is like without explaining why you have labeled him/her that way. Evaluations are often interpreted as negative attacks or criticism of the person(s) they are directed at.

Observation: Stating what happened. When you make an *observation*, you are stating in detail what has happened or taken place rather than making a value judgment about the situation or person. These statements are better received because they are more objective and constructive given that they are based on facts rather than judgments (see the following examples).

A. Evaluation vs. observation

Evaluation	Observation
I can't talk with him, he's a rude negotiator. *You're being unfair.*	I find it difficult to talk with him; he has interrupted me five times in the last 20 minutes. • Your proposal only offers one concession. • We have offered three concessions but you only offered one.

Finger pointing

Another common mistake in negotiation communication comes from what is known as 'finger pointing.' Finger pointing occurs when you place blame on the other person/party or accuse him/her/them of something. However, when you use certain words in English, even if your intention is not to 'finger point,' your counterpart could feel criticized or blamed. Statements with the word 'you' are aggressive and often too direct. When possible, avoid saying 'you.'

B. Avoiding finger pointing

Avoid	Recommended
You don't understand me.	*Perhaps I'm not making myself clear.*
You didn't explain this point.	*I didn't understand this point.*
You need to give us a better price.	*We're looking for a better price.*

Defusing volatile situations

Even the best efforts to avoid conflict may not be successful. Therefore, if conflict threatens to bring the negotiation process to a grinding halt, utilization of just the right words can defuse a seemingly unmanageable situation. As mentioned before, there are many reasons tensions can rise during a negotiation. Sometimes it is the lack of compromise from one or both parties, a cultural misunderstanding, or maybe even the language itself.

Regardless of the reason for conflict, effective communication is vital to successful negotiation. (see Chapter 2 in this volume). When conflicts arise people automatically become guarded and (sometimes literally) raise defense barriers. These walls are put in place to 'protect' people who feel a threat. Unfortunately, barriers also block communication. According to Jack R. Gibb (1961: 141),

> Defensive behavior is defined as that behavior which occurs when an individual perceives threat or anticipates threat in the group. As a person becomes more and more defensive, he or she becomes less and less able to perceive accurately the motives, the values and the emotions of the sender.

In order to defuse a volatile situation, you will need the right language that helps lower shields and brings everyone back to the negotiating table. If the situation is not resolved, then negotiations cannot continue because (as previously mentioned) people will be unwilling to listen and/or are suspicious of what is said. The following sections are specifically tailored to bring people from an emotionally distrustful state to a logical and open one so communication can continue.

C. Defusing volatility

Technique	Language
Empathize (See Chapter 3 in this volume)	• Would you share with us how you* see...? • You* might be feeling...because... • I can understand why you* feel... • I can understand you* might be feeling... • I realize that you* feel...because... • I can see why...could make you* feel... • I can sense that you're* feeling...
Reframe	• What would it look like to you* if we were able to...? • If we succeed in...what differences would you* notice? • How would it be if we (were able to)...?
Getting Back to Need	• What interests need to be served in this situation? • What values are important to you* here? • What's the outcome / result you're* looking for? • Why does that seem to be the best solution / option / action to you*?

*As previously mentioned, be especially careful using 'you'. If formality requires, use a 'third person' title such as your team/delegation/country/etc.

Sample 1: Empathize

A: **I can sense that you're feeling** unsure about this Memorandum of Understanding.

A: **I realize you feel** apprehensive of the second operative clause of the resolution. Allow me to explain our reasoning behind it.

A: **I can understand you might be feeling disappointed because** this contract wasn't what you expected.

Sample 2: Reframe/Getting back to Need

A: Please allow me to ask you a question; if we agree to proposal 4 of the memorandum, **what's the end result** (of the agreement) **you're looking for?**

A: **I can see why** a two week delay **could make your delegation feel** we are purposely dragging our feet. **How would it be if we were able to** compensate for the delay? If that's still not acceptable, **what other interests need to be served now?**

A: I understand your desire to see an increase in subsidies for agricultural goods. If I could just ask, **why does that seem to be the best solution to you?**

Getting back to common ground

After concerns that have resulted in high tensions have been addressed and eased, a good transition to move forward is to get back to common ground. Begin by reminding all parties of the shared interests they have. Use the following process and language to get back to the common ground you had established earlier in the negotiation process.

D. Common ground

Confirm Differences are Settled	• Are we all in agreement concerning...? • Have we addressed everyone's concerns? • Is there anything we missed? • Have we settled on...? • Does everybody agree on...?
Bringing up any Missed Topics/Issues/Concerns	• Please allow me to voice my concerns regarding...a little more. • Could we have a little more discussion regarding...? • I'm afraid we may have missed... • If we could just go over...again that would be great.
Returning to Previous Subjects	• Shall we continue on with...? • Perhaps it's time to discuss...again. • If we could, let's talk about...again. • Let's return to the topic of... • Where did we leave off?

Sample 1: Confirm Differences have been settled/Missed topics

A: Ok, it seems we're settled on the matter of trade volume. **Have we addressed everyone's concerns?**

B: **I'm afraid we may have missed** some points regarding anti-dumping duties. **Could we have a little more discussion regarding** the maximum fees?

Sample 2: Returning to Previous Subjects

A: Great, it appears we've clarified those misunderstandings. **Let's return to the topic of** licensing and distribution rights, shall we?

A: Now that we've come to an agreement on the issues of trade imbalances **perhaps it's time to discuss** pricing **again.**

A: I'm glad we were able to address everyone's concerns regarding information sharing. **If we could, let's talk about** cyber security **again.**

The key to difficult situations is the way you use them. As counter-intuitive as it seems, a conflict can often be used to improve a negotiation because it allows for better understanding. Again, the key to handling any difficult situation is to use the right words in the right way. In addition, keep in mind that in some Western cultures creating tension is a strategic negotiation tool; the way you react to the tension can be vital to the outcome.

Closing a Negotiation

The way you end a negotiation is just as important as the way you opened it. Even if an agreement is not made, it is important to close the negotiation in a manner that leaves the door open for future negotiation opportunities. By at least coming to an 'agreement to act' you signal to the other party that you are willing to engage in opportunities in the future.

If an agreement is reached, the following language helps to clearly solidify that the negotiation process is complete and to reconfirm the details and nature of any agreements that are made.

A. Reaching agreement

Conclusion & Agreement	• Do we concur on ___?
	• Do we agree on ___?
	• Are we on the same page about ___?
	• We've agreed on the following...
	• So this is what we have agreed on so far.
	• I think this is a good time/point to cover what we've agreed to so far.
	• I'd like to check what we've said/confirmed.
	• Let's go over the agreement one more time.
	• Can we run through what we've agreed on?
Final Agreement	• Yes, we can agree to that.
	• We will accept that.
	• We agree.
	• It seems everyone is happy with the agreement.
	• It looks like everything has been settled.
	• All issues have been agreed on.
	• So we have a deal.

Sample 1: Check to make sure it is time to conclude the negotiation.

A: That about settles it. If your party will cover 30% of the shipping costs, then we think we have a deal.

B: OK, before we finalize everything **can we run through what we've agreed on**?

Sample 2: Confirm details

A: You agreed to a 10% reduction in tariffs on our luxury goods while we will reduce the inspection time for imports of agricultural products. **Do we concur on both points?**

B: That sounds about right, yes **we agree.**

Sample 3: Final Agreement

A: After five days of intense negotiations **it looks like everything has been settled**.

B: Yes it does. We look forward to a mutually beneficial and long-lasting relationship going forward.

Negotiation Simulations for Language Practice

Negotiation simulations are usually used for the purpose of practicing negotiation strategy and tactics. However, they can also provide a format for practicing language skills as well. The best way to accomplish this is to provide a language checklist (see below) to each participant in the simulation and to have them rate the counterpart's use of language and negotiation expressions throughout the entire negotiation process. In order for this activity to concentrate on the use of language, it is best to remind participants that it is more important to focus on and utilize the negotiation language skills shown on the checklist rather than trying to reach an agreement or 'winning' during the simulation. Following the activity, participants should provide detailed constructive feedback to their counterparts on use of language and communication. You can find a sample scenario for the negotiation simulation on the following two pages. *Please make sure each delegation does not read their counterpart's main points given in each scenario prior to beginning the simulation.*

Your Team:		Counterparts:		
1-very poor	2-poor	3-satisfactory	4-good	5-excellent
Criteria				**Score**
Builds rapport/makes proper introduction(s)				
States objectives/reconfirms agenda				
Is a good listener				
Gives reasons for disagreeing first				
Disagrees with ideas not people				
Asks questions to clarify				
Uses presupposition questions				
Observes rather than evaluates				
Uses 'We' instead of 'I'				
Manages interruptions				
Resolves conflict effectively (if applicable)				
Uses 'acceptable'				
Trades concessions with counterpart acting first				
Uses concluding language				

Sample simulation for Mondistan

Title: Commitment of Troops and Supplies to a UN Peacekeeping Mission

Background
The UN is presently organizing a peacekeeping mission in The Republic of Conformistan, where the country's ethnic Conformistanians and Nonconformistanians have been fighting for control of the country. The war ended with a truce between the two sides and a Conformistan-Nonconformistan coalition government was formed.

The peacekeeping mission has already been approved and the UN is gathering support and commitment for troops and supplies.

The new coalition government is particularly concerned with the small groups of rebel Nonconformistan troops operating in the mountains in the northwest of the country, who are receiving weapons from neighboring Korginia. The rebels seem to be committed to continuing a guerrilla war against the coalition government, largely through a campaign of terror and sabotage.

Peacekeepers deployed in the countryside can expect to encounter armed resistance from locals who are hostile to foreigners, and some fighting continues in the mountains in the northwest.

Delegation of Mondistan: Main Points for Negotiation

- Mondistan is prepared to provide up to 400 troops to the peacekeeping mission.
  - At least 300 of them should be stationed in the Conformistan capital city of Vantoa and none of them should be deployed in the mountains in the northwest where some fighting still continues.
- Mondistan will accept *a request* to deploy 100 (of the 400) troops to patrol rural areas in the lowlands (don't necessarily need to offer this).
- Troops must be withdrawn in a fixed period of time, preferably in less than a year.
- Mondistan also wants the UN team to provide translators to accompany the troops while on their mission.
- As an additional concession, Mondistan can offer $3 million in emergency aid to Conformistan, **50% of which must be in the form of food, clothing, and non-military supplies**.
- The Ministry of Foreign Affairs of Mondistan is committed to action on this issue and hopes to establish a good relationship with the new Conformistan government in the future.

Sample simulation for UN delegation

Title: Commitment of Troops and Supplies to a UN Peacekeeping Mission

Background

The UN is presently organizing a peacekeeping mission in The Republic of Conformistan, where the country's ethnic Conformistanians and Nonconformistanians have been fighting for control of the country. The war ended with a truce between the two sides and a Conformistan-Nonconformistan coalition government was formed.

The peacekeeping mission has already been approved and the UN is gathering support and commitment for troops and supplies.

The new coalition government is particularly concerned with the small groups of rebel Nonconformistan troops operating in the mountains in the northwest of the country, who are receiving weapons from neighboring Korginia. The rebels seem to be committed to continuing a guerrilla war against the coalition government, largely through a campaign of terror and sabotage.

Peacekeepers deployed in the countryside can expect to encounter armed resistance from locals who are hostile to foreigners, and some fighting continues in the mountains in the northwest.

UN: Main Points for Negotiation

- The UN wants Mondistan to commit 500 to 700 combat troops, half of which will be deployed in three major cities and the other half in the countryside.
  - The UN wants to send at least 100 Mondistan troops to the mountains in the northwest because of the troops' experience in mountain training and tactics.
- In addition to combat troops, the UN wants Mondistan to provide 50 army engineers to the capital city of Vantoa to help in restoring supply facilities for water and electricity. The country is in dire need of rebuilding and no skilled engineers are available at this time.
- The UN wants a guarantee that Mondistan troops will remain in Conformistan for 12 months; after that there needs to be further assessment of the situation to decide if their presence is still needed.
  - All other countries joining this peace keeping operation so far have agreed to a 12 month stay.
- The UN wants a cash commitment of $5 million and some small arms to re-supply the Conformistan government's own military.
- The UN wishes to emphasize Mondistan's responsibility to support democracy in the region.

Conclusion

A negotiation can be a challenging and complex activity in any language, let alone in English for an increasingly international community. Keep in mind one of the biggest differences between an effective negotiator and an average one is in the way the two communicate. That is, an effective negotiator is very careful in word choice and the manner in which language is used in order to maximize the potential for a successful outcome. On the other hand, an average negotiator allows emotions to take over and does not consider the words put forth which can, at times, create or exacerbate an unnecessarily tense situation.

This does not mean that if English is your second language or additional language you cannot be successful when having to negotiate in English. By utilizing the expressions and methodology provided in this chapter, you should be able to increase the effectiveness of your English communication skills for the purpose of negotiation. The language recommendations advocated here and the manner in which they are used comes from hours of training, interviews, and application by various levels of diplomats who have successfully negotiated in English as a second language.

It is the hope of the authors that the information provided will assist you as you continue to carry out your vital work as a diplomat or instructor to promote positive exchanges and interactions among countries and peoples around the world.

References

Baguley, P. (2000) *Teach Yourself Negotiating*. London: Teach Yourself Books.

Baranyai, T. (2011) The role of translation and interpretation in the diplomatic communication. *SKASE Journal of Translation and Interpretation* 5 (2). Retrieved February 9, 2015, from, http://www.skase.sk/Volumes/JTI06/pdf_doc/01.pdf

Burr, W. (ed.) (1998) *The Kissinger Transcripts: The Top Secret Talks with Beijing and Moscow. New York*: New Press.

Clinton, H.R. (2014) *Hard Choices*. New York: Simon & Schuster.

Gibb, J.R. (1961) Defensive communication. *Journal of Communication* 2 (3), 141.

Hall, E.T. (1976) *Beyond Culture*. Garden City, NY: Anchor Press/Doubleday.

Hennig, J. (2008) *How to Say It: Negotiating to Win*. New York: Prentice Hall Press.

Moore, C. and Woodrow, P. (2010) *Handbook of Global and Multicultural Negotiation*. San Francisco, CA: Jossey-Bass.

Neiuliep, J.W. (2012) *Intercultural Communication: A Contextual Approach* (5th edn). Los Angeles, CA: Sage Publications, Inc.

Negotiation Essentials (2012) Bisk Education, Inc., & University of Notre Dame.

Redmond, L. (2009) When in Riyadh. *The Market* https://www.enterprise-ireland.com/en/Export-Assistance/Market-Research-Centre/ref-45-3-4-Guidetobusinessetiquet teinSaudiArabiaandQatar.pdf

Runion, M. and Windingland, D. (2012) *Perfect Phrases for Icebreakers*. New York: McGraw-Hill Companies, Inc.

Seidlhofer, B. (2005) English as a lingua franca. *ELT Journal* 59 (4), 339–341.

Nagoya Protocol on access to Genetic Resources and the fair and equitable sharing of Benefits arising from their utilization to the convention on Biological Diversity. Convention on Biological Diversity. See http://www.cbd.int/abs/doc/protocol/nagoya-protocol-en.pdf retrieved (9 February 2015)

Recommended Reading

Blavoukos, S. and Bourantonis, D. (2011) *Chairing Multilateral Negotiations: The Case of the United Nations*. New York: Routledge.

Mulholland, J. (1991) *The Language of Negotiation: A Handbook of Practical Strategies for Improving Communication*. New York: Routledge.

Pinet, A. (2011) *The Negotiation Phrase Book*. Avon, MA: Adams Media.

Rodgers, D. (1998) *English for International Negotiations Instructor's Manual: A Cross-Cultural Case Study Approach*. New York: St Martin's Press.

Rodgers, D. (1998) *English for International Negotiations: A Cross-Cultural Case Study Approach*. New York: St Martin's Press.

Appendix

Language of Multilateral Negotiation

As most diplomats are aware multilateral negotiations involve being familiar with conference decorum. An integral part of this decorum is the required formal language used to address other parties during a negotiation. Even for native-English speakers using and mastering this language takes practice. The following are the most commonly heard expressions in the context they are used.

Situation	Expression
Referring to one's self	Always refer to one's self as: this delegate this delegation the delegation of (country) (country name)
Addressing the chair/ president	Mister/Madam Chair Mister/Madam President. Mister/Madam Secretary. Mister/Madam Speaker.
Addressing Fellow Delegates	Always refer to other delegates as 'distinguished' or 'esteemed' delegate from (country) or just the country name. Ex. 'This delegate would like to respond to the question posed by the distinguished delegate from Belgium.'

20 Words to know for Negotiation

Word	Example
Alternatives: any other choices a person or group has, rather than agreeing with the negotiation counterpart	We can ask them to do A if we do B, but they have many **alternatives to consider.**
Arbitration: when a neutral person or group comes in to settle a disagreement	If we can't agree by midnight tomorrow, this case will go to **arbitration**.
Commitment: an obligation to do something or deliver something	We've made a **commitment** on this point. If we don't do it, the agreement will fall apart.
Compromise: an agreement where you get less than you want but also give less than the other person wants	If we don't **compromise**, this deal will never get done.
Concession: accepting less on one specific point in order to get something from the other person on a different point	Okay, you've made a concession on price, so we can make a **concession** on the delivery date.

Word	Example
Confidentiality: an agreement that prevents either side from talking about the agreement in public	I'm sorry but our **confidentiality** agreement prevents me from answering your questions in detail.
Equivalent: a proposed agreement that is different from, but equal in value to, a previous proposal	We can't agree to that proposal, but here we would like to suggest an **equivalent** package for you to consider.
Facilitation: a process where people, called facilitators, try to make it easier for two people to reach an agreement	You may not reach a better agreement with **facilitation**, but you will reach an agreement faster.
Final agreement: the results of the negotiation that everyone agrees to put into action	After six long months, we now have a **final agreement**.
Good faith: being honest about your intentions	If we negotiate in **good faith**, we are sure to reach an agreement eventually.
Impasse: when two sides hold different positions that they are unwilling to change	We were close to an agreement but we suddenly hit an **impasse** over payment terms.
Intermediary: a person who communicates between the two sides of a negotiation (see arbitration)	They've been negotiating through an **intermediary** after that big argument last week.
Issue: a topic that needs to be discussed in a negotiation	Money is the biggest **issue** in this negotiation, but resources and responsibilities are important **issues** too.
Mediation: when a neutral person or group comes in to identify the issues, explore options and clarify goals (see arbitration)	If we use **mediation**, it may help to move the negotiations forward.
Offer: one or more options that is communicated by one negotiator to the other	Let's **offer** them a one-year service contract and see how they respond.
Package deal: a combination of options that has been offered as a solution	John put this **package deal** together last night. Let's look at each option and see if we really want to offer this.
Party: either side in a negotiation is called a party, whether one individual or a whole group	The negotiation was suspended when the host **party** was suddenly called away for an emergency meeting.
Proposal: any suggestion or idea given to one party from the other	We can't agree to that **proposal**, but here we would like to suggest an equivalent package for you to consider.

Word	*Example*
Tentative: anything that depends on some conditions, so that it might not be a final agreement	At last we've reached a **tentative** agreement. Perhaps these long negotiations will be over soon.
Trade-off: an exchange process in which one side gives up partly on some issues in order to gain on other issues	There are always **trade-offs** when negotiating. You can't expect to get everything you want.

24 Idioms and Terms for use During Negotiation

Idiom	*Example*
accept an offer: to agree to an offer or proposal	The EU representative **accepted the offer** made by his counterpart.
bog down: to slow down and make no progress (a bog is an area of land that is wet and muddy - like a swamp)	We don't want to get **bogged down** over the issue of agricultural imports.
breakthrough: a success that comes after overcoming a difficulty	There was a major **breakthrough** in the talks after both sides agreed to make concessions.
bring (something) **to the table**: to have something to offer during a negotiation	We were able to **bring a new offer to the table** during the negotiations.
call off (something) or **call** (something) **off**: to stop or quit or cancel something	We'd like to **call off** the second round of negotiations in order to formulate a new strategy.
come back with an offer: to return to negotiations with a new offer	I'm happy to say we **came back with a new offer** and the negotiations continued smoothly.
common ground: shared beliefs or interests	We'd like to see if there is **common ground** on that issue.
consider an offer: to think about an offer or proposal	We will **consider the offer** carefully before agreeing to it.
cover ground: to talk about the important facts and details of issues	We've been able to **cover much ground** during the meeting today.
draw up (something) or **draw** (something) **up**: to put something (a contract or a plan) in writing	We'd like to **draw up** an outline for the new government development plan.
give and take: to share, to give up part of what you want in order to make an agreement	After much **give and take** we reached an agreement regarding the revised trade agreement.
go back on (something): to not be faithful/loyal to one's word/agreement	It seems that you are **going back on** what you agreed to yesterday.

Idiom	Example
go back to square one: to go back to the beginning	We should resist the urge to **go back to square one** on this as we don't have the time to start over.
hammer out (an agreement or a deal): to negotiate a deal or agreement by discussion and debate	We feel that we have the capacity **to hammer out** an agreement in the coming days.
iron (something) **out/iron out** (something): to solve a problem	We'd like to **iron out** the final details of the contract.
make a concession: to change your position in favor of the other person/ side when you are negotiating	We can **make a concession** on this matter.
make headway: to make progress	We feel that we are **making headway** with the new agreement.
meet (someone) **half way**: to compromise with someone	We can **meet you half way**.
off the record: to be not published or revealed, to be a secret	I can let you know **off the record** that we could extend the negotiations for another month.
reach a compromise: to achieve a compromise with someone	We feel we can **reach a compromise** in order to end the conflict.
reach a deal: to complete or make a deal	It should be possible to **reach a deal** and finalize an agreement on inter-governmental greenhouse gas reduction.
reach an agreement: to complete or make an agreement	We hope to **reach an agreement** even after months of negotiations.
a setback: a change from better to worse, a delay, a reversal	We shouldn't see this recent outbreak of violence as **a setback** for the peace negotiations.
talk (something) **over/ talk over** (something): to discuss something	We asked for some time during the meeting to **talk over** the new proposal.

7 Force and Grace

Biljana Scott

Introduction

Is it possible to disagree without being disagreeable; can one be assertive while remaining gracious? The expression 'a fist of iron in a velvet glove' captures the judicial combination of force and grace explored in this chapter and represents one of the essential skills that a diplomat should master.

Force, I suggest, is achieved through assertion, and grace through attentiveness. Assertion ranges from affirming what is what (i.e. providing semantic categorization and labeling), to determining what words mean (i.e. offering definitions), and stating what 'things' mean (i.e. arriving at the interpretation of facts and events through logical thinking and reasoned argument). The person who proves persuasive in assigning members to categories, defining key terms, and pursuing a well-reasoned argument is likely to maintain control of the topic under discussion. These three types of assertion constitute the iron fist of an argument and are discussed in the section on force below.

Attentiveness, in turn, refers to three activities: acknowledgment of the other party, aggrandizement and what I call 'face-space.' The most basic expressions of acknowledgment are greetings, closely followed by listening: letting the other party have a voice; hearing what they have to say (whether or not you agree with their opinions); not interrupting them or talking over them should they interrupt you. Acknowledgment may also be expressed through phatic expressions such as 'you know', 'as you say', 'you are right', all of which create 'feel-good' (see Noriko Ishihara's contribution to this volume (Chapter 2), especially her section on positive politeness). Feel-good in turn can be enhanced through the aggrandizement of the other party. This second form of attentiveness has been formally incorporated into many languages by means of a different register, most often expressed through the polite form of pronouns, but often through choice of words as well. Finally, attentiveness also requires that one not impose on the other party through overly direct or demanding language. Several linguistic devices, including hedges (e.g. 'to some extent', 'rather'), modals (e.g. 'may', 'could'), counterfactuals (e.g. 'if', the subjunctive), interrogatives and tense (e.g. 'I wanted to ask you', 'will you take a look'), secure 'face-space' for the addressee and indicate a gracious altruism on the part of the speaker. These dynamics, namely acknowledgment, aggrandizement and face-space, are discussed in the section on grace below.

This chapter aims to show the linguistic devices that underlie force and grace respectively and to demonstrate how these are not incompatible categories, but can be judiciously combined as needs be. I begin with an overview of the linguistic devices that help to communicate both force and grace, and then provide an analysis of the language of a former British diplomat, Sir Jeremy Greenstock. Tone of voice, body language and facial expressions also play a role in the dynamics of force and grace, as do strategic maneuvers, but these are not considered here as my focus is primarily on linguistic factors. What *will* be discussed here, however, is the universal relevance of force and grace: it is my contention that the principles of assertiveness and attentiveness outlined above are relevant to all languages, with only relatively minor language-specific distinctions where the linguistic realization of face-space is concerned.

Force

Force may be achieved in communication through the three-forked process of categorization, definition and argumentation. In this section, I consider each of these processes in turn.

Statements such as 'This war is legal but of questionable legitimacy' and questions such as 'Are you a man or a mouse?' or 'Is that a promise or a threat?' provide us with three useful insights: first, that a ready way to make sense of the world is to categorize it through an either-or distinction and second, that each category tells a very different story. Sometimes the category distinctions are relatively fluid, as in the case of the spectrum that includes civic unrest, uprising, insurgence, rebellion, civil war, and revolution. Other times, regardless of plausible fuzziness, boundaries have to be categorical because of the legal ramifications associated with each category, as in the case of 'refugee' versus 'economic migrant', 'war casualties' versus 'victims of genocide,' 'murder' versus 'manslaughter' or, as in the case of Syria, 'civil unrest' versus 'civil war.' A third insight to be gained from the process of categorization involves the validity of arguments used in order to justify membership assignation. Without sound reasoning, good examples and attested facts, any attempt to explain the world comes across as a point-blank assertion rather than a convincing argument.

An assertive speaker will be very clear about the semantic categories he or she is using and why. This, in turn, will involve providing a definition to support the category assignation being made. For instance, it is not sufficient to say 'this person is an economic migrant, full stop.' Justification for categorization will involve mapping the definition of the term to the relevant facts, in this case that the person is seeking employment abroad in order to improve their standard of living, rather than to escape political persecution, which in turn requires a definition of 'persecution' and what factors constitute a threat to life.

Wherever legal consequences arise from category membership, definitions become paramount. Thus the declaration in 2012 of civil-war status for the conflict in Syria by the International Committee of the Red Cross and Red Crescent triggered the application of international humanitarian law and so had legal ramifications for crimes committed. Yet definitions and category distinctions are not always definitive. Thus the criteria that distinguish civil war from civil unrest are open to debate, and whether events on the ground should be interpreted as one or the other may give rise to heated disagreement. Similarly, one dictionary's definition of the term 'poverty' may not coincide with another's, and the criteria adopted by one administration to define 'poverty' may not coincide with those adopted by another, with the result that as the definition of 'poverty' changes, so will the categorization of who qualifies as poor, and what policies they are subject to.

Given this scope for managing definitions, there is an obvious advantage in defining the key terms of the discourse one is engaged in, and sure enough, there is good evidence of this being done in International Affairs. In a 2009 article, Heather Sharp suggests that the Israeli Defence Force's definition of 'legitimate target,' 'civilian' and 'proportionate force' is different from that of the International Red Cross and Red Crescent, which in turn may differ from the definitions resorted to by other players with different interests.[1]

It is not only in the case of legally loaded words that definitions matter, but also where persuasion is at play. Paired terms that denote the same event or entity in the world, but carry different connotations, tell distinct stories loaded with very different values. Examples include 'apartheid wall' and 'security fence;' 'illegal person' and 'undocumented migrant;' 'honour killing' and 'misogynist murder.' A forceful communicator, as we know from persuasive orators, is one who chooses terms carefully and assigns membership convincingly by correlating the story told by the term with the 'facts' on the ground. I place the term 'facts' in scare quotes because of the degree of interpretation that usually mediates between facts and their corralling into the speaker's chosen categories.

The third and final ingredient of assertiveness involves argumentation: providing convincing arguments to demonstrate the 'rightness' of one's interpretation of events. It is surprising how often speakers get away with bare assertions.[2] Statements such as 'the truth is…,' 'let us face the facts,' and 'we must recognize that…' all represent point-blank assertions with no supporting argument. Although we would expect a follow-up explanation and justification of the 'truth' or 'facts' or the presupposition triggered by the factive expression 'recognize,' speakers do not always provide this, thus placing the onus on us as listeners to ask for justifications. Even the opening line of this paragraph, which starts 'It is surprising how often...' is an unsupported assertion.

The aim of this section is not to provide advice on developing arguments and gathering evidence, skills which can readily be found in books on critical thinking and guidelines on debating.[3] My aim here is to remind readers of the importance of argumentation in the process of justifying one's categories and accompanying definitions: without supporting evidence and sound reasoning, a statement becomes an assertion, not an argument, and it is likely to be less convincing for it. I say 'is likely to be less convincing' because other variables may come into play, not least the authority of the speaker. Might the mark of a forceful speaker indeed be *not* to provide supporting arguments, along the lines of the adage 'never explain, never apologize?' I think two forms of forcefulness need to be distinguished here: conviction bolstered by personal authority on the one hand and sound arguments based on verifiable evidence on the other. There is no doubt that authority all too often wins the day over argument, but it is also true that a figure of authority will lose credibility if their assertions do not hold water.

Having set out, defined and illustrated my three categories, I now turn to a discussion of how they interact. Arguments about what the truth is and what the facts are, about what is right and what is wrong, all represent a form of categorization. Similarly, categorizations based on a NOT X BUT Y structure, such as 'we are dealing not with unrest but with a civil war' or 'this is not a refugee but an economic migrant' may equally be used as bare assertions rather than supported arguments. They may, moreover, be guilty of presenting a false choice between X and Y and ignoring the existence of other categories that might be equally relevant, including a superordinate BOTH-AND category. Once again, the onus is on listeners to demand an explanation of the criteria underlying category assignation and to assess the validity of the supporting arguments.

Arguments are often fallacious – indeed, persuasiveness thrives on logical fallacies such as the appeal to emotion, to fear in particular, the slippery-slope argument (often also predicated on fear), gross generalizations, false causality etc. Similarly, a persuasive rebuttal will often recast a valid argument into a fallacious one, as we know from debating. For example, humane considerations may be recast as a propagandist appeal to emotion; wise words of caution may be recast as an appeal to fear; a chain of consequences may be denigrated as a slippery slope fallacy; or a relationship of causality as a fallacy of false cause. To recast a sound argument as a logical fallacy is to recategorize the validity of the argument through denigration. Assertiveness in this case depends on the robustness of one's evidence and the integrity of one's argumentation, but – as noted above – people's evaluation of one's robustness may well be influenced by subjective and possibly fallacious attributes such as seniority or personality.

To summarize this section on how to achieve force in discourse, I have argued that assertiveness through categorization is instrumental in procuring a fist of iron. The categories one advocates need to be well defined, and should preferably be justified by means of sound argumentation. However, given our human predisposition to be swayed by people and values as much as by arguments, factors such as authority and connotations should not be discounted. We find that the elements of force outlined here are universally applicable, demonstrating no language-specific differences, though there may indeed be some cultural variations with regard to the necessity for – and quality of – argumentation expected.

We will return to the use of force when we look at discourse connectives and signaling as a further means of combining force and grace.

Exercises on Force

(1) How would you define and distinguish between the following paired terms:
   a. Propaganda : persuasion
   b. Price : value
   c. Courage : desperation
   d. Concern : consideration

(2) Find an alternative category for the following terms and the stories they tell:
   a. A country's intervention in another: liberation or … [Possible answer: invasion]
   b. Government rhetoric: persuasion or … [propaganda]
   c. Pre-election promises: policies or … [panic]

(3) How would you define the following terms:
   a. Diplomacy
   b. Peace
   c. Battle
   d. Rebel

(4) Now consider the satirical definitions of these same terms[4] – how far can definitions be stretched?
   a. DIPLOMACY, n. The patriotic art of lying for one's country.
   b. PEACE, n. In international affairs, a period of cheating between two periods of fighting.
   c. BATTLE, n. A method of untying with the teeth of a political knot that would not yield to the tongue.
   d. REBEL, n. A proponent of a new misrule who has failed to establish it.

(5) How would you use definitions, categorization and argumentation to debate the following motions:
   a.   This house prefers trade to aid.
   b.   This house believes the internet does more harm than good.
   c.   This house believes the UN has failed.
   d.   This house believes that war nurtures future generations.

Grace

In this section I focus on the linguistic expressions associated with the three principles of attentiveness itemized in the introduction: acknowledgment, aggrandizement and face-space. I argue that graciousness involves the expression of one or more of these principles and that these can be found across all cultures.

The first principle of courtesy, which is to acknowledge the other party, involves, in the first instance, greeting them and giving visual recognition of their presence. To be cut or ignored is a surprisingly painful experience, even when it is done unintentionally. This is no doubt because, as social animals, we find it important that the group recognizes us. However, because of the forceful message it sends, cutting someone off is also at times done intentionally. When a party or country stages a walk-out, as has occurred during several of President Ahmadinejad of Iran's speeches at the UN, the diplomatic rejection signaled by this kind of protest is so strong that it invariably makes the news.[5]

The human need to be acknowledged also explains why, when a country is not given a voice in the UN, a minority people are not represented nationally, or the members of a segment of society find themselves disenfranchised, their exclusion and resentment are deeply felt. This leads us to a further dimension of acknowledgment, which involves listening to the other party both in the sense of hearing them out as well as hearing what they are saying. This premium on attentiveness explains why it is considered more gracious to allow yourself to be interrupted than to interrupt.

It seems that different cultural conventions govern the acceptability of interruptions, with interruptions indicating engagement and enthusiasm for the discussion in some cultures but a sign of rudeness in others. This personal observation does not detract from the universal principle I am proposing here, however, that acknowledging the other party is an expression of courtesy. The discourtesy involved in failing to do so is well illustrated by the film clip of Berlusconi stepping out of his car at a world summit hosted by Angela Merkel.[6] Rather than greeting his host with a handshake and a few words, Berlusconi indicates that he is otherwise engaged and turns his back to her in order to continue a conversation on his mobile phone. Indeed he keeps her waiting so long (as measured by how many cars there are in the cavalcade of heads of state), that Merkel finds herself constrained to give up on greeting Berlusconi, as it would be rude for her in turn to ignore the rest of her guests. Given that the flouting of diplomatic protocol is a form of signaling (rarely incompetence, since this is not tolerated in diplomacy), Berlusconi's behavior was the subject of much speculation as to what he intended to accomplish by failing in this most fundamental act of courtesy.

Linguistically, acknowledgment is expressed through tag-questions (isn't it; aren't you; won't we), through strokes and prompts (as you know; don't you think; as you yourself have explained), through acknowledgment using the second person pronoun 'you', and inclusion using the first person plural 'we', and through the use of titles and appellation (Ishihara's chapter in this volume also addresses these point). Propositionally, acknowledgment involves making mention of the other party's opinions, statements and actions, and perhaps also giving them precedence, as discussed next.

My second postulated principle of courtesy involves aggrandizing the other party. This includes giving them precedence, either physically by letting them pass first, or verbally by addressing their concerns first. Both in letter-writing and in conversation, enquiring after the other person's concerns, thereby acknowledging them and giving them priority, is considered a sign of courtesy, whereas promoting and pressing ahead with one's own agenda, regardless of the other, tends to be considered pushy.

Once again, cultural conventions differ with regard to precedence, and those professional cultures which adopt a 'business first' policy may feel justified in dismissing the niceties of small talk as a waste of time whereas this very disregard of expressions of attentiveness may be judged as lacking in civility by those who emphasize the politeness of giving precedence. I mention professional cultures rather than national ones because the military in all countries promotes clarity and efficiency, which is why military communications often come across as unacceptably brusque in civilian circles. Yet, notably, the military internationally has a strict code of precedence based on rank, indicating that precedence is no less important a feature of social organization.

Just as culture plays a mitigating role with regard to precedence-based aggrandizement, so does context. At issue is not only choosing one's moment – when to be affable and when to be assertive – but also how to interpret a given action or utterance, given the scope for ambiguity. Thus whereas ceding the way to the other party and ushering them through a door first may be interpreted as an expression of deference, it could also be intended as a form of assertiveness: the last person through the door is the most powerful. This alternative dynamic is well illustrated by the tussle that took place at the November 2000 Camp David summit between

Hosni Mubarak and Yasser Arafat once President Clinton, the host, had been urged through the door first.[7]

Praise and promoting the other party's feel-good are a further dimension of aggrandizement, closely related to giving precedence. Linguistically, this is often expressed through phatic expressions and tag questions, the aim of which is to reach out to the other party, partly in order to acknowledge them through inclusion, but also in order to big them up through flattery and deference. Self-deprecation, being the flip side of praising others, is often part of this dynamic of positive politeness. This can be expressed through the respectful form of pronouns, the tentativeness of the modal system, through subjectivity markers such as 'in my humble opinion', and through disclaimers such as 'I'm not an expert, but…'.

The importance of the aggrandizement principle is best illustrated by those instances that flout it. A clear example is to be found in a humorous exchange that took place between Barack Obama and Hillary Clinton during their televised New Hampshire debate in 2008.[8] The interviewer asks Hillary Clinton what she thinks of the likability question, namely that the electorate seems to like Obama more. Clinton responds to the question by saying 'You've hurt my feelings … but I'll try to go on!' at which the interviewer apologizes profusely and the audience laugh appreciatively. As she makes her point, that Obama is indeed very likable, but that she's not that bad, Obama quips 'You're likable enough.'

In context, the exchange is very effective, with both candidates playing to the audience, whose members are clearly loving the entertainment provided by Clinton's exaggerated pain as the injured party and Obama's ironic condescension. However, out of context, the exchange caused a huge upset as the expression 'You're likable enough' is a form of qualified praise – a prototypical instance of 'damning someone with faint praise,' and as such an evident transgression of the principle of aggrandizing the other party.

Another much more serious example of flouting the aggrandizement principle is to be found in attacks *ad hominem*, that is to say attacks on the person rather than the policies, principles or ideas they advocate. Nigel Farage's infamous attack on Herbert van Rompuy on the latter's appointment as President of the European Council demonstrates the shock factor in humiliating the other party publicly.[9] This is a vicious attack *ad hominem*, the verbal equivalent of a physical attack. Farage intentionally fails to acknowledge the other party ('Who are you? Belgium is a non-country'), and denigrates him at every turn ('You have the charisma of a damp rag and the appearance of a low-grade bank clerk').

Nigel Farage was subsequently fined and suspended for bringing the honor of the house into disgrace.[10] When asked to apologize, he apologized to bankers for the negative comparison he had slighted them with. As with all breaches of protocol, one needs to look for ulterior motives, in this case an election at home and Farage's desire to be seen as the strong man who dares to put down the EU President.

As already mentioned, aggrandizement can be formally expressed in most languages through the politeness register: many languages distinguish between a polite and a familiar form, not just with pronouns, but also with other parts of speech and set expressions. Just as linguistic differences exist between languages, so too do conventions differ between cultures. Thus for instance, in France it is considered a common courtesy to greet a shopkeeper on entering, or to greet a person with a good day before making an inquiry. In England, this basic acknowledgment is optional, and may even appear too familiar depending on circumstances and thus potentially rude, but saying 'excuse me, please …' is essential. Similarly, 'thank you' is an appropriate expression of parting in such circumstances, but a 'good day' would be more appropriate in French. These variations of emphasis do not detract from the underlying principle that courtesy requires bigging up the other party and either actually – or by implication – humbling oneself in the process.

Finally, the third principle of courtesy I have proposed and which I think is essential to achieving grace involves what I call 'face-space.' This refers in the first instance to physical space, and we all know how uncomfortable and potentially humiliating it is to have one's personal space invaded. To be 'crowded out' or 'elbowed out', or to have someone 'in your face' or 'breathing down your neck', are all expressions that denote this discomfort. An astonishing example of personal space being violated in a formal setting is provided by a fisticuff that arose between the former Czech Minister of Health, David Rath and the deputy Prime Minister, Miroslav Macek, in which Macek, standing at the lectern, begins by claiming that he has a purely personal matter to settle with Rath, who is seated on the podium. Stepping up to him, Macek slaps Rath hard on the back of the head.[11]

Several details of this attack are noteworthy. First, the injured party responds with great dignity and composure, walking away rather than hitting back. The audience, however, bays for blood and the aide who steps up and whispers in Rath's ear clearly tells him to go back. The aggressor, Macek, then indicates the microphone with a gesture of politeness (giving precedence, palm open), so that Rath's words might be heard by all. This is a surprising move, given that he has just struck the man, and is probably an unconscious gesture of politeness. What happens next is interesting with regard to space, and face space in particular: the injured party uses indirect rhetorical questions rather than direct accusations, until he makes to leave and then walks back again, saying 'you are a coward', not 'what you have done is cowardly' as he did previously. Why does this prompt another attack? The difference between these two ways of expressing the same proposition is that 'you are a coward' refers to a state, and therefore a permanent attribute of the person, whereas 'what you have done is cowardly' refers to an action, possibly a one-off.

In the UK Houses of Parliament, it is possible to say 'what the right honorable gentleman has just said is utterly stupid' but not 'the RHG is utterly stupid.' To accuse someone of committing a wrongful action is less face-threatening than to accuse them of being in the wrong. The latter, in allowing no room for reprieve (and the term 'room' extends into the metaphorical sense of space), is more damning. Thus the categorization of an action as either an event or a state has ramifications on politeness, and on face-space in particular.

Other forms of verbally created face-space include giving the other party choice (note the difference between 'You will do this by tomorrow' versus 'Will you do this by tomorrow'; or even 'What is the time' versus 'Do you know what the time is') (for further examples, see Ford & Kim Luksetich's contribution to this book (Chapter 6). One of the most uncomfortable instances of an interviewer denying his interviewee face-space is the notorious Jeremy Paxman and Michael Howard BBC Newsnight interview in which Paxman asks the same question ('Did you threaten to overrule him?') a dozen times.[12] A Yes-No question, in forcing one to choose between two prescribed options, forces one's hand and denies alternative approaches.

Enhancing choice and therefore allowing room for maneuver may also be expressed through the use of indirect speech acts. These are especially relevant where the face-threatening dynamics of negation are concerned (as in disagreement, refusal, rejection etc...). In response to the question 'Are you free tomorrow?' note the difference between 'No, sorry' versus 'How about the day after?' or 'Perhaps after-tomorrow would be better.' These latter two answers imply that the person is not free, but in indicating this indirectly do so less bluntly. The use of indirectness in order to avoid causing offense is a subject that has been well covered by the literature on Speech Acts, face and politeness (see for example Chapter 2 in this volume), and is not discussed further here.[13]

Face-space can also be secured through all those linguistic devices that soften one's imposition on the other party, such as modals and counterfactuals, which shift the action from the actual world to a possible one, thus relieving pressure on the here and now. Even tense can be used to this end, the past and future tense often being resorted to in order to express present actions (I *wanted* to ask you a question; *will* you sit down please), because use of the present tense is deemed too imposing. Hedges which qualify the certainty of one's utterance (*as it were, perhaps, rather*) and the manner or degree of the thing being described (*in so far as, to some extent, more or less*), are a further linguistic means of softening one's assertions, allowing room for doubt or dissent, and thereby creating face-space. Finally, agentless verbs (*It is required that...*), and impersonal passives (*The decision has been taken...*), as well as impersonal pronouns (*one*, and certain uses of the collective *we*), in removing agency, help to create face-space, since where there is no agency, there is no-one to impose.

Different cultural conventions govern verbal face-space much as they do optimal physical distance, with the North European (possibly excepting the UK) and North American cultures much more frank and in-your-face than Latin, Asian or Eastern ones (see Ishihara's and Ford & Kim Luksetich's discussion of high and low context languages in this volume: Chapters 2 and 6). Although there is some merit in the claim that so-called 'face cultures' are most sensitive to face concerns, I believe that face is relevant to all cultures, and that the linguistic expressions of face-space outlined above are available, with variations, in all languages. Grace is therefore equally accessible to all, and the degree to which it is deployed is ultimately a question of (1) discernment in evaluating the situation, (2) individual choice in deciding how best to respond to and capitalize upon the situation, and (3) personal mastery of the linguistic and communicative conventions for expressing courtesy.

Exercises on Grace

(1)   View the news-clips referred to in this section and discuss (1) the nature of the offense observed in each case, and (2) the range of reactions from the class, from embarrassment to laughter and horror.
(2)   List some additional expressions of acknowledgment:
    a.   *As you know / are aware / have explained...* (add a verb)
    b.   *In response to your ... / Considering your ...* (add a noun)
    c.   List some subjectivity markers (e.g. *In my opinion / I believe...*)
(3)   List hedges that qualify
    d.   The degree of certainty (e.g. *to some extent / rather*)
    e.   The manner of expression (e.g. *To put it simply / generally speaking*)
(4)   Find as many ways as possible to soften the following utterances:
    f.   Sit down
    g.   I don't know what you mean
    h.   We cannot attend
(5)   How is face-space secured in your own language through:
    i.   Linguistic means (modals, counterfactuals, tense, hedges, pronouns, agentless verbs and impersonal passives etc...)
    j.   Coded language (such as indirect speech acts)

Combining Force and Grace

By and large, it is up to the individual to combine force and grace as they see fit. Whereas this chapter may heighten our awareness of the linguistic resources available to us, nothing can replace our personal judgment on how best to respond to a situation and advance our objectives. There is, however, one area of language that inherently combines force and grace, namely linguistic signaling.

The clear signaling of one's argument through discourse connectives promotes assertiveness while ensuring attentiveness. On the one hand, signaling often addresses what it is one is talking about, what we mean by the words we are using, and how the various components of our discourse add up to a coherent argument. Thus expressions such as 'Let me begin by explaining my topic' and 'I am talking about X, not Y or Z' all help us to focus on the category being singled out for discussion. Similarly, expressions such as 'What I mean by X is…' and 'I define X as…' are clear indicators of a working definition. Connectives such as 'therefore', 'in addition', 'nevertheless' and 'notwithstanding', all indicate how the components of an argument fit together coherently. Signaling therefore enhances assertiveness by promoting order and clarity.

On the other hand, this focus on order and clarity acts as a courteous acknowledgment of the other party and their needs. A speaker who makes no effort to signal the relevance of what they have to say to their current audience is guilty of disregard. Similarly, speakers who fail to join up their thinking into a coherent sequence of thoughts are, if not evidently confused, at risk of seeming presumptuous in expecting their audience to do the work for them.

Pitching one's argument to one's audience and 'being in the room', responsive to what is happening in the here in now, further express recognition and respect for one's audience, in a way that delivering a pre-packaged speech or opinion would not. Determining how best to address one's audience, listen to their views, respond to their opinions and adapt to the needs of the moment provide evidence of a discernment that may enhance one's authority. In such cases, grace promotes force. It can thus be seen that force enhances grace where clear signaling promotes other-awareness, and grace enhances force where mindfulness adds to one's competence and authority.

Another example of the combination of force and grace, which draws on inherent features of the language rather than speaker-choice exclusively concerns loaded terms, whether positively as in 'clever,' 'smart power,' 'just war,' 'good disagreements,' and 'security fence,' or negatively as in 'too clever by half', 'hard power' (to some), 'unjust war,' 'bad disagreements,' and 'Apartheid wall.' The positive connotations tend to be so readily accepted as desirable that they are rarely questioned. It would seem then that establishing a positively-branded category and assigning a member to it offers a short-cut to finding common ground: we are all primed to believe in good cholesterol but avoid the bad variant, we are all inclined to support the importance of persuasion but condemn propaganda. The relevance of this observation to our discussion of force and grace lies in the following dynamic: on the one hand, loaded terms define themselves as inherently good or bad, without the need for supporting arguments, and this categorical judgment of what is what in the world epitomizes assertiveness. On the other hand, the appeal to shared values is an effective expression of grace in that it shows an awareness of the other party's beliefs, validating them. Despite the fact that this interaction between force and grace may obscure some questionable assumptions (does the prefix 'smart' always guarantee smartness?), it nevertheless comes across as a winning combination precisely because it so often pre-empts critical thinking.

A final example of the combination of force and action is provided in the case study below.

Exercise in Combining Force and Grace

This three-step exercise is designed for you to practice brute force first, grace through active listening second, then force and grace combined. In groups of two or four, choose a proverb (e.g. *The early bird catches the worm* or *Many hands make light work*).[14]

(1) One party explains and illustrates the proverb. The other party adopt an antagonistic stance, questioning and ridiculing the proverb, and in so doing targeting the definitions, categories, examples and arguments given.
(2) Repeat the exercise this time adopting an interested stance, asking:
    a. Questions of clarification (what do you mean by X)
    b. Questions of interpretation (why do you think that Y)
    c. Questions of implication (If X then is it the case that Y...)
(3) Structure an argument in defense of a proverb (or any other argument) using the following discourse connectives.
    a. To start with; Let me begin by...
    b. By way of example; This may be illustrated by...
    c. Similarly; Just as ... so too; A further example can be found in ...
    d. Furthermore; Moreover; Indeed
    e. Alternatively; It might be argued; A different perspective ...
    f. However; Even though; Nevertheless; In fact...
    g. Thus; on the one hand ... on the other hand
    h. In conclusion; Therefore; Thus we can see; As a result...
(4) Compile as many compound terms as you can in which the modifier is (1) positively charged and (2) negatively charged. Find examples and arguments that question that charge (for instance, are all cases of so-called 'constructive ambiguity' necessarily constructive to all parties, at all times? Similarly, should 'hate speech' be criminalized in the hope of eliminating it, or would such a move deny the democratic right to free speech and discourage us from entering into robust

debates?). Such discussions would be relevant to the 'positivizers' listed in Chapter 1 (Friedrich & Gomes de Matos) and further elaborated in the Pedagogy of Positiveness in Chapter 8 (Gomes de Matos).

Case Study

In the following case study, I analyze the use of force and grace by Sir Jeremy Greenstock, former British ambassador to Washington, in his testimony to the Iraq Inquiry (also known as the Chilcot Inquiry), on the question of the legality of the Iraq war.[15] The reason for providing a detailed analysis is, firstly, to illustrate the various linguistic resources outlined above as they interact in a single context by a given speaker and, secondly, to draw attention to the diverse reactions which one and the same data can give rise to. The advantage of analyzing an inquiry transcript, moreover, is that the exchanges are recorded (a rare occurrence in diplomatic interaction), are of considerable formality and gravity (thus requiring both force and grace), and yet they remain impromptu (allowing for the dynamism of dialogue rather than the premeditation of prepared speeches).

A Fist of Iron

The clear-cut category distinction Sir Jeremy draws between legality and legitimacy is, I suggest, an example of force. He states the following: 'I regarded our invasion of Iraq – our participation in the military action against Iraq in March 2003 – as legal but of questionable legitimacy...'[16]

Next, Sir Jeremy follows the presentation of this distinction with a definition of 'legitimacy':

> [...] in that it didn't have the democratically observable backing of a great majority of member states or even perhaps of a majority of people inside the United Kingdom. So there was a failure to establish legitimacy,...[17]

This definition, in turn, builds on one Sir Jeremy had introduced in the lead-up to his categorization, where he explains:

> When you get to legitimacy, it is a very fair way of describing that if you have got broad opinion behind you, broad, reasonable opinion behind you, you are doing something that is defensible in a democratic environment.[18]

Having categorized the war as being of 'questionable legitimacy' and provided a definition of 'legitimacy' (as actions which earn broad reasonable support, in this case both internationally and domestically), he goes on to establish the war as legal, once again defining the operative term 'legal' there and then by means of his 'to the degree' clause:

> So there was a failure to establish legitimacy, although I think we successfully established legality [...] to the degree at least that we were never challenged in the Security Council or in the International Court of Justice, for those actions.[19]

This unexpected definition of 'legality' builds on a preceding discussion in which Sir Jeremy explains that in International law, one and the same action may be considered legal by some yet illegal by others, and that ultimately the distinction boils down to a matter of opinion.[20]

If, in the judgment of key international organizations, the decision to go to war was not challenged as illegal, this therefore constitutes justification enough to categorize it as legal, or so his argument would suggest. The fact that he has prepared the ground for this conclusion by explaining the workings of legality at an international level is part of the effectiveness of his argumentation: Sir Jeremy leads us by the hand to the conclusion he wants us to reach.

What these extracts show is that Sir Jeremy Greenstock ticks all the boxes of assertiveness: he introduces a key distinction between legality and legitimacy, provides a working definition of each, assigns the Iraq war to one category not the other, justifying his categorization largely by means of his own definitions. In addition to these definitions and categories, Sir Jeremy introduces his 'legal because not illegal' argument. In terms of 'what's what in the world', this is the way the things are, he asserts!

Since we know, from his own account, that Sir Jeremy was sufficiently uncomfortable about the prospect of invasion in the absence of a new and unambiguous UN Security Council resolution as to think of resigning,[21] the affirmative way in which he establishes the legality of the war during his evidence to the Inquiry is particularly striking, requiring a degree of assertiveness which, in all likelihood, surpassed his own convictions.

There are numerous other examples in the evidence provided by Sir Jeremy that illustrate the use of verbal force. One is his renaming of the 'invasion of Iraq' as 'our participation in the military action against Iraq in March 2003'.[22] This re-categorization puts a different slant on the activities under discussion since the connotations of 'invasion' are probably more reprehensible than those of the softer 'participation in the military action,' with its implications of collective responsibility.

Another canonical example of the definition-categorization-justification triptych can be found in the following extract:

> [...] when you mention the smart sanctions, let's be clear what we are talking about; we are talking about changing the sanctions process

from a list which allowed things to go into Iraq, … the green list, into a list which said, 'These are the things which are not allowed into Iraq', the goods review list. That was a sensible way to go, because …[23]

Here, the term 'smart sanctions' is defined as constituting a 'goods review list' in contradistinction to the preceding 'green list', and a justification for their adoption is provided in the argument that follows (not cited here).

Another example, this one focusing on his interpretation of political practice rather than his definition of terms, involves his interpretation of American foreign policy under Bush:

[…] as I observed it, it was the practice of the Bush administration to seek allies only when they needed allies for a particular piece of policy. If they could do it on their own, they would do it on their own. If they couldn't do it on their own, they would collect allies, but then retreat to a piece of territory where they could again do things on their own … They were selective in their alliances[…][24]

Force is achieved here through the categorical description he provides of the selective alliances practiced by the Bush administration. The repetitive tone of his description adds emphasis and authority to his words, with the effect of turning an interpretation into a pronouncement.

Revision Exercise of the 'Definition-Categorization-Justification' triptych:

(1) Provide a working definition of the term 'legal' and 'legitimate' which helps to distinguish between them.
(2) Why might the Iraq invasion of 2003 be considered EITHER (a) legal but not legitimate OR (b) legitimate but not legal?
(3) Can the distinction 'legal but of questionable legitimacy' be usefully applied to any other war or event of your choosing?
(4) To what extent do we tell a different story by using the term 'war', 'intervention', 'invasion' or 'military activity'?

Notice that this exercise can be conducted in any language since defining terms, assigning events to categories and justifying one's categorization are logically rather than linguistically driven processes.

A Glove of Velvet

As mentioned earlier, grace in discourse is primarily achieved through attentiveness, and in particular by means of acknowledgment, aggrandizement and face-space. In the extracts cited so far from Sir Jeremy Greenstock's testimony, we find several examples of acknowledgment in the following italicized expressions: *'when you get to* legitimacy'; *'when you mention* the smart sanctions'; *'as you can see* from the outcome.' Other examples include 'Because – *and this came into your previous question* – there were different views …'[25]

Just as each of these expressions makes mention of the other party by means of the second person pronoun 'you,' the first person plural 'we' may serve the same purpose. The following extract shows both pronouns at play in the process of acknowledging the other party (italics mine):[26]

> Fine. *We* will get on to it in due course, but I'm saying that because the approach to smart sanctions was eventually successful and the cross-voter, *if you like*, the marginal voter, that made it possible to go from failure to success on this was, *as you surmise*, Russia, and *if you want* to go into detail, *we could talk about* why Russia opposed the smart sanctions regime in mid-2001.

The second form of attentiveness mentioned above is aggrandizement, and although expressions such as 'if you like' and 'as you surmise' might be understood as mild forms of enhancing the importance and feel-good of the other party, there are no significant instances of Sir Jeremy bigging up his interlocutors and giving them precedence. This is to be expected under the circumstances, given that he is under interrogation by an official inquiry, and therefore needs to give his version and interpretation of events rather than flatter his questioners. However, since the converse of aggrandizing others is to diminish oneself, expressions of self-deprecation may, by implication, big-up the other party, as illustrated by the use of qualifiers such as 'in my view', 'as I understand it' etc… Diminishing the force of one's own utterances in order not to impose on the other party belongs to 'face-space', as discussed next.

The third form of attentiveness, face-space, is amply illustrated in Sir Jeremy's discourse, through the use of modals such as 'may', 'might' and 'could', for example, which he uses in order to introduce an element of epistemic uncertainty, thus allowing for alternative claims. Similarly, the use of the conditional in the previous extract, as illustrated by 'if you like' and 'if you want', implicitly allow for choice, thus increasing the other party's room for maneuver.

Another means of creating face-space is to qualify one's remarks with hedges such as 'rather', 'perhaps', 'to some extent', 'in so far as' and so forth, all of which detract from the force of the proposition which follows by qualifying the certainty with which it is communicated or the extent to which it applies. Consider the difference between 'It is necessary to…' and 'I rather regarded it as necessary to …'[27]

Similarly, as noted above, the expression 'in my view' allows for the possibility that one's view is mistaken or marginal, for example,[28] '... there needed, *in my view*, politically and legally, to be [...]. *In my view* – and this was my advice to London – there needed to be a new explicit resolution ....'

Sir Jeremy makes extensive use of the phrases 'in my view', 'as I observed it' and 'I regarded', all of which emphasize the personal nature of the perspective being conveyed, thus allowing for differences in opinion. Opening the field up to alternative perspectives is a way of securing face-space.

The examples above offer a clear illustration of the use of acknowledgment and face space as expressions of courtesy. There are some uses of qualifiers and hedges, however, which come across as more ambiguous. Most notably, Sir Jeremy's use of 'to some extent' in the following phrase is ambiguous between a softener and strategic hedging:[29]

> To some extent, the United Nations is a democratic environment. It is a forum of equal states equally signed up by treaty to the United Nations Charter, and each of those states have an opinion.

This statement immediately raises the question of what the democratic deficit of the United Nations might be. To some, especially those who may be on their guard against any tricksy argumentation, this qualifier acts as a warning signal: is Sir Jeremy perhaps passing the buck to the United Nations for responsibilities which lie elsewhere? He explains the thinking behind his qualification in the following sentence:[30] 'If you do something internationally that the majority of UN member states think is wrong or illegitimate or politically unjustifiable, you are taking a risk in my view ...' and then goes on to recommend, 'I think one of the lessons you may want to look at as an Inquiry is on the importance of legitimacy in geopolitical affairs nowadays.' Here too, the skeptical observer will feel that despite the polite hedging involved (the conditional 'if'; the personal perspectives 'in my view' and 'I think'; the modal 'you may want'), it is presumptuous of a witness in an inquiry to tell his panel what they should consider doing.

In the final example to be analyzed in this case study, I consider how force and grace are combined to questionable effect.

Revision Exercise on the Acknowledgment – Aggrandizement – Face-space Triptych:

(1) Watch the video of Sir Jeremy's testimony to the Iraq Inquiry and make a note of all the modals, conditionals, hedges, subjectivity markers, expressions of inclusion and other softeners he uses: http://www.telegraph.co.uk/news/newsvideo/6670545/Iraq-inquiry-war-not-legitimate-says-Sir-Jeremy-Greenstock.html

(2) What is your personal reaction to Sir Jeremy's manner:
  a. How would you rate his forcefulness out of 10?
  b. How would you rate his graciousness out of 10?
  c. How does this compare with that of your colleagues?

A Fist of Iron in a Glove of Velvet?

The following example raises the question of balance between force and grace, and the possibility that Sir Jeremy errs on the side of force to the detriment of grace. In discussing UN Security Council Resolution 1441, Sir Jeremy makes mention of the categories 'clever diplomacy' and 'too clever for its own good', neither of which he defines:

> This is where diplomacy gets clever and, as you can see from the outcome, from 1441, too clever for its own good, but diplomacy got clever and it produced a text in 1441 that was equivocal on two issues…[31]

When challenged on what he means by these terms, Sir Jeremy rejects the description that is offered him and challenges the questioner's language in turn: [32]

> **Baroness Usha Prashar:** You said earlier that 'diplomacy got clever.' Did that actually mean that 1441 was a successful example of keeping the show on the road and a substitute for a policy? There was no agreement on policy, but it was the words that were used to get an agreement?
> **Sir Jeremy Greenstock**: No. I don't agree with the formulation of that question, Lady Prashar. There was no show on the road. I don't know what you mean by 'show on the road.'
> **Baroness Usha Prashar**: What I mean is that this was …

This stand-off regarding which term best describes a situation is typical of the battle for dominance in a discourse. The frustration here is that Baroness Prashar does not ask an open question as to what Sir Jeremy means by 'clever diplomacy' and why UNSCR 1441 might have been 'too clever.' Instead, by adhering to her own terms ('show on the road' and 'bar set too high'), and by not being as clear as she might be about what she means, she conducts an exchange in which Sir Jeremy makes no mention of her questions and simply asserts his own speaking points:[33]

> **Baroness Usha Prashar**: What I mean is that this was a follow-on from the speech that President Bush made, that it was an attempt to get a resolution, … but there was no fundamental policy agreement.

Sir Jeremy Greenstock: What we felt that 1441 had achieved was the return of the inspectors.
Baroness Usha Prashar: But the bar was set too high.
Sir Jeremy Greenstock: It was an important opportunity for establishing whether or not Iraq possessed WMD or was trying to obtain WMD, and for the United Kingdom this was all about WMD.

Sir Jeremy seems to have the upper hand in this exchange as his clarity and precision, backed by definitions and arguments, and further bolstered by his refusal to adopt any terminology other than his own, gives his utterances a compelling assertiveness and forcefulness. But what of grace? Is Sir Jeremy proving ungracious in his assertiveness? There are indeed several instances of possible discourtesy. First, his 'No, I don't agree with the formulation of that question' and 'I don't know what you mean by…' are clear face-threats. Second, his refusal to answer directly the questions he is being asked represents a failure of acknowledgment. The same holds for his refusal to engage with the expressions being used by Baroness Prashar, notably 'show on the road'. Finally, when Baroness Prashar interjects 'but the bar was set too high', she is in fact citing something Sir Jeremy himself had said earlier, but he does not acknowledge this by explaining or elaborating on his earlier formulation, choosing instead to press ahead with his speaking point about WMDs, in effect snubbing her.

This snub appears all the more damaging when we review the exchange Lady Prashar is clearly alluding to, where Sir Jeremy had said:[34]

Because -- and this came into your previous question -- there were different views in Washington as to what they were trying to do with this draft resolution, setting the bar too high, I wanted to make it clear that, if this was just a Potemkin exercise at going to the UN, I was not going to be part of it…

The 'show on the road' is clearly an allusion to Sir Jeremy's mention of the Potemkin exercise,[35] and the 'bar set too high' a reference to his own words. Under these circumstances, for Sir Jeremy to have stone-walled Lady Prashar in the way he did seems very discourteous indeed. The advantage he gained through clarity and assertiveness is at risk of being overturned by the disregard he evinces here. Judgments, however, will differ between those who are inclined to admire his force, and those who are more inclined to lament his discourtesy.

To conclude this case study, we have seen how Sir Jeremy achieves a fist of iron through the combination of clear categorization, corroborating definitions and supporting argumentation. His use of clear-cut categories is particularly distinctive of his style and a signature of his assertiveness.

He achieves the soft touch of a velvet glove through his repeated acknowledgment of the other party, including the use of aggrandizing tag phrases and insertions. In particular, the graciousness of his style is secured through his deference to the face-space of his interlocutors, expressed through the use of hedges and modals as well as through the repeated use of subjectivity markers which make space for other possible views and interpretations of the evidence he is providing.

Sir Jeremy evidently combines both force and grace, as exemplified by many of the extracts provided above in which assertiveness and acknowledgment clearly co-occur. However, we have also seen an example of a hedge used less as a softener or subjectivity marker and more as a strategic maneuver in argument building ('To some extent the UN is a democratic environment'), as well as an example in which force outweighs grace (the exchange on clever diplomacy). An important insight to be gained from this case study, and in particular from the controversial examples cited at the end, concerns the divergent reactions that one and the same discourse may elicit in different audiences.

Conclusion

This chapter has set out to identify those elements of language that contribute to forcefulness and those that contribute to graciousness respectively. I have illustrated the importance of categorization, definitions and argumentation through a variety of examples, and have illustrated the normative influence of acknowldgment, aggrandizement and face-space by means of examples in which each of these principles was flouted. In the second half of the chapter, I provided a case study to demonstrate how force and grace have been combined in the language of a former diplomat, Sir Jeremy Greenstock. This case study was chosen both for the public availability of the transcript, unusual in diplomatic exchanges, and for the particular fluency which Sir Jeremy demonstrates, not only as a seasoned British diplomat, but as a man under pressure, in order to communicate his message as forcefully as possible while nevertheless delivering to the requirements of grace and deference required by a formal inquiry.

To the initial question of whether it is possible to combine force and grace, and to disagree without being disagreeable, I hope to have demonstrated that it is indeed feasible, since assertiveness can coincide with attentiveness. It is up to the speaker to decide how and in what measure they wish to combine force and grace.

I also hope to have shown that the principles involved are readily available in all languages. Language-specific dimensions arise primarily in relation to grammatical elements. Thus in the case of aggrandizement we find that not all languages have a polite pronominal form, and in some languages the formal register determines vocabulary choice more extensively than in others. With regard to face-space, not all languages have the subjunctive, and some languages have greater recourse to modals than others. In addition, we find cross-cultural variations where the coded language of politeness is concerned, with those cultures which prefer indirectness (the high context languages discussed by Ford & Kim Luksetich in Chapter 6) resorting to more coded usage.

While allowing for such variations, the cross-linguistic and cross-cultural similarities of the principles of underlying force and grace are significant for diplomatic practice in that mastering these principles in one language will enable a diplomat to recognize them at play in other languages as well. The challenge facing diplomats is not so much to overcome differences across languages and cultures, but to bring to awareness dimensions of their own native language that are often insufficiently recognized. It is hoped that this chapter will have helped to reveal what these dimensions are with regard to force and grace, and will have shown how to combine them in order to achieve a fist of iron in a velvet glove.

Notes

(1)   Sharp, H. (5 January 2009) Gaza conflict: Who is a civilian. *BBC News*. See http://news.bbc.co.uk/go/pr/fr/-/1/hi/world/middle_east/7811386.stm   (retrieved   31 January 2015).

(2)   Scott, B. (2013) Framing an Argument. In Jovan Kurbalija (ed.) *Persuasion: the essence of diplomacy* (pp. 47–64) Malta: DiploFoundation and MEDAC.

(3)   See, for instance, Cottrell, S. (2012) *Critical Thinking Skills: Developing Effective Analysis and Argument (Palgrave Study Skills)*. London: Palgrave Macmillan (2nd edn); Newman, D. and Woolgar, B. (eds) (2013) *Pros and Cons: A Debater's Handbook (19th edn)*. Oxford: Routledge.

(4)   Ambrose Bierce, *The Devil's Dictionary*, 1911. See http://www.gutenberg.org/files/972/972-h/972-h.htm (retrieved 31 January 2015).

(5)   See, for example, Borger, J. (21 April 2009) Mahmoud Ahmadinejad's attack on Israel triggers walkout at UN racism conference. *The Guardian*. See http://www.theguardian.com/world/2009/apr/21/ahmadinejad-geneva-speech-israel (retrieved 31 January 2015).; MacAskill, E. (24 September) Mahmoud Ahmadinejad's renewed attack on Israel hastens walkout.' *The Guardian*. See http://www.theguardian.com/world/2009/sep/24/mahmoud-ahmadinejadun-speech-criticised. For a film-clip, see Mahmoud Ahmadinejad speech sparksUN walkout. See https://www.youtube.com/watch?v=AeqBv6nR-tc (retrieved 31 January 2015).

(6)   Berlusconi call puts Nato on hold. *BBC News*, 4 April 2009. See See http://news.bbc.co.uk/1/hi/world/europe/7983043.stm (retrieved 31 January 2015).

(7)   See clip on The Secrets of Body Language, part 3, 91ilargia: See http://www.youtube.com/watch?v=wGd-nfID6bE. Clip 4 on President Bush and Tony Blair at 10 Downing Street shows a similar dynamic where the guest dominates the host by ushering him through the door first (retrieved 31 January 2015).

(8)   'Not   so   Likable'   in   Top   Ten   Obama   Backlash   Moments,   *TIME* Magazine.   See   http://content.time.com/time/specials/packages/article/0,28804,1929415_1929418_1929431,00.html (retrieved 31 January 2015).

(9)   Ukip's Nigel Farage tells Van Rompuy: You have the Charisma of a Damp Rag. *The Guardian*, 25 February 2010. See http://www.theguardian.com/world/2010/feb/25/nigel-farage-herman-van-rompuy-damp-rag (retrieved 31 January 2015).

(10) Nigel Farage fined for verbal attack on EU President. *The Guardian*, 2 March 2010. See http://www.theguardian.com/politics/2010/mar/02/nigel-faragefined-mep-rompuy (retrieved 31 January 2015).

(11) Czech politicians exchange blows. *BBC News*, 21 May 2006. See http://news.bbc.co.uk/1/hi/world/europe/5001414.stm (retrieved 31 January 2015).

(12) Jeremy Paxman interviews Michael Howard. *BBC 2 Newsnight*. First broadcast 13 May 1997. See http://news.bbc.co.uk/1/hi/programmes/newsnight/7740130.stm (retrieved 31 January 2015).

(13) See for example Austin, J.L. (1975) *How To Do Things With Words* (2nd edn). Oxford, UK: Oxford University Press; Watts, R.J. (2003) *Politeness*. Cambridge, UK: Cambridge University Press.

(14) The reason for using a proverb in this exercise is to help participants focus on their use of language rather than the merits of the argument. Since most proverbs have a counter-proverb (for instance, 'Many hands make like verb' advises the opposite of 'Too many cooks spoil the broth'), we do not need to believe in a proverb in order to advocate it. Moreover, the ridiculing jibes are less likely to be taken personally.

(15) For the full video and transcript of Sir Jeremy Greenstock's evidence, see the official website of the Iraq Inquiry, entry for 27 November 2009. See http://www.iraqinquiry.org.uk/transcripts/oralevidence-bydate/091127.aspx. The discussion on legality versus legitimacy begins on p.34, line 14. A video of the relevant extract is available here: http://www.telegraph.co.uk/news/newsvideo/6670545/Iraq-inquiry-warnot-legitimate-says-Sir-Jeremy-Greenstock.html (retrieved 31 January 2015).

(16) Iraq Inquiry transcript, See http://www.iraqinquiry.org.uk/transcripts/oralevidencebydate/091127.aspx, p. 38, lines 9–11.

(17) *Iraq* Inquiry transcript, See http://www.iraqinquiry.org.uk/transcripts/oralevidencebydate/091127.aspx, p. 38, lines 11–15.

(18) *Iraq* Inquiry transcript, See http://www.iraqinquiry.org.uk/transcripts/oralevidencebydate/091127.aspx, p. 37, lines 15–23.

(19) *Iraq* Inquiry transcript, See http://www.iraqinquiry.org.uk/transcripts/oralevidencebydate/091127.aspx, p. 38, lines 15–21.

(20) *Iraq* Inquiry transcript, See http://www.iraqinquiry.org.uk/transcripts/oralevidencebydate/091127.aspx, p. 37, lines 7–18.

(21) *Iraq* Inquiry transcript, See http://www.iraqinquiry.org.uk/transcripts/oralevidencebydate/091127.aspx, p. 35, lines 8–10: 'In my view – and this was my advice to London – there needed to be a new explicit resolution saying that Iraq was in material breach of the resolutions.' And page 36, lines 17–19: 'Therefore, I said I might not be able to continue as ambassador in New York if there was no further updated basis for regarding Iraq as being in material breach.'

(22) *Iraq* Inquiry transcript, See http://www.iraqinquiry.org.uk/transcripts/oralevidencebydate/091127.aspx, p. 38, lines 10–11.

(23) *Iraq* Inquiry transcript, See http://www.iraqinquiry.org.uk/transcripts/oralevidencebydate/091127.aspx, p. 10, lines 2–9.

(24) *Iraq* Inquiry transcript, See http://www.iraqinquiry.org.uk/transcripts/oralevidencebydate/091127.aspx, p. 18, lines 8–18.

(25) *Iraq* Inquiry transcript, See http://www.iraqinquiry.org.uk/transcripts/oralevidencebydate/091127.aspx, p. 36, lines 7–8.

(26) *Iraq* Inquiry transcript, See http://www.iraqinquiry.org.uk/transcripts/oralevidencebydate/091127.aspx, p. 16, lines 13–20.

(27) *Iraq* Inquiry transcript, See http://www.iraqinquiry.org.uk/transcripts/
   oralevidencebydate/091127.aspx, p. 34, lines 17–19: 'I rather regarded it as
   necessary, politically and legally, to have one new resolution or at least one new
   resolution for the following reason'.
(28) *Iraq* Inquiry transcript, See http://www.iraqinquiry.org.uk/transcripts/
   oralevidencebydate/091127.aspx, p. 35, lines 2–10.
(29) *Iraq* Inquiry transcript, See http://www.iraqinquiry.org.uk/transcripts/
   oralevidencebydate/091127.aspx, p. 37, lines 23–6.
(30) *Iraq* Inquiry transcript, See http://www.iraqinquiry.org.uk/transcripts/
   oralevidencebydate/091127.aspx, p. 38, lines 2–5.
(31) *Iraq* Inquiry transcript, See http://www.iraqinquiry.org.uk/transcripts/
   oralevidencebydate/091127.aspx, p. 40, lines 21–24.
(32) *Iraq* Inquiry transcript, See http://www.iraqinquiry.org.uk/transcripts/
   oralevidencebydate/091127.aspx, p. 42, lines 15–25.
(33) *Iraq* Inquiry transcript, See http://www.iraqinquiry.org.uk/transcripts/
   oralevidencebydate/091127.aspx, p. 42, line 25 to page 43, line 13.
(34) *Iraq* Inquiry transcript, See http://www.iraqinquiry.org.uk/transcripts/
   oralevidencebydate/091127.aspx, p. 36, lines 7–16.
(35) This expression refers to fake settlements erected by Grigory Potemkin along the
   banks of the Dnieper in order to impress Empress Catherine, and is used to denote
   a political or economic measure aimed to deceive.

References

Greenstock, J. (2009) Oral Evidence to the Iraq Inquiry. http://www.iraqinquiry.org.uk/
   transcripts/oralevidence-bydate/091127.aspx
Scott, B. (2013) Framing an argument. In J. Kurbalija (ed.) *Persuasion: The Essence of
   Diplomacy* (pp. 47–64). Malta: DiploFoundation and MEDAC.
Watts, R.J. (2003) *Politeness*. Cambridge: Cambridge University Press.

8 Pedagogy of Positiveness Applied to English for Diplomatic Purposes

Francisco Gomes de Matos

Besides English, a diplomat should also speak the languages of the great powers whose
interests bear most heavily on the state s(h)e is representing.
Ambassador Chas. Freeman Jr, *The Diplomat's Dictionary*, 2010: 121.

Diplomats,
When positively you communicate
Your diplomatic work you elevate
When you use your English for diplomatic positivity
It will enhance cordiality, mutual trust and dignity
Francisco Gomes de Matos

Introduction

An early application

The intersection of English and diplomacy is an important one I have already explored in other works. In Gomes de Matos (2001), for example, I provided an overview of the nature of diplomatic communication; in addition, I drew a distinction between communicating positively and negatively. Also provided was an 18-item checklist on principles underlying a Pedagogy of Positiveness Applied to Diplomatic Communication. Such listing, focused on language use, includes the following notions:

- Diplomatic communication can be a humanizing form of interaction;
- Communicative Peace is an important aspect of diplomatic interactions;
- The diplomatic profession can and should be viewed positively;
- Linguistic probity is the quality of being communicatively honest, truthful.

On the other hand, communicative fallibility in this context means showing inability in using vocabulary appropriately, accurately, positively.

In the five-item section on Pleas/Recommendations, I provide a bit of advice on the semantic preparation of diplomats through their sensitization to the functions of 'positivizers' in diplomatic discourse – verbs, nouns, and adjectives that reflect/enhance inherently positive actions and attributes or qualities in human beings.

In my closing paragraph therein, I make a case for transforming diplomatic communication into dignified and dignifying discourse and express my conviction that communicating well diplomatically means communicating for the well-being of diplomatic interlocutors and, more broadly, for the well-being of humankind. For my current views on communicative dignity, you can refer to my poster on that core-concept, downloadable at www.estudenaaba.com. For the author's comprehensive perspective on dignity, refer to Gomes de Matos (2013).

Now, 13 years after the publication of that precursory chapter, I have provided an updated, expanded text for this pioneering volume. The new focus is on how to engage diplomats and international relations professionals in enhancing their English, especially their vocabulary, in challenging and creative ways, inspired by the Pedagogy of Positiveness. Accordingly, this contribution will be of a practical nature, through activities aimed at challenging the book's users to identify/produce/react to some key-concepts in diplomacy, as expressed through the medium of English. Each activity will have a title and instructions. Suggested answers to activities will be provided in Appendix II of this chapter.

Such aids notwithstanding, readers are asked to go beyond the suggested solutions, thus further dignifying their own communicative decisions. Due to space limitations, activities have been made relatively short. When used in workshops or similar professional preparation contexts, such experiences can be expanded and cross-culturally adapted, thus capitalizing on the pedagogical creativity of diplomat-training-education mentors. This chapter is offered in the same spirit of Vivian Cook's (2002: 341) affirmation that 'the purpose of language teaching is to change the student positively.'

Activities

Introduction

Before engaging readers in 20 activities designed especially for this chapter, I will provide some clarification on my coinage of the term 'Positivizers.' In descriptive grammars of English, a terminological tradition was started of labeling some lexicogrammatical concepts with nouns ending in – er. Thus, amplifier (e.g. completely, extremely) and downtoner (e.g. barely, slightly) stand as instances of such practice. Inspired by that usage, I coined 'positivizers' to refer to nouns, verbs, adjectives, and adverbs that convey positiveness, a positive attitude or perception. My conviction in the communicative force of such positively oriented words led to drafting 'A plea for using positivizers' (Gomes de Matos, 2007). Two of the seven stanzas in that rhymed reflection are shared here:

Let's use words that help build self-confidence
and encourage people everywhere to cooperate
Let's express to encourage a strong interdependence
and a spirit of planetary citizenship to celebrate
Let's use nouns, verbs, adjectives and adverbs as positivizing vocabulary
for the words we use in speaking, writing, or signing can play a significant part
in helping Humankind perceive and practice Communicative Peace as necessary
Please, users of mental marvels for meaning-makers, let's communicate from
      the heart

My approach to Pedagogy -known in Portuguese as *Pedagogia da Positividade*- is briefly described in the entry on Pedagogy of Positiveness available widely on the internet. The coining of positivizers should be a reminder to users of English that, alas, there are negativizing uses of lexical items that could be labeled negativizers. In this chapter, the major focus will be on learning to enhance one's repertoire of positivizers as related to diplomacy. One way of starting one's lexical (re)education as a user of diplomatic positivizers could be to list positive nouns which co-occur with the adjective diplomatic.

A search in Davies and Gardner (2010: entry 3944, p. 228) will show that 'diplomatic' typically precedes these nouns: relation, effort, solution, recognition, mission, tie, initiative, support, negotiation, correspondent. Interestingly, those two corpus linguists-lexicographers provide a list of 29 adjectives that express positive emotions (Davies & Gardner, 2010: 36). Among adjectival positivizers are the following: confident, hopeful, sympathetic, humble, enthusiastic, cheerful, and appreciative. Those words surely refer to positive qualities characterizing diplomats in action.

For a 14-item list of verbal positivizers, you can refer to Gomes de Matos (2012). Included there are the following verbs: affirm, appreciate, dignify, beautify, edify, humanize, nourish, promote, protect, save, spiritualize, support, and sustain.

How about positivizing adverbs? Readers might enjoy composing their lists, which could include: diplomatically, tactfully, conciliatorily, harmonizingly, constructively, peacefully, dignifyingly.

I hope to have made a cogent case for the vital role played by positivizers in everyday communication and that using English diplomatically may also mean using that global language positively as hereby stressed.

Now it is time for readers to engage in applying the Pedagogy of Positiveness to their professional uses of English as diplomats or international relations experts. Here are activities that can be implemented in English for Diplomatic Purposes courses and expanded and modified to fulfill the needs of specific audiences: answers to activities are given.

Activities

Activity 1

Positive ISMS in diplomacy

Complete each -ism on the list below. Sometimes more than one term can be created.

- Opt
- Prag
- Glo
- Idea
- Multi

Add a couple of *isms* and justify your additions.

Write sentences or short dialogues where these words might appear. Decide which can be used as positivizers.

Role-play the dialogues with a partner.

Activity 2

Identifying positivizers

Read each statement (from an imaginary diplomat's internet English) and identify the positivizers used.

Give a near-synonym for each positivizing word. Justify your synonymy.

- It was a great pleasure to receive your warm message, kindly forwarded by our mutual friend **X**.
- I have the very highest regard for **Y**, whom I haven't seen for over ten years, and I appreciate your putting me in touch with that distinguished colleague.
- I am grateful for your suggestion especially about the recent sources on cyberdiplomacy. They will be most relevant to my overview of current trends in dignifying diplomatic communication across cultures.
- Among the qualities expected of a diplomat, probity stands out. Above all, s(h)e must be truthful and show a sustainable commitment to integrity.
- There are several advantages to carrying out globalizing practices: spreading cell phone communication, disseminating powerful and effective vaccines, strengthening intercultural ties among nations, and

raising standards of professional performance in many areas of human endeavor.
- In TV series, diplomats should also be given erudite and influential roles.

Share your answers with your colleagues or group facilitator.

Activity 3

Positivizers: Nouns in – ation

- Conciliation
- Cooperation
- Demilitarization
- Negotiation
- Mediation

Explain each of these words to a layperson. Then add 5 nouns ending in -*ation* that express positive diplomatic actions. Use them in context. Justify your additions.

Activity 4

Positivizers: Verbs in – ate
Some verbs in diplomatic communication end in -*ate*. Fill in each blank. Uses three verbs that seem to be frequently used. Use your verbs in contexts.

Fill in each blank.

- I'd like to stress this point, so let me re____ ate it.
- This proposal should be presented to the community, so I'll ar_____ ate it.
- After exchanging points of view, are we read to ne____ate?
- In country X, how are public protests to _____ ated?
- Successful diplomatic efforts have made it possible for violence in conflicts to be mi_____ated.

Activity 5

Your interlocutor
Challenging your lexicombining ability
One of the most frequently used words in English is **relationship**. In English used for diplomatic purposes, that noun occurs typically preceded by several positive verbs. See the list below and challenge your ability to combine verb + relationships. How many positive verbs can you find to make up a larger combinatorial set? Test your intuition, look up dictionaries and ask your friends and peers to contribute, too.

In diplomacy it is important to build relationships

cement
consolidate
cultivate
create
deepen
develop
diversify
enhance
foster
nurture
reaffirm
strengthen
(make your own additions to this list)

Activity 6

Your communicative dignity

Read and react positively to the items in this lexical set, all expressing the idea of 'poor persons, collectively.' Compare your feedback to that/those in the diplomatic/international relations context where you work. How do you react to each of the euphemisms below? Which of the euphemisms most strongly violates Communicative Dignity? Why?

(a)   the less fortunate
(b)   persons of modest economic background
(c)   the unfortunate
(d)   the needy
(e)   the indigent
(f)   the lowly

Create sentences that use the two euphemisms that you believe better express a concern for human dignity. Find other expressions for equally sensitive terminology naming other collective categories (e.g. countries in various stages of development). Look for their use in the media or in international relations channels.

Activity 7

The positiveness of your English

Read each statement and decide if you agree or disagree. In disagreeing, explain why.

(1) Using English effectively for diplomatic or other international relations purposes calls for one type of competence: communicating empathically.

AGREE/DISAGREE

(2) When at the negotiating table you disagree with your interlocutor, to support your opinion, you should express your disagreement as vehemently as possible.

AGREE/DISAGREE

(3) In persuading someone, a key consideration is **point of view**. As a diplomatic persuader, you should do your best for your interlocutor to support your opinion, rather than oppose it.

AGREE/DISAGREE

Activity 8

From everyday usage to diplomatic terminology
Fill in the blanks.

(1) The financial generosity of countries with sizeable resources = foreign _____
(2) A connection of countries for a joint action = an a_____
(3) Two countries making concessions to each other = a c_____
(4) Reducing tension between countries through mutual understanding = c_____
(5) Trying to solve a conflict peacefully = n_____
    Create sentences or short dialogue exchanges where there terms are featured.

Activity 9

Your communicative reactions
    Match each communicative reaction and corresponding verb. Identify reactions you should avoid and justify your feedback.

- To criticize sharply
- To refute by offering opposing evidence
- To prove to be false
- To reply in a quick, sarcastic way
- To refuse to accept or to believe
- To find fault with

(a) Rebuke
(b) Refute
(c) Rebut
(d) Retort
(e) Reject
(f) Reprove

Activity 10

Identifying and paraphrasing positivizers
Read the paragraph and identify positivizers. Then paraphrase each positivizer with an equivalent expression.

Urgency and impatience have both advantages and disadvantages for a diplomat. On the positive side, such attitudes may encourage the government official to work harder to create diplomatic momentum and resolve challenging issues.

Activity 11

Alliterations on interactions
Below is a set of alliterations aimed at actions typically performed by diplomats and other international relations professionals. On the basis of the English alphabet, add other alliterations and justify your creations. Be sure to use key verbs in diplomacy.

AAA - Advocate agreement and app _____
BBB - Better your bargaining ability in business rel _____
CCC - Communicate cooperatively and cor _____
DDD - Dignify all diplomatic dia _____
MMM - Mediate with a magnanimous min _____
NNN - Nurture Nonkilling among all nat _____
PPP - Persuade patiently and pea _____
RRR - Reassure respectful rel _____
SSS - _____ sustainable ser _____
TTT - Treat tensions tac _____
UUU - Universalize for union and und_____

Activity 12

Languages for diplomatic purposes.
Complete each statement. Justify your choice.

(1) Using a language effectively for diplomatic and other international relations purposes calls for two types of interpersonal ability: _____ and _____.

(2) At the negotiation table when a diplomat feels the need to rely on an interpreter, s(he) should do so in a spirit of hum _____.

(3) In a diplomatic or international business negotiation, languages should be used primarily to _____.

(4) The more languages a diplomat knows/uses the more _____ s(he) will be.

Activity 13

Mini-dialogue: Translating negativizers into neutral language

Read the mini-dialogue below and replace negativizers with neutral language. Discuss the two points of view with a diplomatic colleague and role-play the dialogue.

Subject: Diplomatic writing in the digital age

Characters: two diplomats, A and B

A: I hate to write my diplomatic texts with paper and pencil. That old-fashioned practice is such a waste of time. Computer composing is here to stay...Alternate forms of writing should be banned.

B: We wouldn't see eye-to-eye on this, A. To me, that will depend on the nature and goal of the piece. You sound too negatively radical.

Activity 14

Positivizing your communicative intention: A checklist

Read each pair of statements. The first statement is a communicative intention to be changed. The second statement is the suggested change. With a diplomatic partner, discuss each of the pairs from 1 to 5.

Context: In a negotiation or international relations interaction

(1) Instead of rudely reprimanding
     I humbly opt for recommending
(2) Instead of criticizing
     I opt for emphasizing
(3) Instead of complaining
     I opt for explaining
(4) Instead of an idea rejecting
     I opt for an idea correcting
(5) Instead of a proposal hating
     I opt for a proposal negotiating

Now complete the last word in pairs 6 to 10. Verb initials are given. Be sure to rhyme.

(6) Instead of an agreement imposing
     A dignifying decision: an agreement pro_____

(7) Instead of my interlocutor insulting
      A dignifying decision: my interlocutor con_____
(8) Instead of an incident abominating
      A dignifying decision: an incident inv_____
(9) Instead of both discussants tiring
      A dignifying decision: both discussants ins_____
(10) Instead of my interlocutor intimidating
      A dignifying decision: with my interlocutor con_____

Activity 15

Talking about nonkilling linguistics and diplomacy
   A dialogue for in-depth discussion with a friend. Act out the two roles and comment on the views expressed.
   Two graduate students in International Relations, A & B, are talking about emerging branches of linguistics and their potential application to diplomatic communication in English.
   Here is a fragment of their conversation:

A: A friend of mine who identifies himself as a nonkilling linguist says that from the perspective of Nonkilling Linguistics, diplomats have the right to thrive linguistically and to use language to foster understanding and peace.
B: What do you mean by that? Can you explain it to me?
A: Sure. Well, as you know, diplomats should be given due recognition for their extraordinary service to world peace and, as a result, they have the right to thrive in a world free from violence, where they can negotiate and share ideas.
B: I see... Then what are nonkilling linguists committed to?
A: To a nonkilling peace, or to put it more precisely, to nonkilling communicative peace.
B: You mean to say that languages can kill communicatively?
A: Languages can't, but I'm sad to say, language users can. An example will help make my point clearer: a person could harm another when intimidating in a life-threatening way... A heart attack can be caused that way ... More figuratively, a person may feel their voice has been silenced if their ideas are not given full consideration.
B: How can I learn more about what you call 'killing communicatively' and more importantly its opposite, how to foster peaceful communication?
A: That's easy. New literature on Peace Linguistics and Nonkilling Linguistics is coming out now. A quick internet search using those terms will reveal many good sources.
B: Will do. Thanks a lot. So, there is Peace Linguistics and also a Nonkilling Linguistics. Don't they share a challenging goal?

A: Yes, they do. Both are committed to helping educate language users for communicative peace and dignity, or to put it another way, to educate human beings as users of languages for peaceful, nonkilling purposes. A nonkilling peace is urgently needed everywhere.

B: I appreciate your sharing all this with me. Communicating nonkillingly, peacefully should be a part of professional preparation, shouldn't it?

A: Absolutely. And I would add positively, too, because communication should be a constructive process. From now on, I'll monitor my vocabulary and whenever possible opt for what do peace linguists call it? Positivizers.

B: Positiveness in diplomatic communicative life is a sustainable goal, my friend!

Ask students to identify the positivizers in the text. Then encourage students to create other dialogues discussing language, English, and diplomacy. Suggest that they use positivizers when creating the dialogues. Have the students role-play their own texts or swap them with other pairs. Follow up each presentation with class discussions.

Activity 16

A positive view of risk-taking in diplomacy

Read the statement below – an email from Ambassador Chas W. Freeman Jr. and discuss his view with a colleague of yours. How would you define a diplomat's honor? Why? What positivizers could you use?

'...I also think that part of the honor of diplomats is that they, like soldiers, accept special risks. It is that willing acceptance of risk in the interest of a larger cause than one's own, rather than indignation at abuses of diplomatic immunity, that I tend to regard as most important.' Ambassador Chas W. Freeman. Personal communication, April 6, 2014.

Activity 17

A diplomat's communicative responsibilities

In their communicatively engaging profession, diplomats are expected to fulfill several responsibilities, in speaking or writing. The items below could be included on a list of such linguistic duties. Complete each statement. Word initials are given. Then compare your answers with those of a colleague and discuss the point made in each message.

(1) Diplomats are expected to use effective neg_____ sty_____.
(2) Also expected of those government officials: an ability to plan and write acc_____ re_____ in English or in other languages used in the particular diplomatic exchanges.

(3) In a negotiation, diplomats may be challenged to use ges_____ more
judiciously, more spa_____.
(4) In making a diplomatic point, a diplomat may opt for a ded_____ or
an ind_____ argumentative approach.
(5) Today's diplomats seem to prioritize fa_____ and other concrete
fac_____ rather than abs_____ prin_____.

Activity 18

The continuum of positiveness

Label each of the statements below to indicate their place in the
continuum of communicative positiveness. Use these abbreviations:

VN (very negatively expressed)
N   negatively expressed)
P   (positively expressed)
VP (very positively expressed)

Imagine a dialogue between two diplomats, A and B, in which A would
say:

1a: I'm sure you're telling the truth (   )
1b: You must be telling the truth (   )
1c: Aren't you ashamed not to be telling the truth? ( )
1d: You're not telling the truth ( )

Then, add a statement that would express the comment most positively.

B would reply:

2a: You know me: I would never tell a lie (   )
2b: If there is anyone here telling a lie, that would be you ( )
2c: I can prove to you I'm being truthful (   )
2d: Do take my word: what I'm saying is absolutely true ( )

Activity 19

D-words in diplomacy

List 10 words beginning with D that have to do with or are related to
diplomacy. Word initials are given. Then use each word in context.

(1) Def_____   (2) Dem_____   (3) Dem_____
(4) Dev_____   (5) Dét_____   (6) Dia_____
(7) Dig_____   (8) Dig_____   (9) Div_____   (10) Du_____

Activity 20

Enhancing the positiveness of a statement

Complete each statement below by enhancing its positiveness. An example is given. Then exchange your completion with a colleague and discuss the core concepts in each statement from a diplomatic perspective.

Example: 'Wars begin in the minds of men but Peace begins in their hearts.' (UNESCO Charter)

(1) Discourtesy and impoliteness may keep diplomatic doors shut, but using English cordially _____.
(2) If results test actions, in diplomacy, good results _____
_____.
(3) Diplomacy should have more than the last word in peacemaking; it should_____.
(4) If independence is an indispensable quality for the survival of nations, interdependence is equally _____
_____.
(5) Cultural misperceptions of nations may be changed into accurate cultural interpretations if we_____
_____.

Conclusion

In the section 'How do we communicate orally?' in Gomes de Matos (2001), I state that as humans we can communicate by expressing either positive or negative (questionable) perceptions, by delivering either good or bad news, or by highlighting or leaving out the positive side of an issue. We can communicate in socially responsible or irresponsible ways. In other words, communicatively we can generate communicative dignity/harmony or communicative indignity/disharmony. In that text, I ask what positive features are being associated to the way diplomats communicate in speaking and in writing and ask what would seem to be missing in the linguistic and/or communicative education of diplomats. Then I present an 18-item checklist on Applying the Pedagogy of Positiveness to Diplomatic Communication. Given the relevance of such text for concluding this chapter, I would like to share five of the items therein:

(1) Learn to identify and avoid potentially aggressive, insensitive, offensive, destructive uses of language(s).
(2) Think of each language you use as a peace-building-making-promoting force.
(3) At all times, do your very best to view the diplomatic profession positively.

(4) Consider what parts of a diplomat's vocabulary can be systematized for constructive communicative purposes.
(5) Educate yourself in identifying positivizers in spoken and written English for diplomatic purposes and challenge yourself to make increasing use of such constructive, human-dignifying nouns, verbs, adjectives and adverbs.

Finally, I would like to paraphrase my concluding remarks from that chapter and say that communicating well in a variety of World Englishes for Diplomatic Purposes means communicating for the well-being of diplomatic interlocutors as well as for the good of humankind. May I also add that among the professional competencies in which diplomats and diplomats-to-be can excel, one could stand out: communicating positively.

I hope this chapter in this pioneering volume will prove of interest and use to you in your relevant work as a diplomat or an international relations professional in related areas. Having started this chapter with a rhymed reflection, let me close by adding another rhymed message:

Dear Diplomat,
As a user of English, a vocabulary you can activate
Does your choice of words help human dignity elevate?

As a user of English, a positive vocabulary how can you select?
By checking if the words you choose can create a positive effect

As a user of English, a positive diplomatic vocabulary you can prioritize
Such positively oriented words and expressions how can you optimize?

By using:
Nouns that communicative dignity will help elevate
Verbs that communicative Peace will help consolidate
Adjectives that positive human emotions will help translate

Acknowledgments

I am indebted to Patricia Friedrich for including me among the contributing authors in this ground-breaking, pioneering volume and for her competent critical reading of two drafts of my chapter, helping me enhance the pedagogical activities and improve my academic style.

I would also like to thank Ambassador Chas W. Freeman Jr. for granting permission for me to quote from his *Diplomat's Dictionary* and from an email message of his on a topic of relevance to my positive approach to diplomatic communication.

References

Cook, V. (2002) Language teaching methodology and the L2 user perspective. In V. Cook (ed.) *Portraits of the L2 User* (pp. 325–344). Clevedon: Multilingual Matters.

Davies, M. and Gardner, D. (2010) *A Frequency Dictionary of Contemporary American English.* London and New York: Routledge.

Freeman Jr., C.W. (2010) *The Diplomat's Dictionary.* Washington, DC: United States Institute of Peace Press.

Gomes de Matos, F. (2001) Applying the pedagogy of positiveness to diplomatic communication. In J. Kurbalija and H. Slavik (eds) *Language and Diplomacy* (pp. 281–289). Malta: University of Malta, Mediterranean Academy of Diplomatic Studies.

Gomes de Matos, F. (2007) A Plea for using Positivizers. *Braz-TESOL Pernambuco Newsletter*, November.

Gomes de Matos, F. (2012) Life Plus: The life-improving force of peaceful language use. In P. Coleman and M. Deutsch (eds) *Psychological Components of Sustainable Peace.* New York: Springer.

Gomes de Matos, F. (2013) *Dignity: A MultidimensionalView.* Oregon: Dignity Press.

Appendix I

A plea for using positivizers

F. Gomes de Matos

Let's learn to use words that create affect
and their role in doing good let's weigh
for kindness has a communicative effect
on how constructively we live every day

Let's use words that can help dignify
and make people seek reconciliation
Let's use words that can truly magnify
our ways to express deep appreciation

Let's use warm words that forgive
and interact with other persons well
the communicative example we give
may become an edifying story to tell
Let's use words that humanize
And help Justice to restore
Let's use words that positivize
And say to harm: Never more!

Let's use vocabulary that conveys integrity
and humanizing rights let's CREactivate
Let's always seek words' moral quality
compassion in communication, let's celebrate

Let's use words that help build self-confidence
and encourage people everywhere to cooperate

Let's learn to express a strong interdependence
and a spirit of planetary citizenship celebrate

Let's use nouns, verbs, adjectives, adverbs, pronouns as positivizing vocabulary
for the words we use in speaking, writing, or signing can play a significant part
in helping humankind perceive and practice Communicative Peace as necessary
Please, users of mental marvels for meaning-making,
Let's communicate from the heart!

Appendix II

Answers to activities

Suggested answers are given to all activities but 15, 16, and 20 because respondents' solutions may vary.

Activity 1

Answers: Optimism, Pragmatism, Globalism, Idealism, Multilateralism. Additional -isms: Inter (or Cross) culturalism, Multilingualism, Internationalism

Activity 2

Pleasure = satisfaction; warm = enthusiastic; kindly = sympathetic, regard = respect; appreciate = am thankful for; distinguished = eminent; grateful = appreciative; relevant = appropriate;dignifying = enhancing; qualities = virtues; stands out =is prominent; truthful = honest; commitment = dedication; advantages = benefits; spreading = universalizing; disseminating = sharing; strengthening = consolidating; ties = relations; raising = elevating; endeavor = initiative; erudite = learned; influential = important

Activity 3

Conciliation = overcoming distrust; cooperation = working together demilitarization = absence of military forces or installations; negotiation = action for resolving differences between two persons/countries . Additional nouns in -ation: classification (of documents, materials), pacification, translation, interpretation, relation

Activity 4

(1) reiterate; (2) articulate; (3) negotiate; (4) tolerated; (5) mitigated

Activity 5

Additional verbs: improve, better, optimize, dignify, elevate, maximize

Activity 6

Item (f) strongly violates communicative dignity by referring to the poor as low in (economic) condition. This reflects rankism.

Activity 7

(1) AGREE. Diplomatically, empathy means putting oneself in the place of one's negotiating partner
(2) DISAGREE. Rather than vehemently, cordially, mutually respectfully
(3) AGREE. You should lead your interlocutor to accept your proposal amicably

Activity 8

(1) aid; (2) alliance; (3) compromise; (4) conflict resolution; (5) negotiation

Activity 9

1a; 2c; 3b; 4d; 5e; 6f

Activity 10

POSITIVIZERS: advantages (benefits), encourage (inspire), harder (more intensively), create (generate), momentum (impetus), challenging (creative)

Activity 11

AAA   -   appeasement
BBB   -   relationships
CCC   -   cordially
DDD   -   dialogue
MMM -   mindset
NNN   -   nations
PPP   -   peacefully
RRR   -   relations
SSS   -   support, serenity
TTT   -   tactfully
UUU   -   union, understanding

Activity 12

(1) empathy, dignity (2) humility (3) dignify (4) creative, professional

Activity 13

Hate= don't like; old fashioned = not current; waste of time= time not well; used ban = not allow

Activity 14

(6) proposing (7) consulting (8) investigating (9) inspiring (10) conciliating

Activity 17

(1) negotiating styles
(2) accurate reports
(3) gestures sparingly
(4) deductive or inductive
(5) facts factors abstract principles

Activity 18

(1a) VP; (1b) P; (1c) VN; (1d) N
2a - P; (2b) VN; (2c) VP; (2d) VP

Activity 19

(1) 1-defense (2) demand (3) democracy (4) development (5) détente
(6) dialogue (7) dignity (8) dignitary (9) diversity (10) duty

9 Conclusion

Patricia Friedrich

As I hope this volume has made clear, many are the opportunities and ideas to be explored in English for Diplomatic Purposes. The recognition that diplomacy is a unique realm of use, which nonetheless relies on well-known and important elements of linguistic dynamics, opens the door to many innovative practices and creative pedagogical activities (of which we clearly are only starting to scratch the surface). It is the goal of the contributors to this volume that instructors, students and diplomatic education centers join us in devising plans that allow the full range of possibilities in diplomacy to be realized. In the same spirit, we hope other researchers will invest time in further unveiling elements of communication that foster greater communicative peace.

In these concluding remarks, I would like to offer ideas for reflection and prompts to generate dialogue among instructors, among students, and between these two groups. I invite you to add to these ideas and create opportunities, through workshops, meetings and retreats, for your peers to ponder and contemplate these items. Some possible self-reflective questions are as follows:

Ideas for teachers to explore
(1) Given World Englishes knowledge and contribution and a framework of peace, what activities or tasks can students engage with in the classroom so that English for Diplomacy better fulfills these students' needs for communicative competence?
(2) Utilizing the vocabulary that students already bring to class, what steps can be taken to ensure a positive addition to their linguistic vocabulary so that it can be peace fostering and consensus seeking?
(3) What activities can you envision to teach empathy to your students of diplomatic English?
(4) What linguistic elements can you teach your students so that they can balance force and grace when using diplomatic English(es)?
(5) We often acknowledge that the strategic level of linguistic competence helps learners make up for 'imperfect' linguistic knowledge. In a way, all knowledge of language is imperfect (nobody knows 'the whole' language), so it is more positive to focus on strategies to fill in these linguistic gaps than to consider the 'imperfections' themselves. How

can we help our students productively engage with the strategic level to supplement linguistic knowledge? What are good ways to teach circumlocution, repetition, clarification questions, etc.? How do students feel about using the strategic level? Do they see it positively or as a sign of their shortcomings?

(6) Language can at times be quite unpredictable, even in situations of communication, such as diplomatic interaction where a certain protocol is in place. When we practice language for negotiation, phrases and expressions can become seemingly fixed. When learners of English use language in real life, they may become disoriented by the more fluid way in which linguistic expression happens. How do we avoid this gap between teaching and language use in the real world?

(7) One of our chapters has presented a view of English in the more specific context of ASEAN countries. Are there specific characteristics of the region where you come from (e.g. South America, Western Europe, Northern Africa) that should be taken into consideration when applying English to diplomatic communication?

(8) Since Englishes have multiplied and many areas of knowledge have invested in describing variation and diversity, how does a classroom teacher address such concepts as 'error,' 'mistake,' and 'standard language,' without on the one hand limiting individual expression and on the other conveying the message that there are no contextual rules to be followed? How can balance be achieved in this case?

(9) How can politeness be manifested in different Englishes and what linguistic forms are essential to negotiating politeness in context?

(10) How can you make your classroom into a laboratory of ideas, a place where students feel safe to experiment with linguistic expression so as to be prepared for real-word interactions?

(11) Are there competing understandings of diplomacy that need to be addressed in the English language classroom? If there are, how do they manifest in a world that often uses English for international communication?

An important consideration here is that the English classroom can work not only as a place of linguistic awareness, but perhaps more importantly of sociolinguistic knowledge. Because words are never detached from some form of cultural meaning, exploring these elements – the linguistic and the social together – can create important opportunities for improvement in communication. The classroom in this sense is a microcosm of the dynamics that occur outside of it.

Activity suggested by Francisco Gomes de Matos (personal communication)

Choose a piece of diplomatic communication (a speech or address for example)

Listen carefully and identify the following items.

(1) Positivizers used (these can be nouns, verbs, or adjectives): e.g. peace, protect, dialogue, community.
(2) Key-concepts or common diplomatic terms: e.g. negotiation, peace, joint-effort, mediated.
(3) Positive phrases: e.g. 'we have come to an agreement regarding...'
(4) Negative 'isms:' e.g. cynicism, despotism, radicalism (note: not all 'isms' are negative, so students can discuss what makes an 'ism' negative).
(5) Mentions of diplomacy, diplomatic, diplomat and derived terms.
(6) Mentions of problems: e.g. the issue of...., the problem of...
(7) Uses of modals to indicate opinion or advice: 'We should do better...,' It would be advisable...'

After collecting such an inventory, discuss with students which of these uses make the speech/address more effective and which detract from those goals. Reuse the most relevant vocabulary in other classroom practices.

Ideas for students to explore

(1) How do I see my role as a communicator in diplomatic circles?
(2) What are some of the elements of communication that challenge me the most?
(3) What are some attitudes or utterances by other parties that could trigger a negative verbal response in me? How can I address those in a more positive manner?
(4) What new kinds of linguistic interaction can I try?

Activity

Keeping a journal

As you embark on this learning process of not only using English for Diplomatic Purposes but also of choosing language and expressions that will generate goodwill and cooperation, try to keep a written journal describing the practices that you feel the most comfortable with and the ones that seem to work the best. Refer back to your journal entries when you need inspiration.

Ideas for teachers and students

If dialogue among teachers is very important, communication between teachers and students is essential. Here are a few questions that can be addressed collectively in the spirit of dialogue.

(1) What knowledge do I bring to the classroom that can benefit my instructor in their role as class lead? What knowledge do I bring to the classroom that can benefit my students in their role as (future) diplomatic workers?
(2) How can I provide my instructor with hints to the kinds of language and skills I need?
(3) How can the idea of compassionate communication already work in the classroom?
(4) How can I conduct diagnostic analyses of the linguistic needs of my students?
(5) What can my students teach me about diplomacy?
(6) What can my instructor teach me about the role of Englishes in different environments?
(7) What activities can we, teachers and students, devise together to better practice?

Keeping a Glossary of Terms

Because certain words and expressions will occur often within the realm of diplomacy, it is a good idea to keep a list of terms. However, writing them down only once will likely not be enough to make them available to you when you need them. Instead, actively look for opportunities to use them. One way to get started is to employ them in written communications. Since when you write you (often) have a chance to stop and look for the best vocabulary items, using your glossary to compose written messages helps take words from your passive vocabulary (those words you can recognize if you see them but would not ordinarily use) to your active vocabulary (the pool of words you actually use more spontaneously in communication). Following this practice, you can try and incorporate the items to your oral communications as well.

Because diplomacy is a highly interactive realm of language use, the more opportunities a learner has to interact with others the better.

If you are using this book to learn about aspects of diplomatic English that could potentially apply to your profession and practice, these are a few reflections worth carrying out:

(1) What aspects of my professional practice resemble those of diplomatic communications and what elements differ significantly?

(2) What aspect of my professional communications do I want to improve? What do I value in a communication counterpart?
(3) What are some of my challenges when communicating with others?
(4) What aspects of communication present the least challenge to me?
(5) What are some of the ways of communicating compassionately in my practice?
(6) What are some of the ways of communicating peacefully in my practice? How do compassion and peace interact in communication?

It is our hope that this volume has contributed to the important mission of teaching English to those who engage in the delicate job of communicating diplomatically in a second or foreign language. May we use language to negotiate, to uplift, to understand and to be understood.

Index